Mandate to Humanity

Edwin McNeill Poteat

MANDATE

to

*An Inquiry into the
History and Meaning of the
Ten Commandments
and Their Relation to
Contemporary Culture*

HUMANITY

ABINGDON-COKESBURY PRESS
New York • *Nashville*

MANDATE TO HUMANITY

Copyright MCMLIII by Pierce & Washabaugh

Library of Congress Catalog Card Number: 53-5399

All direct quotations from the Bible unless otherwise designated are from the American Standard
Version of the Revised Bible, copyright, 1929, by
the International Council of Religious Education.

SET UP, PRINTED, AND BOUND BY THE
PARTHENON   PRESS,   AT   NASHVILLE,
TENNESSEE, UNITED STATES OF AMERICA

DEDICATED

TO

THE CONGREGATION

OF

PULLEN MEMORIAL BAPTIST CHURCH

*Whose Interest in Much of the Material
Here Discussed Encouraged the Effort to Expand It*

Foreword

I ACKNOWLEDGE gratefully the permission of the following publishers allowing me to use materials held under their copyright: Harper and Brothers, New York; Macmillan Company, New York; *Crozer Quarterly*, Chester, Pa.; Charles Scribner's Sons, New York; Westminster Press, Philadelphia; Alfred A. Knopf, Inc., New York; Little, Brown and Company, Boston; W. W. Norton and Company, Inc., New York; *The Saturday Review of Literature*, New York; *The Notre Dame Lawyer*, Indiana.

These have read part or all of the manuscript and offered suggestions which have been incorporated, in whole or in part, in the book: W. F. Stinespring, Ph.D.; Nell Hirschberg, Ph.D.; B. F. Brown, Ph.D.; William H. Poteat, Ph.D.; and Mary Ayscue. I record my gratitude to them for the time and effort they spent in trying to improve the product. And where their suggestions are used, initials identify the source.

My special thanks to Mrs. Betsy Senter Wooden, who once again as in times past has cheerfully taken time from her routine responsibilities to put the typescript in order.

Edwin McNeill Poteat

Raleigh, N.C., 1953

Contents

Introduction

1

NOWADAYS any effort to set forth what the biblical record has to say must begin with an understanding of a literary problem that is involved in its "history." Until fairly recent decades it was a simple matter to consult the biblical timetable prepared by the Protestant Archbishop of the Irish diocese of Armagh, James Ussher (1581-1656), and learn, to begin with, that the creation occurred on October 4, 4004 B.C. at 9 A.M. Less spectacular events and dates fall neatly into line in the honest archbishop's schedule, so that individual patriarchs and heroes, as well as national catastrophes and triumphs, are properly pegged on a calendar of over 5,900 years' duration.

To the uncritical who accepted this it did not occur that the time calculation Ussher used was a mistaken one. Mathematicians and astronomers had been struggling for centuries with the vagaries of calendar making while the sun and moon moved with invariable constancy above them. Their arguments occasioned such scandal and schism in the early Church that a man could be condemned as a heretic if he was found to have perverse opinions about the week, the month, and the lunar year. The Julian Calendar, named for Julius Caesar, was early discovered to be mistaken; but not until 1582 was it corrected by order of Pope Gregory XIII. This was one year after Ussher was born, but not until 1752 was the Gregorian correction legally acknowledged in Great Britain. Ussher doubtless was never aware of the errors into which his chronology fell, and had he heard about the pope's tampering with time, he would perhaps have dismissed it as papistical presumption, stout Irish Protestant that he was. His was an exercise in piety, not astronomy, and thus both accepted and confirmed the popular misconceptions that stood so long in the way of the general acceptance of the corrected calculations of the watchers of the sky.

Ussher's figures

If the archbishop was innocent of the aberrations of his trusted time scheme, he was less troubled by the possibilities of error in the history he undertook to date. Abram, he calculated, was born 1996 B.C., Moses four and a quarter centuries later. It would have been impious for him to entertain the thought that these great figures could have been more legendary than historic, heroes of folklore rather than solid men whose records were established beyond the need for examination. And yet it is to this point that the research of modern historical and literary criticism has brought us. There is disagreement among the scholars today, but this does not lend credence to the opinions held uncritically in Ussher's time, opinions which for reasons held by trustworthy modern scholars either are no longer credible at all or are subject to considerable modification on the basis of carefully established evidence.

2

The relation of this to a study of the Ten Commandments is so obvious that there is no need here for more than a statement of the historic and literary problem involved in their consideration. The book of Exodus was written in the middle of the fifth century B.C. as part of the editorial undertaking of Hebrew patriots during the Babylonian exile. "Ezekiel gave us the Torah" (the Pentateuch, or the first five books), said the early rabbis; and he was only one of those wise and devoted men who in the thralldom and leisure of bondage sought to capture the record of past ages in permanent writings. What materials they had other than the great oral tradition is not known. There may have been scraps of crude record, preserved in a somewhat polyglot tongue. Whether these were "documents," as was assumed for many years in the documentary hypothesis (J, E, D, and P), or collections of traditions formally accepted and written is something for the experts to pursue further. For our purposes it is enough to accept the fairly late date of their editorial task and to recognize what this involves as we address ourselves to the Mosaic Code.

It is because ideas are living that this necessity confronts us. It has little to do with our theories about how we know what we know, whether revelation or reason is the source of proximate and efficient knowledge. That which is revealed comes through the screen of

12

reason. He is a dupe who believes, and a bigot who defends, nonsense by assigning it a purely private origin. Similarly it may be said that he who accredits all he knows to the simple—or complex—operations of the rational process is blind to the initial fact that to know that one knows is not a logical deduction. Prior to knowing there must be communicable knowledge. Mind may not always be superior to matter, but the datum is always prior to the idea. And all thought is vital, which means that ideas germinate and grow and bear fruit and seed, and sometimes even die, which oddly enough may be properly understood to be part of the vital process.

3

The Ten Commandments are living ideas. This means not only that they have survived for a long time in the sometimes friendly and often hostile environment of social change, but that they had their origin in experience. This experience can be just as accurately described as revelation for the scribe of the code as the spectacular portents above Mount Sinai were revelatory to the awestruck people below. It is of no very great importance whether we understand the story of the finger of Yahweh writing on stone tablets as literal or figurative so long as we do not assume that what was graven there had no reference to the past experience of the nomads at the base of the mountain, or that it was fixed in stone so that no subsequent experience could alter or erode it. Surely the sculptured stones were not the symbol of dead ideas. The whole history of the Mandate from its origin to the present is a denial of that. By means of its still thunderous imperatives it speaks to our own times, though not always and everywhere in accents identical to those that accompanied their first pronouncement.

This may seem to be giving ground to what today we call moral relativism, the notion that we can read the Ten Commandments seriously only if we keep our fingers crossed. I will give attention to this aspect of the matter as we get along with our study, but for the moment I may observe that much of what is both the advocacy, on one hand, and the fear, on the other, of moral relativism comes close, in its own way, to being moral absolutism. It says: There is no absolute anything, forgetting for the moment that in so speaking it elevates relativism to the status of an absolute. There is no absolute but relativism: that is dangerous nonsense.[1]

More simply stated, however, is the relation of this to the subject of this inquiry. Those who wrote the history of the moral beginnings of the Hebrew people believed that Moses had been the medium through which the Mandate to Humanity was transmitted. The highly dramatic record of its presentation to him is one of the great stories of all times, but the meaning and value of the revelation are hardly related to the physical portents that were said to have accompanied the ascent of Moses to the fulgurant summit of the mountain or his labored descent from the cloud cap, bearing two tables engrossed by the divine digit.

4

The Hebrews were a mixed race. For generations they had been caught in the crosscurrents of the cultures of nations already fairly well advanced. A chosen people they unquestionably were, but not a pure or isolated people living in a cultural enclave. Archaeology and anthropology have established this beyond question. This, furthermore, is a fact that lends importance to the epic of the escape of these doughty rebels from the bondage of Egypt. For the living God to communicate effectively his divine purposes to a segregated race would have been, we assume, a far less formidable undertaking than speaking to a mixed folk among aliens. For the same reason the divine success was more impressive.

The root word *abar*, from which the word "Hebrew" has come to us, means "one who crosses, a nomad." Abram's earliest distinction would seem to have been his mobility. Traces of his wandering descendants have turned up in many ancient inscriptions. "The *Apiru* wherever found are clearly aliens, adventurers, wanderers, and the name is foreign and not Egyptian, identical in every respect with the

---

[1] Observe the invasion of the judicial branch of our government by this idea. A recent decision by the United States Supreme Court had the chief justice saying: "Nothing is more certain in modern society than the principle that there are no absolutes; that a name, a phrase, a standard has meaning only when associated with the considerations which gave birth to the nomenclature. To those who would paralyze our government in the face of impending threat by encasing it in a semantic straitjacket, we must reply that all concepts are relative."

Hebrew *Ibri* and the cuneiform *Habiru*." These people were a long time settling down and for that reason a long time developing a culture of their own. The wonder is that out of their experience should have come the set of moral maxims that have become the core of the ethical idealism of the Western world.

5

Our concern is limited to these ethical rudiments of their culture as they are set forth in the Decalogue. It is perhaps not popular to say so in a time such as our own when the economic factor in social development is thought to be determinative, but there are still timeworn arguments to be made in favor of the primacy of the ethical component in culture. It is then necessary to ask whence came this compact body of law, ten directives for human behavior that encompass both the religious and moral aspects of experience.

There was a point, we assume, at which the inchoate tribes were co-ordinated into a new people, identifiable in habitation, name, and character. This cohesion in all likelihood was stabilized when what came to be known as a covenant and a simple covenant code were acknowledged between God and his people. Then *Bene Yisra el*, or the Israelites, became self-consciously existent. We must keep in mind that what we have in the first three books of the Bible is not history as we know this discipline today, any more than the dates we use today in pegging events in the story of the Hebrew people are the sort of dates Ussher used. The construction of what we may properly call the ancient history of the Jews is still going on. If it is ever finished, it will be due not to the assiduous study of the Old Testament alone, but to the slow and highly technical work of that small body of scholars who, in order to piece together its fragments,

---

Theophile James Meek, *Hebrew Origins* (rev. ed.; New York: Harper & Bros., 1950), p. 13. Used by permission. This book is indispensable for those who would know what recent studies have turned up in this field. "The words 'Hebrew' (English), *ibri* (Hebrew), *habiru* (cuneiform), and *apiru* (Egyptian) may be the same word in different languages; but scholars are not agreed on this point." W.F.S.

By religious we mean specifically man's awareness of and relation to God through rational intuition and immediate experience; by moral we mean man's awareness of and relation to his fellow man as they are determined and accepted by judgments of value and obligation, however they may be established. W.H.P.

have had to be familiar with the culture and the records of all the peoples who jostled together in the cradle of civilizations we today call the Near East.

It has been within recent years that the spades of archaeologists have dug up codes and assigned to them dates both earlier and later than the Mosaic Code. The Code of Hammurabi (ca 1728-1676 B.C.) was discovered around A.D. 1900; German excavators at Ashur found an Assyrian Code (ca 1112-1074 B.C.) fourteen years later. The Hittite Code (ca 1400-1200 B.C.) was found in 1906 and deciphered in 1915 by a Czech scholar in Prague. In 1947 among tablets in the University of Pennsylvania Museum, fragments of a Sumerian Code were found. The most recent discovery has turned up the earliest of all the ancient codes, that of Bilalama (ca 1930 B.C.), unearthed by an expedition in Iraq only four years ago. All of these codes are earlier than the date assigned to the promulgation of the Hebrew Code; all of them have both old and new materials indicating that the experience of the code makers was constantly altering the details of the laws they codified. This parallels the experience of the development of the Torah, which is not the work of a single lawgiver, Moses. Aside from the fact that law in general does not have its origin that way, accumulated evidence supports the conclusion that the law of the Hebrews is a corpus that gradually came into being during many centuries and is a compendium of the Book of the Covenant, the Deuteronomic Code, the Holiness Code, and the Priestly Code. Thus the Torah is the accrescence of many years of social experience and thinking. It is difficult to imagine such an impressive development taking place in isolation, that is to say, insulated from the experience of neighbor peoples. Cross fertilization is clear in any comparative study of these ancient codes. There are identities that are interesting; there are dissimilarities that are striking. While the Hebrew people borrowed indirectly from Hittite and Canaanite and Babylonian law, it is remarkable that the characteristic features of Hebrew law were uniquely their own and the product of their own experience. What they borrowed, they adapted until in the end it acquired, under the influence of their sublimated and sensitized moral consciousness, a quality that has set it over against, indeed higher than, the codes of other cultures. We must not lose sight of this significant circumstance.

16

6

The Ten Commandments were perhaps put down for the first time in the written form we have about 550 B.C. It is unlikely that research will ever discover hints as to the interest, or even excitement, that must have attended this editorial *tour de force*. There were scribes who had a lively sense of the dramatic and an understanding of the important fact that the teaching process is more than mere dogmatizing. Others exhibited a bold economy of line; others, perhaps, had a sense of humor that was far from flippancy. Yet we cannot say with certainty that they sought simply to preserve intact a tradition. Did they regard it as sacrosanct, or inerrant? Hardly.

We may be certain, however, that the moral sensitiveness of the Hebrew people was much more acute and profound when the editing was done in 550 B.C. than it was in the fifteenth century B.C. of Moses. If ideas are alive, considerable growth can be detected over a period of 850 years, the difference between the date for Moses and for the compilation of the book of the Exodus. One need only reflect what has happened to the ideas within which the Christian testimony has moved since A.D. 1100. The name and influence of one man, Thomas Aquinas (1225-74), is reminder enough. The Angelic Doctor is for most of Christendom today as definitive as Moses is for Jewry.

Assuming the vitality of ideas, we are confronted at once with an interesting question. Did the ideas of the Ten Commandments—and I shall confine my inquiry strictly to the Decalogue from here on—have any development between Moses and the editors of the Exile? We must assume that they had grown conspicuously before they were collated by Moses as reported in the dramatic episode at Mount Sinai. The Old Testament shows us the answer: Great advance is seen in ethical sensitiveness between Moses and Second Isaiah. Indeed we cannot avoid the conclusion that the process of refining and elevating moral directives was a steady one, that living ideas concerning man's

---

* It needs to be said that not all modern scholars agree on the late date of the coding of the Torah, either in terms of the date of Moses or in the editorial work of the later scribes. Cf. W. F. Albright, *From the Stone Age to Christianity*, who argues for an early date for the written law. There is also strong support for the idea that some of the injunctions, such as those against murder, theft, and so on, are much older than Moses even though the redaction of the Ten Commandments was late. W.F.S.

religious and moral conduct were nourished by experiences of all sorts and grew greater and more profound. A part of this growth was the sloughing off of irrelevancies and inferences of dubious value.

One wishes it were possible to know whether the editors were aware of this. Did they undertake to set down slavishly a tradition about the giving of the law to Moses, disregarding the fact that the spiritual sensitiveness of their own times was uncomfortable in the presence of some of the demands that the law contained? Not that conscience had grown dull, but that it had grown acute. What, for example, did they make of the threat of vengeance on impiety to the third and fourth generations? Jeremiah, who died *ca* 585 B.C., had already discredited that notion. Another question: Was their effort directed by a historical or a didactic interest? Here again we are at a loss for an answer. What we have a right to assume, however, is that they knew what they were about. Their effort and their success were considerable. It is for those of us who are within the stream of that great ethical inheritance to set their effort and their ideas within the perspectives, both historic and cultural, which our modern methods of study have made possible for us. If we find ourselves restive under some of the religious ideas in the first five commandments, we will not feel it a sign of superiority. We shall be all the more grateful for the resources that modern historical study have made available to us.

7

It is only within some such pattern of study that we can rightly understand the levels on which the commandments rest. That there are different levels is obvious. A proscription against covetousness deals with a mood and involves insights more subtle than the rugged prohibition against killing. Making graven images to worship is easily identified as a sin, but image making as the function of the imagination is as necessary as it is inescapable. The moral gradations that we shall encounter are to be accounted for either as valid in terms of a fiat order, however inscrutable it may be, or as valid only when understood in terms of the development of the consciousness of God and the relations that this involved in human society. The nomads who became the Hebrew people were moral primitives. That they could by the time of Moses have become aware of elementary principles and maxims that have been refined into the ethical framework of

18

our civilization is a development of enormous importance. That this came about by a unique and radical sense of the divine in human experience makes place for revelation as a medium of moral knowledge. That there are varying levels of sensitivity and a moral insight gives room to the component of human experience, the trial and error by which the rational function is educated in precision and steadiness.

It is commonplace to observe that the Ten Commandments are divided in two equal parts. The first five have to do with man's relation to God. This is what we describe as a religious concern. The second five have to do with man's relation to his fellows and is what we call a moral concern. What is not so generally recognized, however, is that while the moral quintet by and large are regarded today as normative, the religious quintet are accepted in the form preserved in Exod. 21:2-17 and Deut. 5:6-21 only with reservations. Such religion as we have is, generally speaking, monotheistic; but it is doubtful that Moses, judged by the commandments about God, believed in the existence or the idea of only one God. By the time of the exile editors a monotheism was emergent, but in some respects it was incomplete. The development of the idea of deity from its first tentative and tribal aspects to the intimacy of the God and Father of our Lord Jesus Christ and the magnificence of the creator and sustainer of the universe we now know, has been epic in vigor and dimension. Indeed the easy reversion to tribal and national and racial and social gods of which we in our times are guilty is proof enough, if any were needed, that the struggle to sustain a credible faith in one God is never adjourned, either in the hearts of individuals or in the practice of groups.

It may be that the immediate future will see the moral half of the Commandments abandoned or modified out of recognition. Within our Western cultural ethos it would perhaps prove to be as impossible as it seems absurd to try to dismiss by formal legislation the authority of this ancient moral law in our culture. The centuries have not eroded these mighty prohibitions, but the relatively new and hostile culture behind the Iron Curtain has sought to erase them.

The victory of the proletarian revolution is a victory of the new morality—the morality of the communist society. Our morality is subordinated to the interests of the class struggle of the proletariat. From the point of view of the communist morality, ethical or moral can be

19

only what forms a means to annihilate the old world, the world of exploitation and what strengthens the new socialist revolution.[5]

We may want to shout this down as nonsense or warn the Kremlin King Canute of the ineffectiveness of his remonstrance against the endless insurgence of the tides of what he contemptuously calls "bourgeois morality," but in ways more subtle than many of us detect, the self-proclaimed morality of the Soviets is influencing the morals of the West even as the diplomacy of the Kremlin subtly influences the defensive decisions made in the departments of state of the countries that openly oppose it.

8

We are confronted then by what must be regarded as an amazing fact no matter from what point of view it is approached. A code of maxims, ten in number, have come down from a legendary past and given shape to the moral idealism of what is still the most virile culture in the world. Its concern with both religion and morals is singular in the light of the fact that many codes have to do with only one or the other or see no difference in the two. How does it happen that when we think of moral commandments, we think not of Hammurabi or Bilalama, or Ashur or Babylon, but of Moses and the wilderness of Sinai? The quick and therefore the doubtful answer is that we are in the cultural stream of the Hebrew folk. But why that? Deep in the same ancient Levantine world other codes were born and nurtured to maturity. But the cultural floods of Assyria and Babylon have long since dried up in the Eastern deserts, and there are no folk today who know them as their parent codes or follow them.

The explanation of this can easily be smug and not a little patronizing. Whether we claim that our code is a divine revelation or the product of social experience, we do not escape the risk of oversimplification. Similarly to say it is both does not dismiss the matter. Since the moral rudiments of a cultural order are more important even than the rituals within which the religious experience is contained, their

---

[5] *Kratki Filosofski Slovar*, ed. P. Rosenbaum and P. Yudin (2nd ed.; Moscow: Politizdat of the Central Committee of the All-Soviet Communist Party, 1940), p. 177. Quoted by Hans Kohn, *The Twentieth Century* (New York: Macmillan Co., 1949), p. 117. Used by permission of Macmillan Co.

survival must be explained by excavating to deep levels, a sort of spiritual or psychological archaeology.

This is all the more necessary now that the validity of the moral basis of Western culture has been repudiated and is being deliberately undermined by the pretensions of the Marxist order. When after 1859 the biological theories of Darwin were applied to society, Herbert Spencer wrote of the survival of the fittest among societies and even among ideas. A few years before (1848) Marx had predicted through what he claimed was an infallible understanding of history what the fittest was sure to be. It was the strong culture that would survive, the culture that, because its inner tensions had been resolved by violence, would by violence resolve all exernal tensions and win its way to dominance. Power needed no justification except its muscles. It was exempt from the judgments of good and evil. Bismarck for purely political reasons took this seriously and by 1870 had made a success of changing the direction of German history and defeating the liberal movement that had begun to take morals seriously. This does not mean that Bismarck himself was indifferent to morality. On the contrary he was in his own gruff way proud of his piety, but he saw German progress in terms of power—military not moral power. And in the succession of Bismarck we see Hitler, Mussolini, Tojo, Lenin and his Kremlin heirs, and countless lesser figures. Most disturbing, however, is the general moral malaise that has infected our own culture. Do we not find it easy to kill, to corrupt, to steal, to perjure, if the act is committed in the nation's interest? We would not for a moment confess that we, like our adversaries, have scrapped Moses for Marx; but we cannot fail to note that we rest more and more complacently within what we call the modern necessities for breaking the code.

This sort of thing can be rationalized or laughed off, but it does not give us spiritual security to do so. Deeply the heart of modern man is touched with guilt, and the fury of his denials is as clear proof of it as his preoccupation with killing and stealing is evidence that he dares not face up to himself. He holds in his heart—because he is the child of his culture—ten short admonitions. When he has the curiosity to lift them into the light of scrutiny, they seem to have the faded pallor of ashes; when he tastes them, they are denatured of their pristine pungency. And the sound of the thunder over Sinai is the

21

faraway echo of a faint rumble. Moses comes down from the mount and finds some people averting their faces. Many have gone off into the wilderness on their own.

9

This is the problem to which a study of the Mandate to Humanity invites us today. To its understanding must be brought all that can be had of the resources of literary and historical criticism, as well as the lofty sense of idealism that has invested it for centuries. It will be necessary to ask whether Moses was right. This in the minds of some is the same as asking if God was right, and that puts the questioner in an unenviable position. Suppose he should decide God was wrong. Some have. We think that such a dismissal has been due to a faulty understanding of what the code actually says, or an unwillingness to concede that in the development of the divine law, as of every other sort, the experience of human fallibility and perverseness must be allowed as a conditioning factor.

There is one assumption, however, upon which must rest all that is said in this study. It is an assumption because nowhere in the deliverance of the law is it explicitly stated. It has to do with the intention behind this astonishing development in human history. Before the primitive mind had articulated its dim faith in a God with whom it had to do, it must have felt that there was an intention behind what was going on. It is too much to say that a purpose had been clearly discerned, that a teleology had been marked out. We are still puzzled about such matters. But was there not an intention that was vaguely felt? It is clear that the more men came to know of God, the sharper became the outlines of this intention. Today we call it familiarly the will of God, although he who is most sensitive to it will perhaps be most restrained in his talk about it.

It can be simply put. God was undertaking in the transfer of his law to mankind to bring individuals to a realization of the qualities of himself with which man had been endowed when at his creation there was breathed into him the breath of life and he became a living soul. Correlative to that was the design for a society within which men could live together in such a fashion as would aid their growth toward godliness. Eden had been abandoned because innocence had insufficient protection. Outside Eden, Abel had died at the hand of his brother. The lie had been told to avert the divine suspicion of the theft of forbidden fruit. This is the language of myth, but of myth that carries a freight of profound wisdom into the problem of human society. If men were to live together, they had to be told how to do it. How was sin to be distinguished from innocence? How was society to cohere? The understandings of sin were to be sharpened through the experience of every living person and every growing society. When Yahweh God "gave the law," it was not the first edition man had been confronted with nor the last edition society was to face up to. Creation is a continuing process, and this is just as true in the moral as in the physical experience of the race.

10

To summarize: In these introductory paragraphs I have set forth the perspectives within which our study of the Mandate to Humanity will proceed. The years of painstaking research by excavators and linguists and interpreters have given the Bible a new dimension. It is no longer simply linear, as it was to the good Archbishop. It has the breadth, height, and depth that an understanding of the neighbor cultures of the Hebrew people has made possible. The Ten Commandments were so important to those who first put together the epic of the *Habiru* that the episode of their pronouncement was preserved in all the dramatic intensity of the folk tales that had carried it for centuries. For this reason we are compelled to look at the story less as a historic account than as a dramatized portrayal of the gradual emergence of a great moral and religious ideal.[6] The moral and religious culture of the West must now defend the Ten Commandments against slow erosion and violent assault, and this defense will not be

*This important consideration has been cogently presented by Dillard S. Gardner, Marshal Librarian of the Supreme Court of North Carolina, in an article in the *Notre Dame Lawyer, A Quarterly Law Review,* Fall, 1951, entitled "The Almost-Forgotten Law Book." He says, discussing the moral and religious bases of the Ten Commandments: "*First,* they are based on a religious premise. . . . *Second,* they are founded on exalted ethical and moral concepts. . . . *Third,* they reflect a spiritual idealism and are not to be obeyed as ends in themselves . . . but as guides to conduct acceptable to Jehovah. . . . *Fourth,* the basic commandments are universal and timeless. . . . *Fifth,* these commands have an absolute finality that is startling to our age that regards everything as relative." (Pp. 60-61.) Used by permission. Cf. also Gardner's article "Ancient Vision and Modern Yardstick," *American Bar Association Journal,* Jan., 1953. Cf. also *The Spirit of Jewish Law,* by George Horowitz, Central Book Co., N. Y.

in terms of the historic accuracy of a record but of its individual and social practicability. Sentimentalized "history" may be more dramatic, but the realization of the development of the divine intention in a particular type of person, living in a particular type of society, is the ultimate credential of our ethical system.

How does it happen that the moral ideals of Vishnu—the tradition is older than Moses—or of Marduk, or of the bull god of Canaan, have not supplied us the rules by which we are to deal with our fellows or the rubrics by which we address ourselves to the Deity? It is not enough to say that the Ten Commandments were spoken by the Almighty God and that the demand of Vishnu for sacrificial victims is the perversion of the soul of man by a false god. Our answers must rest on deeper levels, even though in exposing these levels we find things that do not fit easily within the patterns of much conventional thinking about the matter.

CHAPTER I

The Right to Command

BEFORE we can address ourselves to the specific commands in the Decalogue, it is necessary to consider in some detail two matters: What right did God have to lay down the rules by which man and society were to be governed? What right did man have to abdicate his freedom to make his own rules? The easy answer to the first is that of the Psalmist: "Let us kneel before the Lord our maker. For he is our God; and we are the people of his pasture, and the sheep of his hand." (Ps. 95:6-7.) Here is equated the right to command with the right of possession. This poetic expression is one that has long been cherished for its simplicity and picturesqueness, but as a statement of the reason for God commanding and man following it is unsatisfactory. If man is as docile as a sheep—which he rarely is—and if his regulation is no more complex than shepherding—which it never is—we might accept the poet's charming explanation. Furthermore the fact is clearly true that in the realm of personal and social behavior man in his unregenerate state does not *belong* to God. His difficulty lies just there. It is of the essence of moral action that it is the result of self-will. It is uncoerced; it is the act of one who is convinced that he owns himself and can do as he likes.

1

It is interesting at this point to remember that comparisons between the Babylonian Code and the Hebrew Code show an important difference. Those who wrote the laws of the former were political rulers. Their concern was largely with the regulation of economic and political affairs. The prosperity of Babylon had to be maintained, and penalties were condign and severe when there was heedlessness or defiance. The Hebrew lawmakers were priests. Melchizedek was both the "king of Salem" and the "priest of the most high God" (Gen. 14:18). Moses, scorned as prince and judge by the quarreling men who, as he sought to separate them, identified him as the slayer of an Egyptian the day before, regarded himself as a priest after he became son-in-law to Jethro, the priest of Midian. There is an element in the formulation of the Hebrew law that is, for this reason, distinctly religious. The fact that in the Exod. 20 account of the Decalogue penalties are not attached, though consequences both good and bad are predicted, indicates a humaneness lacking in the codes of the forerunners and the contemporaries of the Hebrew people, a humaneness that stems directly from a religious sense.

Moses was a lawgiver though it is difficult to trace his influence in the code as we have it in its present form. But his sense of God seems to have been very deep. It is said of him that he renounced royal status in order to become the leader of Yahweh's disorganized and tatterdemalion people. His face lit up with ecstasy in the presence of God, he could burn with fury at the infidelity of the people, and he was willing to have his own life blotted out if his rebellious charges could thereby be saved from destruction. This sounds little like the reactions of a political ruler; it sounds very much like the anxieties of a compassionate man. What made the difference?

It was more than temperament. The codes of Babylon and Sinai were not different because of so superficial a circumstance. The cause and the significance lay in the fact of covenant. God's right to command lay in an agreement into which he and the Hebrew people had been drawn.

So important a relation is this that the code should have had, we might suppose, a clear statement in a sort of preamble. One thinks of the paragraph that introduces the Declaration of Independence wherein was set forth the right of the colonies to institute government and to lay "its foundation on such principles and [organize] its powers in such form, as to them shall seem most likely to effect their Safety and Happiness." The fact is, however, that the covenant relation, while definitive, is vaguely understood and recorded. The Ten Commandments begin with a resounding reminder that it was the God who had fetched the Hebrew children out of the bondage of Egypt who was talking. It does not say that this was the result of a pact between him and them. Indeed it was not long before the reluctance some had felt in leaving their bonds became a general murmuring and a rebellious nostalgia for the fleshpots they had bartered for the dubious freedom of the wilderness.

2

The word "covenant" (*beriyth*) is used extensively in the Bible to describe agreements of various sorts. It occurs first in the story of Noah's emergence from the ark to survey the dry face of the ground upon which he was to make a new beginning. The burnt offering he made as his first ritual act was pleasant to the nostrils of Yahweh, who promised never again to bring plenary destruction upon the earth because "the imagination of man's heart is evil from his youth." This was less a compact than a promise. Nothing was exacted of Noah either for himself or for his seed. Yahweh appeared in a mood of ruefulness over what had been done to the earth, and to assure Noah that his new efforts were not to be aborted by a repeat performance, he told him: "I do set my bow in the cloud, and it shall be for a token of a covenant between me and the earth" (Gen. 9:13). There is even the quaint suggestion that Yahweh felt the need of a reminder quite as much as Noah, if not more. "And the bow shall be in the cloud; and I will look upon it, that I may remember the everlasting covenant between God and every living creature of all flesh that is upon the earth." (Gen. 9:16.)

This was clearly not a legal contract, much less a moral one. It was a promise of immunity from destruction and applied no less to all flesh than to Noah. Noah may have felt for the moment some moral compunctions about presuming too generously upon it, though something in his later experience as a viniculturist sullied the good reputation he had made as a mariner. But moral concerns could not have bothered "every living creature of all flesh that is upon the earth" to which the rainbow was cited as a guarantee against their extermination also.

The next time the word is encountered it has moved from the

broad area of a simple promise to the narrower confines of an agreement, though the terms are still unexplicit. Abram, we are told in the seventeenth chapter of Genesis, verse one, at the age of ninety-nine was accosted by Jehovah who, after identifying himself, admonished him thus: "Walk before me, and be thou perfect." This was followed by a promise, in verse two: "I will make my covenant between me and thee, and will multiply thee exceedingly." The assumption is that Abram considered the compact a reasonable one for he fell on his face in assent, whereupon his name was changed to Abraham, signifying that he stood in a new relation to the purposes of the Almighty.

Beyond the demand for perfection, which we agree was formidable enough even though it was matched by a promise to make him the sire of kings and nations, the moral aspects of the compact are vague. Furthermore, instead of a rainbow as proof of God's faithfulness to Noah, Abraham was required to accept the rite of circumcision as proof of his fidelity. This was as painful a portent as the rainbow was beautiful. Nor is there any confidence as to what its significance was, moral or otherwise. We know it to have been a custom widely practiced in the ancient world among peoples earlier than the Hebrews and that today primitive tribes in South America and Africa perform the operation with pretentious ritual accompaniment. Its symbolism, however, is never identified with moral connotations. In other words, the demand that Abraham be circumcised had nothing to do with the demand that he be perfect. As a tribal badge, as a test of the courage of a neophyte being initiated into the group, as a matter of hygiene, or as preparation for connubium it has had meaning; but as part of a code of conduct for which Yahweh was to offer fabulous compensation to Abraham and his descendants it seems to be insignificant. Obviously Moses himself was unimpressed by any moral connotations in this covenant symbol and risked his life by neglecting to have his own son circumcised. Zipporah, his wife, saved the situation by performing the operation with a flint. This has been taken by some scholars to indicate a very early age for the tradition, putting it back into an age before even scalpels were made of bronze. Whatever may be thought of that, it is clear (cf. Gen. 17:14) that ostracism was the fate of the uncircumcised male because by failing to have accepted that symbol he had denied covenant with God.

3

We still have not come upon the precise terms of contract, but that it was concerned with a moral medium if not specifically with moral maxims is intimated by our next encounter with the word. For reasons that shall engage us later, the observance of the Sabbath was of more importance than the simple matter of physical relaxation. The Sabbath is described as a perpetual covenant, and the penalty for its breach was death. This was such radical treatment that one wonders what undisclosed reasons explain it. The only clue to be had from the passage (Exod. 31:12-17) indicates that the day was thought to be holy and was designated as a sign. Here sign is similar to token, the word that describes the symbolic value of the rainbow. Holiness, however, is an advance on simple symbolism and is the first suggestion we have of the spiritual significance of covenant. For holy is a word descriptive of a quality higher than the symbolism of rainbow and the rite of circumcision. If it is not specifically moral, it is certainly religious in its suggestion.

There is one more reference that brings us closer to what we seek. A gruesome story (Num. 25:1-14) tells about a strange moral prophylaxis that abated a plague that had already taken 24,000 victims in the camp of Israel. Phinehas, grandson of Aaron, observed an Israelite dallying in the company of a Midianite woman in front of the congregation while the people were weeping for the bitterness of the epidemic in the camp. He made of this casual alliance a symbol of the sin of the tribe and following the pair into the pavilion, drove a spear through them. This abated the horrid epidemic and won for Phinehas an everlasting distinction. Yahweh is reported as having told Moses that the act of Phinehas was godlike: "he was jealous with my jealousy." As a reward he was given God's covenant of peace, and to his seed was granted "the covenant of an everlasting priesthood." Here the idea of covenant is symbolized by a unique relation to Yahweh, a priestly rank that carried with it the ritual responsibilities of the order.

By the time the nomads had been a little more than two years in the wilderness, the covenant was represented in what was called an ark. This was a sort of cabinet within which sacred articles were kept and which was a talisman for the success of Israel in her conflicts with other tribes, as well as the sign of God's presence. That it was thought to have magic powers is clear from the stories that are told about it, but its chief meaning was the symbol of the proximity of Yahweh. Thus the ark of the covenant was added to the other symbols that had in one way or another come to stand for the agreement between God and his people.

4

We must be careful not to regard the sequence of the covenant symbols sketched here as an actual record of the development of the covenant idea. It is altogether possible that there were other symbols and that many such efforts to externalize the fact of the compact were employed simultaneously. What we see is, not so much the development of an idea in terms of a series of symbols, as the enlargement of an idea in a series of relationships. There is very little logic in the development of a rainbow into an ark, passing through the intermediate stages of circumcision, a day of rest, and a priestly rank to be held in perpetuity. At the same time there appears to be an enlargement of the compass of the covenant idea. It began in a portent in the sky, the half arc of the rainbow, but a symbol void of any moral reference. It grew into a more complete circumference, each segment of which seemed to pick up more and more of moral suggestion as it developed. The full round provides us with the unique factor in all the law of Israel.

God's right to command lay ultimately in the belief of these simple folk in the fact and importance of God, though, to begin with, their ideas about him must have differed quantitatively very little from their neighbors. It was the quality of moralness in their God that was important if not indeed determinative. All religions can be said to have at least three strata in their composition. The upper and most obvious level contains their writings, their ritual observances, their institutions, and their priests. Beneath that, and less visible even to their votaries, are their history, their distinctive ideas, and their mysteries. On the lowest level rest the compulsions that stir the individual and the group to action, and that unite them against assaults of propaganda or trespass. It is on this third level that is found the essence of faith. Not faith in a formalized sense that satisfies the mind, but faith in a compelling sense that directs behavior. It is, in other words, the moral depth of religion and will be found to express itself in various ways, as often by symbol and token as by the formal dictum. John Morley, when Great Britain was threatening the tiny Boer republic of South Africa, warned his countrymen in a speech at Manchester:

You may carry fire and sword into the midst of peace and industry: it will be wrong. A war of the strongest government in the world with untold wealth and inexhaustible reserves against this little republic will bring you no glory: it will be wrong. You may make thousands of women widows, and thousands of children fatherless: it will be wrong. It may add a new province to your empire: it will be wrong.[1]

Morley was not a professing Christian, but his mind reacted toward this proposed policy of his country in terms of the moral depths that lay beneath the surface manifestations of a Christianity to which he did not subscribe.

Part of this moral factor is the belief that human actions stand in relation to some transcendent order of judgment which rewards or penalizes them. No act stands in moral isolation. The refinements through which this idea has passed constitute the record of the growth of the moral conscience in our culture. To begin with, it was crude. The ox that killed a man had to be stoned. This was not alone to protect others against further caprice of bovine irresponsibility; it was to punish the beast for misbehaving. Seen in its proper perspective this is an important reaction. In the words of Morley it was wrong, and what is wrong is punished.

The exaction of penalty as a social utility may be something quite different from reward and retribution in a moral order. In the former the offense is regarded as against the group, the tribe, the nation; in the latter it is against an order that is superior to all the fortuitous groupings in which men find themselves. It may be simple humaneness that dictates the law and fixes the consequence. Here humanity is regarded as more important than group and a man is dealt with because he is a man. It may be a simple ethical norm

---

[1] Quoted by George W. Davis in "Liberalism and a Theology of Depth," *Crozer Quarterly*, July, 1951. Quoted by permission.

that is superior even to the claims of humanity. Albert Schweitzer has made reverence for life—all life—the basis of his own profound moral responsiveness to the world of his experience. Again it may be an elaborate and complex codification of all man's actual and possible reactions to moral situations and a scrupulous effort to make reparation for damaged eye and tooth both exact and satisfying.

5

What I am saying is that the idea of covenant as it arose within the primitive culture of Israel provided and supported a moral awareness that lay at the heart of its moral code. This is the factor that distinguishes it from codes that were contemporary to it and from which there were inevitable borrowings. This is also what makes the morality of Western culture unique, and though this judgment is given in advance of my argument, it is this factor alone that is our hope of the survival of our Western moral ethos in the face of its present-day assailants.

We cannot be sure that our moral apprehensions have reached the ultimate in depth or in utility. Room must be left for the growth of our souls in the direction of the perfection to which Abram was directed. The rainbow is for us no longer the assurance of man's covenant with God; nor is circumcision, or a priesthood, or an ark. Nor was it thus with the Hebrew people as they developed in their apprehension of God and their moral responsibilities to him. Nothing is clearer than this in the record of the development of the covenant idea in later Hebrew thought.[2]

It is obvious that the covenant did not hold fast. God was endlessly reminding his people that he had not broken his agreement even when calamity overwhelmed them. Indeed this was the exercise of the responsibilities that his contract had laid upon him. It was the prophet Jeremiah (626-585 B.C.) whose concern over the repudiation of the covenant led to a refinement of the idea that has hardly been improved upon since his day. Not only had the covenant been openly flouted; the men of Judah and Jerusalem were no longer inclined to listen to it. Jeremiah puts it characteristically:

[2] Jews (today) put the greatest stress on the covenant idea as expressed in Deut.: e.g., 26:18; 29:1, 12. It is repeated in every service and taught as *the* specific and permanent covenant (pact). N.H.

The word that came to Jeremiah from Jehovah, saying, Hear ye the words of this covenant, and speak unto the men of Judah, and to the inhabitants of Jerusalem; and say thou unto them, Thus saith Jehovah, the God of Israel: Cursed be the man that heareth not the words of this covenant, which I commanded your fathers in the day that I brought them forth out of the land of Egypt, out of the iron furnace, saying, Obey my voice, and do them, according to all which I command you: so shall ye be my people, and I will be your God; that I may establish the oath which I sware unto your fathers, to give them a land flowing with milk and honey, as at this day. (Jer. 11:1-5.)

The response of Jeremiah to this is without equivocation. With vigorous and assertive piety the record states: "Then answered I, and said, Amen, O Jehovah."

Jeremiah was not going back on the covenant, and he got himself into epic difficulties because he kept thundering at those who had. It was to one so completely committed to the covenant that a deeper insight into the covenant relation was vouchsafed. We observe that in the speech quoted above, the word "covenant" is used as a synonym for command. It would seem therefore that by the time of Jeremiah the transition from the early symbols of the covenant to law as the symbol had been clearly made. No longer did the seers and prophets talk of rainbows and arks, and the great insight for which Jeremiah was primarily if not initially responsible was the transference of the law (covenant) from an external matter to an inner one (conscience). "This people hath a revolting and a rebellious heart; they are revolted and gone." (Jer. 5:23.) Set this over against the great word in 9:23-24: "Thus saith Jehovah, Let not the wise man glory in his wisdom, neither let the mighty man glory in his might, let not the rich man glory in his riches; but let him that glorieth glory in this, that he hath understanding, and knoweth *me*, that I am Jehovah who exerciseth lovingkindness, justice, and righteousness, in the earth: for in these things I delight."

He has come a long way from Noah and the rainbow, from Zipporah and the bloody flint. He represents Yahweh as saying, "All the house of Israel are uncircumcised in heart" (9:26); and it is this fresh emphasis upon the heart as the locus of the covenant that has won for Jeremiah the name of *the* prophet. For it is the heart that comprehends lovingkindness, as it is the mind that apprehends justice and the will that asserts the necessity of righteousness.

Jeremiah's greatest statement of the matter is found elsewhere. "Behold, the days come, saith Jehovah, that I will make a new covenant with the house of Israel, and with the house of Judah: not according to the covenant that I made with their fathers in the day that I took them by the hand to bring them out of the land of Egypt; which my covenant they brake, although I was a husband unto them, saith Jehovah." (31:31-32.) Note here another symbolism for the covenant relation. It is similar to that employed by Hosea.

But this is the covenant that I will make with the house of Israel after those days, saith Jehovah: I will put my law in their inward parts, and in their heart will I write it; and I will be their God, and they shall be my people. And they shall teach no more every man his neighbor, . . . saying, Know Jehovah; for they shall all know me, from the least of them unto the greatest of them, saith Jehovah: for I will forgive their iniquity, and their sin will I remember no more. (Jer. 31:33-34.)

Covenant has become conscience; the bow in the sky that promised the earth protection against the devastations of another deluge has become the promise of forgiveness; instead of the ark, the repository of magic symbols, the heart has been opened to the knowledge of God, and instead of an excruciating physical rite is a "law in their inward parts."

6

This understanding of man's moral relationship to God is familiar to those who are within the Christian tradition, and numerous citations will come readily to mind in support of it. It is exactly this familiarity that has dulled our sensitivity to the enormous development that was accomplished between man's first intimations of such relationships and the revelation of them that has come to us through Jesus Christ. To Moses circumcision was a mandate not to be disregarded except at the risk of one's life. To Paul, who could call himself a Hebrew of the Hebrews, "neither circumcision availeth anything, nor uncircumcision; but faith working through love" (Gal. 5:6). That was written to a little enclave of Christian Jews who were for the moment "bewitched" by the idea that the older covenant relations still held for those who had entered the fellowship of Christ. Some of Paul's contemporaries thought this was heresy, but one can imagine that Jeremiah would have found the idea altogether congenial.

Now it is this that provided God with his credentials for command. It is the commonest of experiences that sees one who assumes the prerogative of issuing orders being asked to show his right to do so. Diplomas and certificates decorate the walls of the offices of the doctors to whom we go for orders about pains and pills, and the druggist who compounds the pills takes pains to assure us by his license that he knows what he is up to. It is the insignia of our rank, whether we are in the army, the classroom, the bank, the sheriff's office, or on the bridge of a ship, that we appeal to as our right to order others about. It is therefore nothing to be angry about if in our time we, as the advocates of the Christian moral system, are asked to show the certificate of its authority.

We must be sure about it when we are asked. As I have been saying, this core of ethical idealism that we call the Ten Commandments has so long been unchallenged that we are not very well prepared to defend it for reasons other than its great and venerable age. The history of Israel, so far as it can be put together, is written within the framework of her faithfulness or her infidelity to the law of God. When good fortune attended her, it was reward for the nation's probity; and her poets were quick to point out that this was as obvious to her enemies as it was gratifying to herself. When things fared ill for her, it was due to her faithlessness; and her misery was the judgment of God upon her. It was not always as easy, to be sure, to see and admit the latter; but her most sensitive spokesmen said so.

Today we do not write history within the framework of moral struggle. This need not be attributed entirely to the Marxist influence in historical interpretation. At the same time all secular historians are for the most part as little likely to understand history moralistically as are the Marxists. There is a superciliousness that regards moralizing within the strict historic disciplines as naïveté. The Marxist analysis and prediction of history have no place for the moral factor, as we have understood the words. History is an amoral dialectical struggle between materialist forces concreted sometimes in groups and sometimes in things. When non-Marxist historians

35

agree with the adversary in throwing out the moral factor, they are left with less to explain human vagaries than the Marxists are.

This is no plea for sentimental history. It must be agreed that the subtleties of moral experience make it exceedingly difficult to assess it as a determinative factor. Thus some fall into the pit of sheer sentimentality. This was true of the record keepers of Israel and is one reason why modern historical research has such difficulty in dissecting the true story out of the plexus of moralizing and emotionalism. While all this is true, it should not be allowed to push us into the opposite morass. To those who believe that the meaning of life is to be seen in the value and creativity of those moral actions it can evoke, there is an obligation to guard against letting dialectical materialism establish our values and chart our course.

History is the story of individual personalities confronting God and each other as units or as groups. Before one fact can be attached to another in a record of events, account must be taken of the things that constitute personality. Every man brings the sum total of his ideas, feelings, hopes, ideals, to every experience. Bringing these often contradictory elements into some sort of integrated pattern is the moral struggle within him; bringing this integrated pattern into some sort of harmony—or disharmony as the case may be—is the moral struggle outside him. And the disorder into which these so-called orders can so easily fall is the basic cause for a pessimistic view of the human drama today.

We cannot, for all this, abdicate our responsibility to justify the ways of God to men in moral terms or to insist that God's right to command rests on moral presuppositions. Fortunately this point of view is being stoutly advocated by certain modern historians who have seen the debacle of the last half century as a moral one. The approach of Arnold Toynbee to his *Study of History* is well enough known. That what has befallen certain modern nations is of the nature of the moral judgment is powerfully argued by a professor of modern history in Cambridge:

If Germany came under judgment, then the ancient Russia did the same, meeting a doom more terrible, more swift, more assuredly permanent than that of Germany herself. . . . It is a dangerous illusion to imagine that if Germany can be proved to have sinned those who were fighting against her may be assumed to have been righteous. We are hoaxing ourselves if we think that because judgment came upon Germany through the victory of our arms, we—being the instruments of God in this matter—may count ourselves as having qualified for virtue; or as having even found special favour in His sight. If such an argument were valid God must have a great and unusual favour for Communism, which, besides being the chief beneficiary in two world wars, could outbid us in the claim to have been the most terrible instrument of Divine judgment in our generation. But the truth is that a God who could use even the Philistines in order to chastise His chosen people may similarly use us for the purpose of chastening Germany, while reserving for us a terrible judgment later. Indeed you cannot introduce the idea of judgment into history without quickly meeting with situations of a paradoxical kind.[3]

This is anything but sentimentality; it is the grounding of all human experience upon a moral foundation under the judgment of God. It was this, I have been trying to say, that the earliest code makers of our cultural forebears recognized as God's right to command. As is the habit of the primitive mind, it expressed this giant concept in symbols—rainbow, rite, ark, priesthood, and no doubt many others—but it always recognized that these symbols represented a covenant between God and his people. He had a right to command; he had the right to judge. This stands out boldly over against the known codes of all other early cultures. To forfeit it today would be to abandon the ethical stream alongside which our culture has for twenty-five centuries built its huts and palaces, its temples and its market places.

I asked another question at the beginning of this chapter: What right has man to abdicate his freedom to the point of allowing God to order him around? This too must be answered.

[3] Herbert Butterfield, *Christianity and History* (New York: Charles Scribner's Sons, 1950), p. 52. Used by permission.

CHAPTER II

Man Meets God

IN THE Greek myth of Prometheus and Pandora we discover an interesting attempt by the most sophisticated imagination of the ancient world to dramatize the creation of man. After tidying up the primeval chaos made by gods whose identity unhappily is lost, Prometheus undertook to create a being capable of keeping the created earth in respectable order. He took a handful of earth, moistened it with a proper amount of water, and kneaded it into an image of the gods. The distinguishing characteristic of this image was his upright stature, which enabled him to keep his eyes on the stars while the other animals were forced immutably to look downward forever toward the earth.

Epimetheus, the brother of Prometheus, was responsible for endowing all the creatures with the faculties they needed for survival. Acordingly he dealt out with such prodigal generosity the qualities of courage, swiftness, cunning, wings, talons, and fangs to the lower animals that he had nothing left with which to equip man, destined to be the greatest of the creatures. Minerva, who was the goddess of wisdom, came to the aid of the baffled god and accompanied by Prometheus went up to heaven and lit his torch for him at the chariot of the sun. Whereupon he fetched back the fire, which was promptly turned over to man. This gift made man more than a match for the other animals. He could make weapons with which to subdue them, tools for cultivating the ground; he could warm his dwelling, cook his food, mold coins, and set himself up in business.

Epimetheus received his wife, Pandora, ready-made and lavishly endowed, direct from heaven. She was the composite product of all the creative arts of Venus, Mercury, Apollo, and other nameless gods who wanted to have a hand in the enterprise. Finally she was conveyed to earth and delivered to Epimetheus who in the meantime had been warned by his brother that Jupiter, angered by the theft of fire, might bear watching the next time he turned up with a gift for earth's denizens. It was while Pandora was staying in the house of Epimetheus that she chanced upon a sealed jar within which her chaperon and sponsor had secreted some compounds unused in the process of performing his creative chores. Her curiosity was not satisfied until she broke the cover open and looked inside. Forthwith there escaped all the evils that had been discarded as unnecessary for the making of man: gout, colic, envy, spite, vengefulness, fear, guilt. Before she could clap the lid on the jar, all these noxious things had escaped. Only one thing was not gone. Epimetheus never explained why he had left it out of the man Prometheus had given him to equip, but it was discovered at the bottom of the jar. It was hope. The moral, so the Greek tellers of tales said, was that no matter what evils have been released into the world by the curiosity of man's wife, she can always reassure her unhappy spouse in times of depression that there is still hope if he'll only look for it in the right place.

1

This is only one of the stories that men have told in order to satisfy the questions that have agitated their minds. For this reason myth is very often shot through with insight. Intimations of what have later come to be accepted as solid fact abound in all ancient lore. In its limited way myth shares with legend and folk wisdom the honor of carrying along the vessel into which the truth of man's experience is dropped, bit by bit. For all its whimsy, it adds to the sum total of the things the probing mind of the race is trying to find out about itself.

There were many, we may assume, who moved about the limited areas of the Eastern Mediterranean world in the time of Moses to whom such tales as that of man and his inquisitive Pandora were altogether satisfying. It is important to realize that while the legal lore of the contemporaries of the Hebrew people was borrowed and

adapted and set within the moral framework described in the foregoing chapter, the cosmology of her neighbors was less available to
her use. This is not to say that other known myths about creation and
the flood, for example, do not exhibit parallels with the biblical stories. It says simply—and subject to some qualifications—that while
in Greek thought we encounter mythology, in Hebrew thought we
meet theology. This calls for explanation.

Strictly speaking, theology is what its root components say it is:
the branch of religious science that treats of God. If this were practically possible, by which we mean if it were possible to treat of God
alone, it would be the most technical and specialized of disciplines.
The fact is, however, that God cannot be thought of in isolation,
much less studied thus. The Greeks tried to make their gods into
creatures that lived their lives separate from the world of men. They
had a great time doing this but couldn't make them keep their
distance. The gods were forever invading the human scene and often
behaved so scandalously that it was not always easy to extenuate or
explain their conduct. The reason for the invasion of the gods of
Greek myth into the precincts of the mortals is easy to see. Man
cannot think about God without, by some irresistible impulse, making
him a part of human experience. This is another way of saying that
our knowledge of God is subjective. That is not all it says, for it
also includes the fact that the core of this subjective experience is the
confidence that it is also the experience of an object. The effort of
theologians and philosophers to objectify God as the scientist objecti-
fies the sun, thinking of him as Will, or as Idea, or as something else,
has not been successful. And the reason for this failure lies, we think,
in the fact that God is known in and by experience, even, it might
be added, as the sun intrudes upon the astronomer's telescope as light
and into his room as warmth.

We shall never divide between idea and experience in our treatment
of God. This should not dismay us, for what it costs us in unclearness
of thought, it repays us in the intimacy of fellowship. Though this
may be regarded as a prejudiced opinion, it is not a strange one. There
is no culture that has developed a vital religious element that has not
regarded its gods or God as having close contact with common men
and women. To be sure, this has left the door open for the entrance
of the abuses of superstition and low religious practice; but men, by

and large, will respond more readily to a God though dimly seen or mistakenly apprehended but intimately felt than to a God who is merely a concept, no matter how clearly his outlines stand forth to the inquiring mind or how blazingly his illumination falls upon the up-lifted eye.

2

This is both the challenge and the hazard of all man's thinking about religion. One can never relax his vigilance against making a god out of one's experience or out of values for which one has a peculiar fondness. Similarly one must be careful lest the relation he has to the Divine is that of a premise to a conclusion in a syllogism. God, it has often been said, is more than logic: he is life. It might be simpler for finite human minds if it were otherwise, but if it were otherwise, he would not be God.

If we move forward from this, we find ourselves confronted by two major questions: What has God to do with man, and what has man to do with himself because of God? The second of these questions has already been put in the previous chapter in a different form. What right does man have to abdicate his privilege to command him-self to the commands of something external to himself? This, in the Genesis myth, is one of the first problems man and his woman wrestled with. There was a tree forbidden to them in the garden given to them to tend. Why was it given but denied? It was good of itself, and it promised knowledge. Why should not its fruit be tasted? Was not this also the problem of Pandora? Why should she not look into the sealed jar? And is it not the problem of everyone today? In terms of the Mandate to Humanity why should we be under any compulsion to follow it? Do I not abdicate the very element in me that makes me important both to God and myself, namely my free right to choose the fruit of any tree, if I allow him to tell me what I may and may not do?

In the light of these questions man's confrontation by God, as preserved for us in the story in Exod. 19, is interesting. Those of the wilderness tribe who had escaped from Egypt in a bold but not unusual revolt knew authority in its most crushing form. Their life as bondsmen to the Pharaoh was not under law; it was under the caprice of a monarch whom caprice could render hard or soft as the occasion demanded. The experience of Moses as a member of the royal menage is not known. Just what influences turned him against the palace and toward a ghetto of slaves is similarly obscure. It may have been sheer prudence. Identified as the murderer of an Egyptian he may have had to flee for his life, though princes through the ages have maintained a vested prerogative in homicide that is beyond the reach of the common man's resentment or vengeance. On the other hand his concern for the exploited man may have sprung from a genuinely humanitarian or even religious impulse, an impulse that was both sharpened and deepened when he identified their freedom with his own.

The authority the children of Israel had known was heavy and relentless. When Moses confronted the Pharaoh with the demand "Let my people go," he was asserting in the name of Yahweh an authority that was equally determined. Little wonder there was jockeying between king and renegade prince; the wonder rather is that the prince was not liquidated as the subversive he unquestionably was. In the final moment the slave people were not granted their freedom. Timing their revolt skillfully with an epidemic that had reached all the way to the palace and stricken the heir apparent, they escaped in the night across the marshes that separated Egypt from the wilderness southwest of Canaan and improvised their bivouac under the direction of their new leader.

The growth—if that is the proper word to describe it—of the God-awareness of Moses is another factor in this magnificent saga that is hidden from us. The desert priest Jethro, who sheltered him and gave him his first wife, could have given him very little guidance, if indeed any at all, in the direction of what would today be called theological education. The God he knew and worshiped was a pale intimation of what Moses was to confront in the wilderness, even as the God of Moses is a pale portent of the "train [that] filled the temple" before the eyes of Isaiah. Whatever the process, the result is not in doubt. The authority of the King of Egypt under which Moses had grown up was displeased by the authority of the God of Jethro, the Flame that burned but did not consume, the Voice that commanded and permitted no refusal.

3

For this reason the drama caught in a single verse in the story of the introduction of the People to God is, in its own way, nothing short of spectacular. "And it came to pass on the third day, when it was morning, that there were thunders and lightnings, and a thick cloud upon the mount, and the voice of a trumpet exceeding loud." How often the sound of a trumpet has heralded the approach of authority! "And all the people that were in the camp trembled. *And Moses brought forth the people out of the camp to meet God;* and they stood at the nether part of the mount." (Exod. 19:16-17.)

All necessary allowance is made for the literary quality of the record, but nothing can take from it the sheer drama caught in the picture of Moses leading his frightened charges to a rendezvous with the Eternal. Was there ever a more fateful meeting? Only recently rescued from the tyranny of an earthly monarch, they were led forth to make the acquaintance of their new suzerain, whose credentials were not the whips of the taskmasters by the Nile but thunder and lightning flash about the summit of the mount that had become for the nonce their wilderness shelter.

This is important for us not simply as the story of an experience hidden in antiquity but as the story of the experience of every man and every group since the beginning of time. This may seem to be an extravagant claim, but it is not one difficult to support. It is not said that every man and every group goes to the same smoking shrine and meets the same Deity and has from him the same thundering word. It does say that in some way at some time man the creature meets God the Creator. The introduction may be made in various ways, and the results of the meeting may be similarly varied. But it is, we believe, one of the determinative facts of history that man, to use the words of the text, is led forth out of the camp to meet God. The camp may be the surroundings to which he has become accustomed or even the habits to which he is bound. In one way or another, and in one time or another, man meets God. This is definitive.

4

What was it in the experience of Moses that induced him to accept this fateful agency? There are those who say he was compensating both for a sense of guilt and for a feeling of inferiority. Such modern diggings into the psyche of a legendary figure toss up ideas that we incline to dismiss summarily, but they are not altogether without value. Every great leader in world history has had something uncommon in his make-up that has produced the dimensions by which he has been identified. Moses was, we are told, the son of an unnamed member of the house of Levi. His mother is identified. The ruse by which her foundling babe was transformed into a prince and herself into a nurse in the royal household is a charming story and indicates, perhaps, something more than the protective impulse of a mother.

Clearly in the years when his mother was his nurse and later his tutor, he was given secrets that would have been judged seditious had his foster mother known of them. His true mother built up in him a resentment against the injustices that her people suffered. The conflict between the natural satisfactions provided him as a prince in a palace and the sufferings of the people to whom his attachment was more ideal than real must have been considerable. The picture of it is clear in the story of his murder of the Egyptian gang boss. It was an act of precipitate violence of a restless and divided mind. One wonders how he felt that evening when he returned to his quarters in the palace with blood on his hands. The next day the story was out. Recognized as a prince by two quarreling Hebrews, he was also identified as a murderer. It was not long until Pharaoh heard the report and "sought to slay Moses. But Moses fled from the face of Pharaoh, and dwelt in the land of Midian: and he sat down by a well." (Exod. 2:15.)

The hospitality of the desert shepherds was adequate asylum for the fugitive, and though taken from an Egyptian by the seven shepherdess daughters of Reuel, his chivalrous defense of them and their flocks when interlopers sought to drive them from the water hole won him their gratitude and one of the girls as wife. It was a strange contrast, we may assume, between his recent life as a prince in the palace and this new experience as a member of a shepherd family in the wilderness. With his recollection of an Egyptian dead by his hands and his never-absent fear of detection, one wonders if Zipporah ever startled him from a moment of reverie and was puzzled at his touchiness or his incoherent answer to the playful question she put about the object of his dream or the reason for his sullenness.

It is not, after all, farfetched to think that he was tortured by a sense of guilt. He was a renegade from his people and an apostate to all his mother-nurse had taught him. He had been radically reduced in status, from prince to shepherd. Could he not easily have yielded to the floods of self-pity that are never altogether securely impounded in one's soul? It was to such a man that Yahweh's angel appeared in a flame of fire out of the midst of a bush, to such a person that a voice came calling his name. The portent and the sound were real enough, and the first directive to the wondering, waiting man was to keep his distance. Now he was in the presence of the God of the people he had failed—Abraham, Isaac, and Jacob. "And Moses hid his face; for he was afraid to look upon God. (Exod. 3:6.) Little wonder.

It is unnecessary to introduce further details in the experience of this man who is said to be Israel's first lawgiver. What has been said here is relevant to the general proposition that every man at some time and in a way that is both uniquely and privately his own confronts God. For Moses it meant a final break with the past; both the palace and the pasture were never to see him again except as he defied his one-time royal kinsman who had risen to Egypt's throne, and as he was visited by his herdsmen during forty anxious years of desert wanderings. For him the meeting with God was radical in a very real sense.

5

If evidence of this were needed, it could be had in the simple fact that in spite of the reluctance he confessed and must have deeply felt, Moses finally made his way back to the court of the king and demanded that he release a considerable segment of the working force on which he had depended for the erection of public works. That the demand was made in the name of Yahweh was unimpressive to the monarch, but to Moses it was the heart of the issue. The slaves of Pharaoh were the people of Yehweh. They were, so to speak, expropriated property; and Moses, who had once been a fugitive from the palace, had returned to demand justice for the wretched denizens of the ghetto by the Nile. This took courage of epic dimensions, and Moses' reputation would have been secure if it had had nothing else for support.

The point to consider, however, is not the display of courage but the evidence of a sense of the reality, the immediacy, and the authority of Yahweh. The past had been engulfed in the turgid flood of the present. The power of the Egyptian king had been dwarfed by the majesty of the Deity who had spoken from the flaming bush. The commission to lead God's people to freedom was more pressing than Moses' prudent wish to stay out of reach of those who had once sought him as a murderer. Against every natural impulse to keep free forever of the past, he delivered himself into the bondage of the Almighty for an unpredictable future.

Now it is hardly realistic to think that Moses' assumption of leadership was simply a romantic adventure of a bold man. Nor can we escape the feeling that when in the quaint language of the record, he "brought forth the people out of the camp to meet God," he was bringing them into an experience not unlike his own. In other words what had happened to Moses was to happen to the people he had rescued. God had introduced himself to Moses at the base of the mountain of Gad in Horeb; Moses was to introduce the people to God at the foot of Mount Sinai.

To be sure, we read of much taking place between the exodus from Egypt and the introduction at Sinai; and in not a little of it the suggestion is clear that the people had in various ways been made aware of the agency of God in the routine by which they were fed and guided on their journeyings. But to meet God as the chief commissary officer who could supply manna and quail when other provisions were short was something quite different from meeting Yahweh, whose concern was more with the law than with the larder. And this for the reason that it is a simple matter to accept food for the body from whatever source, but it is far from simple to accept for the totality of man's life moral orders from one central authority.

Indeed we think we have here the nub of the struggle between man and God and the secret of the alliance that can be made between man and God. It provides us with the answer to our question about man's right to abdicate his freedom to do as he pleases to an authority that commands him to do what, as often as not, he may not please to do. To put it in another way: To meet God means to confront the ultimate authority with which man has to deal. It is the question of freedom and authority, and that it lies at the heart of this episode that describes God meeting the people indicates that the question has been around a long time.

6

The enthusiasm with which the children of Israel greeted their newly-won freedom did not last very long. For a moment they had been given recess from making bricks with or without straw. But freedom from excess of anything does not promise full freedom to follow. Freedom as exemption is the most dangerous of illusions since life in its essence is bondage. Man is bound to the simple necessities of food and drink and shelter, and except in some idyllic Eden these are not to be had save by the exchange of the hard currency of toil. Man is bound to the more complex necessities of companionship and intercourse with his fellows, for to be free of them is to perish in isolation. On a still higher level man is under the pressure of necessities that we describe as spiritual. They may lie in the realm of aesthetics or religion. He may want to deny them, but someday a flaming bush will block his pathway and a voice will prescribe limits beyond which he will not dare to trespass.

This is the heart of the moral problem wherever it is encountered. Moses settled it his own way, and it lies within the intentions of the ancient story to indicate that the people of Israel were confronted with the necessity of settling it their way. To be sure, the moral problem cannot be settled by a group for the individuals that compose it. That is why we are endlessly plagued with the ambivalence of individual and social moralities. Such matters were less clear, perhaps, to the primitives than to ourselves, though we cannot claim that our clarity has brought any conspicuous relief to the difficulties they present.

It was just this that had to be understood, albeit in general and imprecise terms, before the giant proscriptions of the Decalogue could be announced and accepted. Once again we must caution ourselves against reading back into the story factors that were not there or hearing overtones of moral sensitivity that were not actually produced. Still and all, man has a right to abdicate the freedom that is his most precious endowment for only the best of reasons. Minerva, to go back to the Greek myth, had a right to steal fire from the chariot of the sun for only the best of reasons. It was in order to give man the freedom by which he could lay the lesser creatures of earth under his dominion. Within the Hebrew-Christian tradition the processes is reversed: man abdicates his freedom in order that he may come under the dominion of a higher One.

This is the paradox of freedom that is at the heart of the moral system around which our ethical culture has developed. Never wholly understood and never consciously accepted by all, this moral monolith has withstood the erosion of the ages and still stands for those to see who have eyes for such seeing. Man does not find his freedom in independence from his fellows, nor does he guarantee his freedom by autonomy. The only true independence is the independence of death; the only true autonomy is the self-rule of anarchy. The ultimate moral question therefore is what authority will man choose as his dependence. He is free to make that choice. He will go ahead then to decide what authority he chooses as the law by which he shall live. He is free to make this choice also.

I do not think I have stretched the matter by insisting that implicitly this was the experience of Moses and the experience into which he conducted the children of Israel as he brought them forth to meet God.

God's right to be the Chosen, which every man has a right to choose or repudiate, was put to the nomads by the mountain in the lovely language of metaphor. Here there was no place for syllogism or abstract theorizing. God was to be chosen because he had made his choice. The agreement was to be mutual and for cause. "Ye have seen what I did unto the Egyptians, and how I bare you on eagles' wings, and brought you unto myself. Now therefore, if ye will obey my voice indeed, and keep my covenant, then ye shall be mine own possession from among all peoples: for all the earth is mine: and ye shall be unto me a kingdom of priests, and a holy nation. These are the words which thou shalt speak unto the children of Israel." (Exod. 19:4-6.) There is no indication that Moses spoke these words to his charges. They would have been surprised to learn that when they thought they were slogging across the Red Sea marshes in panic flight, they were actually taking a ride on the wings of eagles. Nor do we think that the prospect of becoming a nation of priests would have been particularly inviting. That is a type of classless society that few would choose to live in. Nevertheless God

48

was reminding them of a covenant, something we have already seen was not uniformly understood by them; and he was proposing that they, aware of both the fact and the complexities of a recently won freedom, should give themselves to him. That was the path by which the heights of true freedom were to be reached. Has a better way been found in our times?

7

This is precisely what we are are being told, and it is this that gives urgency to any effort to re-examine the moral grounds on which our culture is established. The confidence that activates Marxist propaganda is, ironically, both like and unlike that which we feel does or should inspire us. Freedom as the Marxists understand the word does not mean either independence or autonomy but the liberty to go along with the mandate of history. This is a pallid concept, for it makes freedom nothing more than bondage to impersonal forces which are directing mortal affairs. Since they are impersonal, they are to be welcomed as no person would be. On the other hand the Marxist idea perverts the Hebrew-Christian truth into a heresy by insisting that the way man wins such dubious freedom as he is entitled to is by being lost in the mass. The state consumes the individual with an insatiable hunger, while the individual achieves fulfillment by the process of depersonalization in the group. This is an imitation—though we cannot call it a cheap one—of the concept we have found at the heart of our ethical system. The difference is clear to those who examine it: individual freedom is a delusion; only the state can be free. Therefore the individual must be compelled to accept life as a discipline imposed by the processes of history that shape the state. Enormous energy has been generated by this perverted gospel, and its evangelists frighten the world. Over against this is the older and wiser understanding of freedom as an indefeasible gift to all men but at the same time an endowment that can reach the dimensions intended for it only by a voluntary surrender of itself to the purposes of him who confers it upon all his children. The difference is definitive, and it opens an unbridgeable abyss between the ethical heartlands of the West and the East.

When therefore Moses brought forth the people to meet God, he was re-enacting a scene in the drama that he himself had played. It was out of the wilderness of fear and guilt and spiritual unrest that he went forth to meet God. In this act he became Yahweh's chosen agent in one of the most extraordinary episodes of history. Had he not won freedom by yielding himself to the will of Yahweh? When the people met God at the mountain, they also won a quality of freedom that escape from Egypt had not given them; for they were committing themselves, in ways that were far from clear but which nevertheless were determinative of all subsequent history, to bondage to the Eternal. It would seem to follow that this is normative for all individuals and groups that seek to be free. Every once in so often men have to stop what they are doing and move, it may be, to the edge of terror in order to confront God. Men and nations do not do this easily, and very often the clamorous insistence on their right to hold on to that which always has turned out to be bondage to self is the measure of their spiritual incertitude.

God has a right to command but not to compel. The covenant he shares with the sons of men may take different forms and adopt varying symbols, but it is not a talisman; it works no magic. It rests on the moral grounds on which the universe stands.

Man, then, has a right to accept the commands of God because only by thus yielding to God does he enter into the experience of real freedom—real because it also rests on the moral grounds on which human existence is founded. Having understood this, we are ready to ask what God meant when he spoke to Moses about himself. The centuries have not taken us very far from the smoking mountain, but the days in which we are living seem to invite us again to its foot that once again we may meet God. We shall not light our spiritual fires at the chariot of the sun, but we shall look upward with reverent awe toward the stars and ask the meaning of the play of shadow and flame that crown the summit of the ageless mount of revelation. We are to have no other god. Shall we?

CHAPTER III

No Other Gods

WHAT is the use of having a god? This is not an idle question. Many have considered it important enough to argue about. It has to do, not with the existence, but with the utility of deity. Certain it is that the more self-reliant we become, the less use we think we have for others. Does not this apply also to God? Is he not for use mostly in emergency? "Out of the depths have I cried unto thee, O Jehovah." (Ps. 130:1.) This was spoken by one who was in deep waters. His ready words have been repeated countless times by others over their head in confusion, or pain, or defeat, or shame, and for whom God was a one-man rescue squad. And although it is not implied in the psalm, many who have borrowed the words have perhaps felt that once they were pulled over to shallow water where they could feel terra firma underfoot, they would manage to get along pretty well by themselves. There is, in all candor, a good deal to be said for this attitude. Self-reliance is the aim of the growing body and mind. "When I became a man, I put away childish things." (I Cor. 13:11.) God is occupied with important cosmic affairs. The more I take care of myself, the less he will have to bother with me. The sooner I can reach the point where I am altogether independent of him, the better for both of us. This is the practical view of many self-disciplined persons. It is not that they deny God; they simply have reached the point where they think they can get on without him.

We shall not linger here with this familiar pose since what actually seems to happen to such folk will be dealt with later. To the simple desert wanderers who were admonished to accept Yahweh as their God out of all the other competitors for their loyalty, an introductory comment about the metaphysics of God would have meant very little; but to remind them of rescue made sense.

1

Religion was a practical matter to them, not a theoretical interest. They had to live by accommodating themselves to an environment that was, to say the least, inhospitable; and in doing so, religion was a factor. This, by and large, is the way religion has always come about. There are some spirits, highly sensitized receptors, who can apprehend the truths of religion by what we call revelation; but they have always been in short supply, and no doubt for good reasons. It is clear that God was represented to the children of Israel primarily in terms of his proved utility. "I am Jehovah thy God, who brought thee out of the land of Egypt, out of the house of bondage. Thou shalt have no other gods before me." (Exod. 20:2-3.) No other god had such a record; it was therefore simple decency that his favors should be reciprocated by their exclusive acceptance of him as their god.

The question of polytheism and its relation to the primitive Hebrew religion is a somewhat technical one and is left to the experts. Nevertheless that there was no concept of Yahweh as the only God of the universe is clear even to the casual reader of the Old Testament. References to the God of Abraham, the God of Isaac, and the God of Jacob would be taken, were we not habituated to the monotheism which is the heritage we have from much later periods, to mean three different gods. So sensitive a person as Second Isaiah, who lived in the times when an emergent monotheism was correcting the errors of earlier thinking about God, puts this fact clearly (Isa. 63:15-16). Abraham and Israel (Jacob) had been deified and had forgotten their responsibilities. They were therefore repudiated for Yahweh. "Thou, O Jehovah, art our Father; our Redeemer from everlasting is thy name." (Isa. 63:16.) The references to the multiplicity of gods in the poetry of the people are numerous. "Let God arise, and let his enemies be scattered." (Ps. 68:1.) God had rivals, dangerous ones. "God standeth in the congregation of God; he judgeth among the gods." (Ps. 82:1.) Here God seems to outrank other gods, but he does not stand alone. It is from these earliest fragments of folklore put together into the greatest religious anthology of ancient literature (the Psalms) that we are helped to discover what the thoughts of the ancient worshipers actually were.

The problem that confronted Moses was a practical one, though it had religious overtones. What his religious training had been in the palace, we do not know. There was, we suspect, a cult of Yahweh worshipers, the Levites, in Egypt. The name of Moses' mother, Jochebed, is without doubt a Yahweh name. The tribe of Jethro in Horeb worshiped Yahweh. But the people whom Moses was to lead out of bondage were hardly prepared, had Moses proposed it, to accept the Deity he promised unless they could be sure he would be practically useful.

The cities in Egypt familiar to the slave people all had their favorite gods. Cat, dog, bull, jackal, cow, hawk, ram, served to concrete for them the qualities and capacities most useful to them. The royal family had gods the lesser folk could not worship. What was left for slaves? It is easy to see then how Moses, having fled the palace and found asylum among wilderness herdsmen who belonged to the Yahweh cult of his mother, could with a new sense of mission and confidence go to the children of Israel and assure them that he knew a divine helper who could save them from bondage and give them freedom. What we cannot believe is that anything less than a promise like that could have won them away from such nondescript deities as they had worshiped in their wretched hovels by the Nile. And, we remind ourselves, Moses had to keep making good his promises about what Yahweh would do, all the time he was leader.

2

Not only was there a multiplicity of gods in the Nile basin with whom the Israelites were familiar, but there is good reason to believe that each of the Hebrew tribes had its own god before they were amalgamated into the federation of Israel and Judah. Dan, Gad, and Asher are tribal and god names. Isaiah 65:11 says: "But ye that forsake [Yahweh], that forget my holy mountain, that prepare a table for Fortune [Gad], and that fill up mingled wine unto Destiny

[Meni]." These are late references to the existence within the con-federation of rival gods to Yahweh. It is not surprising then that in the account of Aaron and the golden calf that purports to be much earlier we have the evidence of fanatical devotion to the Canaanite bull god within the camp and among the people to whom Moses was bringing the tablets of the law of Yahweh. No wonder his anger was so violent. During the period of his absence on the mountain the rival of his Deity had stolen a march, and his smashing of the stones was the reaction of one both angered and chagrined by defeat. When he regained the control from his brother Aaron, the severity of his punishment is a measure of his sense of outrage. After the slaughter of three thousand "brothers, companions, and neighbors" by those who had not danced about the calf, Moses called for a re-dedication to Yahweh, a dedication that was designed to go deeper than the ties of kinship that had up to this time united the execu-tioners of the bloody mandate to their brethren.

Time was when a recognition of these facts about the slow develop-ment of the God-awareness of the Hebrew people was an affront to the faithful. But an approach to the matter from another angle would have perhaps softened the shock that the exposure of historic and archaeological data produced. This is the understanding that comes from the directions outlined for us by psychology and anthropology.

What, after all, is a god? This is not to ask: Who is God? If this question had been put to the nomads at Sinai's base, they would perhaps have answered in terms of the common creatures that had been elevated to divine rank. In some ways a cat or a dog or a hawk represented something eerie, but at the same time useful, inscrutable, or powerful to a primitive mind or to an ingenious priest. To a blundering man the stealth and noiselessness of a cat, the speed and ferocity of a dog, the effortless flight of a hawk, represented an as-piration beyond his reach. To this he gave his admiration, and for it he built temples, some of which were masterpieces of the ancient world; and before it he conducted his ritual of worship. The point is that which he called his god was his good, an ideal and unreached good, but nonetheless something useful. It was for him both ideal and advantage. This is the way in which children think of God, and properly so. We would be alarmed at the intellectual precosity of a child who talked wisely about God in the abstract, but no quaintness or novelty in the child's concepts of God as a big person or strange animal should disturb us. The experience of the race is recapitulated in the development of the child.

When we put our question What is a god? to a more sophisticated —or shall we say a more disciplined—mind, we expect a different identity of the object but not a different answer as to its meaning. It will still be in terms of his idea of the good that he is unable to achieve alone. Man, he will say, has an urgency toward what he thinks is good. This is intuitive and will express itself in different ways with different people. In order to think about the good, he must create an idea out of it. Thus good was a cat to one Egyptian, a ram to another. To the Yahweh cult in the deserts of Arabia the good was the storm cloud that brought the rains. To Professor A. N. Whitehead the good is the principle of concretion, and hence God. So every man "dreams up" his idealization of the good into what is essentially for him his deity. This is an advance on an intuitive ex-perience; it is an effort at rational experience. Now this good that man calls his god is never evil, though it will often be inscrutable, inconstant, and contingent. We must allow, furthermore, alongside man's will to good his perversion and destruction of good; but this is not idealized into his god; it is his devil. Or it is in classical terms original sin. There is endless warfare in man's soul between these contrary impulses, and he will perforce seek allies to aid him toward the good and to protect him from the evil. One may imagine that the ancients joined many an argument over which deity was the better—the dog or the hawk. For one who had been bitten by a dog it was a devil, not a god. John Wesley once observed to a companion in dispute that the God he (the companion) worshiped was the devil he (Wesley) hated. We shall never extricate ourselves from such arguments so long as the finite minds we own can only approximate the goods we seek. Thus God, arrived at by this process, will never be wholly satisfying.

3

Yahweh of the children of Israel was not altogether satisfying as he was encountered at Mount Sinai. It took a lot of explaining to keep in line those who had agreed to follow Moses out of Egypt. He was by turns angered and baffled by this necessity. He even wanted to quit. There surely were times when his own faith in Yahweh was grievously tried. What we have in the development of the Hebrew idea of God is the slow and devious progress from a primitive idea of a practical good to a universal and absolute God of wisdom, power, love, and holiness. Unless we conceive of our moral culture and the religious faith that has nurtured it as the result of one instantaneous and complete revelation, we must understand it as a process which has been able to use only man's finite and often perverse mind in bringing it to such perfection as is claimed for it today. This has been a task no tribal god could have undertaken; only such a God as is known to us who are the inheritors of the Hebrew-Christian tradition could have brought off such an enterprise.

For this reason, among others, we hold it is impossible not to believe in God—some sort of God. If God is the externalization of the good, then "no God" means "no good." This would, in effect, deny both man's intuitive outreach for good and his measurable realization of it. Atheism has long been regarded, therefore, not as a denial of good or God, but for what, for any number of reasons, is regarded as an unsatisfactory concretion or idealization of the good. What every man decides, if he makes the effort to rationalize his intuition, is not whether there is good but what represents the good for him. This he does not do in a vacuum or in isolation. All the facts of life impinge upon his thought, and what he comes up with will be original only in the sense that it has its origin in the kind of person he is. Is that good a cat, a jackal, a hawk? Is it the Thunderer, the Judge, the Artist, the Energy, the First Cause, the Magistrate? Is it the Father of our Lord Jesus Christ, the God of Abraham, Isaac, and Jacob?

What took place in what purports to be an episode in the Arabian desert may or may not have occurred according to the details of the record. But of this we may be sure, and it is much more important to know: God was making himself known at Sinai as the God who was to produce for Israel the good they needed in every way, but uniquely in the social, religious, and moral norms by which they were to live. He had recently proved this by freeing them from the despotism of the Pharaoh. All the way back into the dim reaches of their past there were indications that Yahweh had contracted with certain peoples and families who had seen in him the source and meaning of the good, and he had not defaulted on his covenant promises. He had a record of performance no competitor could match. Therefore he could say: "Thou shalt have no other gods before me."

4

Had this command to elect him from the slate of competitor gods been prefaced by a statement that in the nature of the case there could be only one supreme Deity and that all claimants to the office save himself were pretenders or frauds, the words would have had no meaning. Nor do we think they would have won much following. The primitive mind of the times was unprepared for monotheism; it was, in fact, very skimpily prepared for monolatry. This means the worship of one and was a necessary stage in man's intellectual odyssey to monotheism, the worship of the only One.

If religion were purely a practical matter, by which I mean something that could do without the bother of thinking, the worship of many gods might be its most practical device. This assumes, of course, that worship is integral to religious experience. To the question Why any gods at all? the answer might be: If one must have a god in order to give moral authority for what he does, would it not simplify the individual problem for each one to have the god he liked or as many as he thought he needed? Both Isaiah (40:18-26) and Jeremiah (10:3) speak angrily of the making of idols out of trees by skilled workmen for gullible purchasers who were no doubt acting on this basis. This was at a period in Israel's life when a great and noble monotheism was in the making, but aside from the obvious fact that idolatry was even then a bogus substitute for true religion, these prophets had little to say. Religion, some insist, is after all a matter of habit or taste. One will therefore accept or design the kind of deities one needs to keep his religion in repair and to give sanction to his established ways of living. Polytheism, I am saying, has always been inviting because it accommodates the tastes of people in great variety. One wonders whether, after a manner of speaking, each of us does not have his own private pantheon. Certain it is that in one segment of the Christian community the multiplication of saints, each one of whom is allocated to some established human need, comes very close to practical polytheism. This was the convenient pattern practiced by the Greeks.

The difficulty in having many gods is as obvious as is its inviting practicality. The moral problem for each individual lies fundamentally in making his will conform to the will of God. Differences in gods there might be, but there is no difference as to what the rudiment of moral experience is. Many gods, therefore, provided many standards of moral authority. No matter how pleased the individual might be with the god he supplicated in solitude, when he carried into the associations he had with his fellows the private sanctions his god had given him for his behavior, he was likely to get into difficulty.

It was necessary, where individuals were nucleated into groups, to agree upon one god for all the members. This, say the anthropologists, is the origin of the tribal god. He became the authority for all members alike and thus made possible the development of a tribal code under which all conduct was directed and judged. This stage was not easily achieved or sustained. The powerful individuial in the group was always tempted to choose a god to his liking and impose him on his fellows, or even to assume the prerogatives, if not indeed the character, of a god himself. Thus the shaman or the priest. Furthermore all moral commandments grounded in divine sanction were of necessity at the outset broad generalizations. Typical rather than special cases were prescribed for, and a certain latitude of personal choice of practice and interpretation was inevitable. Here was a real danger to social cohesion, something that could be avoided only by the insistence that one deity and one alone would be allowed the group. No matter how many other tribes had how many gods, for "our" tribe—and this was the beginning of the moral evolution of the Hebrew code—there was only one God. This was not monotheism; it was monolatry, and there is little room for doubt that it is this that lay at the root of the first great commandment about God.

5

Nevertheless the difficulty with monolatry is, from our historical perspectives, as easily discerned as that of polytheism. The rivalry of the gods of individuals is simply lifted into a rivalry of the gods of tribes. And because the tribe mind is often more mercurial and more powerful than the mind of the individual in solitude, the rivalries of tribal and national gods became a terrible thing. The evidences of this abound in the literature of the Old Testament. "Let God arise, let his enemies be scattered. Let them also that hate him flee before him." (Ps. 68:1.) Here the reference is to the enemies of God, not of Israel; and if it seems for the moment odd that God should be spoken of in such grossly human terms, we need only to remind ourselves what we say when our God seems to be opposed by the gods of rival societies of nations today. We note, therefore, the necessity in the establishment of a moral authority that polytheism and monolatry should have developed as natural phases in the growing process. And yet, as we have observed, monolatry is not enough, and for a reason as practical as that which disqualified polytheism: it does not eliminate the rivalry of moral systems.

6

It would perhaps be better, if I am to stay within the limits set for this study, to let the matter rest here. Since the belief of Moses as reflected in the Ten Commandments was monolatrous rather than monotheistic, there is no necessity for comment on the latter. It was unknown as an option to the children of Israel at that time. There is, on the contrary, a need for a brief comment here since we can discern a fondness for monolatry today that makes it in a very real way a rival to monotheism. Indeed the earlier phases in the development of a theistic ground for moral idealism are never completely superseded by those that follow logically or historically. Because of the practical necessity every man seems to feel for making God in his own image—or images, for he may have several gods— of the good, we see a pragmatic polytheism of a certain sort rife within our Christian culture. The same thing is seen in the monolatry of our times already referred to. Is there then a place and a reason for monotheism in our times?

By a *place* for monotheism I mean a point within our system of thought where our understanding of the one absolute God can logically fit. It is not my intention to argue that here. There are boundaries we have set for ourselves beyond which we do not propose to wander. But there is a *reason* for monotheism that is not a matter of logic. It is, again, a practical matter where individuals find it necessary to have moral guidance for private and corporate living.

Simply stated it is a need for uniformity with respect to the basic moral concepts that underlie all organized life. It is similar to the sort of thing the United Nations has put together in its Universal Declaration of Rights, a statement that may exhibit fine logical consistency but which came about less by the compulsions of logic than by the pressures of an exigent world situation. One world cannot come about without one law, and one law cannot come about without one source of moral idealism. We would add that that will not come about without belief in and loyalty to one God.

This progression in our tradition from one God to one world is under vigorous assault in our times. There are some who contend that the premises upon which monotheism has so long rested are no longer tenable. Therefore the univocal moral authority of God is lost to us. This is not new. During the eighteenth century Kant argued that the existence of God could not be demonstrated. There followed from this the appalling deduction that no valid and universal morality was possible. To escape from the trap he had sprung, Kant argued that since there was morality, there must be a God who was its source and validation. Thus by the ladder of necessity he thought that he could climb back up to the heights of confidence from which he had tumbled. Those who had followed his descent to a logical Avernus were quick to remind him that a proof of the existence of God that rested only on the idea that he *ought* to exist was wishful syllogizing. It is of the essence of much of the modern temper to insist that just because something *ought* to be true cannot be taken as sufficient grounds for asserting that it *is* true.

To the extent, then, that the belief in God is logically lost to many, their moral choices can no longer be established on the eternal imperative; and they must find their moral sanctions elsewhere. Where? If not in the divine, then in the human—with every man his own moral authority. There is something of nobility in this even though we think it ultimately reduces moral conduct to taste or inclination and thus to chaos. At the same time this secularistic humanism, for such it is, has had eloquent and persuasive advocates, from Marcus Aurelius to Walter Lippmann. These exponents are quick to agree that a morality predicated on belief in man as the source of moral integrity is put to greater strains than that resting on belief in God. It is circumscribed by the secular understanding of history and notes that within the historic continuum moral idealism is often unrealized and righteousness is unrewarded. For the pure humanist there is no post-history adjustment of the moral irregularities encountered within time. Nor is there a transcendent and therefore eternal judgment on the behavior of man. The humanist judge of his own or his fellows' behavior has no credentials save his own integrity and his wish to be just. He has no authority except his own wisdom, and the wiser he grows, the less inclined he is to claim infallibility for it. So he will not thunder commands. He will examine and reach conclusions and then try to persuade others of his disinterestedness and of the plausibility of his reasoning. There is not a little irony therefore in the fact that the sophisticated mind of our generation that repudiates polytheism and monolatry as naïve, and monotheism as rationally unsupportable, has turned in the direction of an elegant polytheism in which every man is in his own god or makes a god out of every compulsion that presses him into moral activity. This polytheism would scorn to talk of gods, one or many; but its moral guides are numerous and are known by the familiar names: Necessity, Contingency, Ambiguity, Opportunism, Improvisation, to mention only a few. And what is the net result of this for the moral life of the world? An exaltation of man in his own eyes and a confusion among men as to how they shall treat one another. It is not enough to talk of the dignity of man since one man's dignity may be another man's denigration. It seems that the age-old problem of the absolute and the relative will not rest in the graves men have dug for it. Perhaps we might as well acknowledge its indestructibility, confer immortality upon it, and then live with it as best we can.

7

The dither into which Kant put the philosophers two hundred years ago is nothing as compared with what the amoralism[1] of Marx

---

[1] "Antihuman morals" is a more exact characterization. The Marxist "ethical principle—the only 'good' is what best serves the working class—hides at its core a contempt for the individual and his needs unless his hardships can be dramatized for propaganda"—William Lindsay Graham in *These Found the Way*, ed. D. W. Soper (Philadelphia: Westminster Press, 1951), p. 71. Used by permission. It is interesting to note that Marxist "moral" judgment leveled against Western sins are Christian rather than Marxist. Marxist denial of free will makes morality impossible, but when capitalism exploits the worker, the Marxist regards this as immoral, not in terms

has done to the practical, moral mind of today. Here is an understanding of the moral base on which life rests that has nothing to do
with gods, whatever their number or character. Man behaves in one
way or another in terms of the social environment in which he is nurtured. Environment changes; therefore the sanctions of conduct
change. Because environment has this authority, it is more important
than man. The state, which is the formalized environment within
which most men in aggregate live, is therefore the ultimate moral
authority. What the state allows is right; what it disapproves is
wrong. States change because of the dialectic of history within which
they are caught. Therefore the moral concepts of the state may
change also. But the locus of ultimate authority in the state never
changes. It cannot change. It is written in the stars' bright diagram.[2]

This is the bold new concept that has become articulate and aggressive in our day. If it used the language of theology, which it
scrupulously eschews, it would deny the validity of many gods, of
the worship of one god among many, since it demands complete and
undeviating allegiance to the one true state. Then it would slyly

of Marxism that can annihilate the individual in the interests of the state, but in terms
of the Christian ethic that allows man the inherent and prior right to inviolability. Cf.
Chap. XI.

[2] This is, of course, the Marxist totalitarian state credo. The state is a sort of
continuing power, overlord, or god, not responsible to human beings—except for
their "good" as interpreted in Marxist values—but to which human beings are very
much responsible. Relations between individuals are not very important; justice
is a laughing matter—"settle it anyway you please"—but relations between the individual and the state are very important—settled if necessary by liquidation,
Siberia, and the concentration camp. There is no god but the state, and its leader is
his prophet. In this hen and egg dilemma the hen (the state) came first, and the
egg (the people) came later.

In the Western view, particularly the American form of it, the people create the
state. They own it and set it up as a system to regulate their relations, and they can
always "alter or abolish it." They do not have to wait, if they do not like the state,
for the slow dialectical processes to erode it. Thus while the people are *under* it,
they are at the same time *over* it.

Those who speak about what our government is doing *to* us are unconsciously
adopting the Marxist view of the state. They regard it as a separate entity against
which we had better protect ourselves. With us, in the Protestant Christian tradition,
relations between individuals are very important; while the relations of the individual to the state (society) are meagerly set forth. For every word in law prescrib-
ing the individual's duties toward society in general, there are hundreds setting
forth in great detail man's duties toward his fellows—contracts, torts, damages, and
so on. The Federal Fair Employment Practices Act, for example, does not govern the
relations between the "shearers and the sheared"; it deals only with the relations among
the shearers, to make them fair in dividing the wool. B.F.B.

say that some good day will dawn and reveal that the great god State has withered away, and man will stand alone in naked amoral grandeur in the heaven of the classless society.[3] Somehow we will have to come to terms with this braggart faith. Will it be by destroying it by force of arms? Our monolatrous loyalties are easily activated. Of all the gods of earth today we are worshiping democracy with fine frenzy. Let others bow at their chosen shrines, but let them not trespass in our temple. But how shall we contain the state god with the democratic god? This is no flippant question. In the realm of practical politics today we are monolatrists. Religiously we come dangerously near to accepting a similar pattern. It is as if we had never escaped from the wilderness of Sinai. Or have we in panic gone back again?

<h1 style="text-align:center">8</h1>

"Thou shalt have no other gods before me." This was an important step. Had the first mandate been a general proposition about the being of God, it would have missed the multitude toward which Yahweh was moving. "There is only one God"; that would have mystified those who had known any number of other gods elsewhere. No; the storm-god Yahweh, first worshiped in Arabia, was to be adopted by Israel as its tribal deity; and then as Judah (Israel) enlarged its influence, the influence of its god was to be extended. Moses by espousing the daughter of Jethro became a worshiper of the god he had perhaps learned about from his mother, and when he went back to Egypt, he was able to persuade the Levites there that their freedom was bound up in the transfer of their loyalty to the Yahweh he worshiped. Moses made good his promise of deliverance, and Yahweh became their deity. Though this was primarily a political victory, when Moses and his fellow tribesmen became the priestly order of Israel, the new movement launched in the wilderness became in a profound way a religious one and established the moral grounds upon which their future was to be built.

When, therefore, the chronicle of this dimly remembered episode set forth as the first of Yahweh's commands that he was to be first

---

[3] Note the contradiction in holding the welfare of the state to the norm of moral action while predicting its ultimate disappearance. The result: not only a "stateless" society but a "moral-less" society.

among all other gods, we see what was meant. It was as far as the mind could have gone at this time, and it was the beginning rather than the end of the most spectacular moral and religious development of all time.

We must listen to this first commandment accompanied by the rumbling of Sinai in eruption and within the developing moral and religious experience of the multitudes at its foot. The wonder is not that from our perspective so little was demanded but that from their perspective so much was expected. Furthermore we observe here the focus that is at the heart of the moral experience of every man. "Thou" is a collective noun and surely meant the whole community to whom the first commandment was addressed. But it sharpened the sense of Yahweh's relationship to them in an inescapable fashion. It was not even implied that others than they would do well to recognize Yahweh as their god also. In the course of time that became the impulse of a propagandist or missionary movement that with its fulfillment in the Christian evangel was to sweep the globe. For the moment, however, it was enough that they recognize and accept Yahweh as their own.

When every man confronts the living God, it is just such an experience that makes religion a vital matter for him. It is *he* who stands before God; it is *he* to whom God speaks his awesome word; it is *he* who must decide where his God will be. Once he has heard the word "thou," there can be no dallying with other gods, many or few. "Thou" and "me" are the initial and terminal words of the first commandment. With stark clarity they set forth the divine-human encounter. Man may think he can walk alone and pick his way sure-footedly past the moral pitfalls that imperil his advance, but before he has gone far or stumbled often, he will supplicate one god or another. What will be the name he calls?

CHAPTER IV

Man's Other God

BECAUSE this chapter is something of a parenthesis, it may serve the purpose of keeping our continuity clear to give a quick run-down of what I have been saying up to this point. It was necessary at first to accept the established viewpoint of biblical scholarship with respect to the date and structure of the records that contain the Ten Commandments and to point out the reason for the tenacity with which these ancient directives have held on to the moral conscience of our culture. It was the grounding of code on the deep foundations of morality and the correlation of morality and religious practices that were the unique quality the Hebrew law exhibited among the codes of neighbor cultures. God, I said, had a right to command because he was dealing with man on the most important level of experience; and man has a right to abdicate self-direction to the directing of God because only thus is the paradox of freedom accommodated. The religious factor in this significant equation is the fact of God, and for that reason the First Commandment had to do with man's response to God when they confronted each other. God would therefore demand that he alone be the God of the children of Israel. This was not a revelation of what we call monotheism; it is more accurately designated monolatry. There had been quite a considerable history of conflict between the Yahweh and other cults, contests that were to continue for centuries. Yahweh versus Egyptian occultism, versus the Moabite Chemosh (cf., "Then did Solomon build a high place for Chemosh the abomination of Moab, in the mount that is before Jerusalem, and for Molech the abomination of the children of Ammon." [I Kings 11:7.]), versus the bull gods of Canaan—this is a chronicle of competitive struggle we easily lose sight of. Even the spectacular battle between Yahweh-Elijah and the priests of Baal at Mount Carmel is rarely set within the correct perspectives of the constant warfare among the gods for Israel's patronage. We are able to see within this struggle the incipient ethical monotheism that was eventually to emerge, and with it a moral seriousness that stands in clear contrast to the moral irresponsibility of polytheism. It was to take a long time, however, for the religious-ethical antithesis between Yahweh and his adversaries to be composed into the ethico-religious monotheism which is the heart of the religious culture of the West. That this heart beats feebly today is a common lament. Some have blamed this on an inadvertence of Kant, others on Descartes. Professor Hajo Holborn of Yale has said: "The collapse of religious unity and the catastrophe of the wars of religion dethroned religion as the regulating force of Western culture. Philosophy and science took its place." [1] And now we are confronted by an aggressive politico-economic culture that reserves its angriest scorn for all religion and particularly for the bourgeois morality of the Hebrew-Christian tradition.

1

This much by way of recapitulation. Yet for all this emergence and struggle and decline, man still is confronted, in one way or another, by what to him is a god, the idealization of the good he has or wants. To the disciplined religious mind the problem of monotheism is no longer difficult. Those who see the ground of moral experience level with the ground of religious devotion find that monotheism supplies the only practical alternative to the ethical pluralism of polytheism and monolatry. In the light of this it is puzzling to many that in ever-widening areas of modern life religion seems less and less to provide our moral sanctions, and it is partly this that has given Marxist irreligion the opportunity it has not been slow to capitalize. Into the dry barrens of man's soul the new freshet is flowng, and one

[1] *The Political Collapse of Europe* (New York: Alfred A. Knopf, Inc., 1951).

wonders whether it will become a flood to revivify the earth or to drown it.

What has happened to the modern mind? In so far as it has given itself to reflection, it has become increasingly preoccupied with itself. Buddha sitting cross-legged on the calyx of a lotus blossom, contemplating his navel in imperturbable calm, has his counterpart in modern man's fascination with his ego. There is a difference: Modern man's perch suggests little of the languid serenity of a lotus flower; nor is his concentration upon himself as leisurely and undisturbed as that of an ancient sage. But both take themselves very seriously.

It is because our study not only is oriented to the history of the Mandate to Humanity and its meaning at the time it was pronounced, but is also concerned to inquire what its flinty essence is that has defied the erosion of the ages and what its relation is to the modern world, that we insert a parenthesis at this point. It deals with man's other god as he is worshiped or feared but never ignored.

Our difficulty, I have said, is not with rational support for the hypothesis or faith of monotheism. The direction of our world's spinning moral vortex is centripetal. More and more men are being compelled by the momentum of life to accept the unities that can bind them lest their diversities spin outward into the wild tangents of political, economic, and moral dissolution. So we are monotheists after a fashion simply because of the pressure of our times. Our problem is not *unideism*; it is *alterdeism*. We believe in one god, but is it the God our fathers and their fathers worshiped?

2

The late Carl Jung in a book that was widely read and quoted in the mid-thirties said that modern man has turned his attention from material things to his own subjective processes and that he has done so first, because he has lost the certainties that his medieval brother had and, second, because he has found that the ideals of material security, general welfare, and humanness have proved illusory (that was a depression and pre–World War II judgment), and in the third place, he has been led to expect something from the psychic life which he has not received from the outer world, something which our religions doubtless ought to contain, but no longer do contain—

at least for the modern man.[2] In other words, modern man's other god is his ego, his psyche.

Jung was right only in so far as he meant modern man's preoccupation is with the understanding of the self made possible by the formal disciplines of depth psychology. Man has always been interested in himself; his ego has always been as obvious as his navel. The most important experience that man has ever had has been making the image that he has always formed of himself, a process started the moment he first became aware of himself. It was not good for man to be alone even within the innocence of Eden. God made a woman to be a helpmeet, and the likelihood is that the first aid she offered was in correcting some notions he had formed about himself in the interval of his solitude between his creation and hers. This is part of the Genesis *mythos* and indicates clearly that as a religious problem— for the Genesis story *is* a religious insight—man's awareness of self got him into complications very soon. The state of innocence attributed to him at first can hardly be thought of as being devoid of self-awareness. That would have been a state of idiosyncrasy. His ego may not have got man into trouble during that incorrupted period, but it was there just the same, and it was developing ideas about itself, willy-nilly, right and wrong.

Within the orbit of primitive religion the understanding of the self was both simple and complex, the former because it was not subject to critical analysis, the latter because it appeared to behave in unpredictable and incomprehensible ways. Man was created out of the dust of the ground, and into his nostrils was breathed the breath of life, and he became a living soul. Here is the simplest of all explanations: Man's soul was the vital breath of God. There may be more precise names for the ego, but soul is certainly the most commonly used. If it is an endowment of a life principle, it is certainly more than that; for it outlasts death and during life gathers to itself all man's nonphysical functions. It is the soul that feels, thinks, wills. It is the heart and the mind. Complete devotion to God demanded that it bring with it all the mind, heart, soul, and strength. This was only saying man's love for God must employ all of his personality. Con-

[2] *Modern Man in Search of a Soul* (New York: Harcourt, Brace & Co., 1934), pp. 226-54.

versely man's addiction to evil was the result of the complete offering of his soul, mind, heart, and strength to unrighteousness.

This was the unanalyzed notion men had of the self in the early experience of religion. It is, one is tempted to say, as far as the average man's idea of the nature of his ego has taken him today. Nor are we inclined at this point to feel very disturbed about it. Since the Hebrews were moralists rather than philosophers, they saw the self more in action than in reflection, since an act is always easier to see and judge than the hidden energies that propel it, their general concept of the ego, or soul, or self, was uncomplicated. For that matter the ego is still easier to understand in action than in essence.

3

The Greek neighbors of the Hebrews took the self more seriously as a subject for thought. Plato is said to have admonished his followers: "Know thyself." This claims no particular distinction for him since everyone who has thought about behavior has said the same thing or wanted to, particularly when the behavior of another was irritating. And yet the philosopher who exhorts is the first to warn that his exhortation asks the all but impossible. One cannot know one's self. The moment one is sure of his data, he has already made a mistaken deduction. Why? There is something inside him that throws his self-analysis out of kilter.

The man of simple, unreflective religious faith would call this a devil, perhaps. The Greeks came close to this by saying every man has his daemon, by which they sometimes meant a morally neutral spirit and sometimes a man's essential genius—which was his ego. But the assignment of a name solved no problems. Because a man was what he was, he could not understand himself correctly. Very often he was more easily deceived about himself than about others, but even in judging others that inscrutable magnet of the self pulled the needle off the true direction of inquiry.

It did more and worse than this. Man, the subject, gives color to everything he thinks and does. This is called ego-centrism, and it means that all experience is screened through the mind of the experiencer. There is nothing bad about this until it goes to the extreme of saying that the only thing that is real is the idea of the subject who is thinking. Nothing is real, it is said, except as an idea. The Soviet Union exists not as a fact but as a notion.

To be sure, this is dangerous nonsense to the harassed gentlemen in departments of state and in armed services; but it is nonsense for which the ego is responsible. There are answers to it, all right, but one almost detects the mischievous glee which the ego has in the predicament that it has created. Professor Ralph Barton Perry of Harvard popularized a phrase that described the way in which man's effort to think, in distinction from his effort to act, is plagued by the "egocentric predicament." It has been taken so seriously by some of those who have believed in pure subjectivism that two Latin words were brought out of a convenient lexicon to dignify the idea. *Solus* and *ipse* were put together, and "solipsism" became the term by which the doctrine that the self alone exists was known. This was taking in a lot of territory, but it only goes to show what mischief the ego can get itself into. Not satisfied with complicating man's understanding of what he does and how he thinks, the ego finally usurped the claim of being the only thing that was.

4

Now it is the hand of psychology that has been offered to man with the promise that it can help him find his way out of this wilderness. And this engendered hope is all the more alluring because of the apparent failure of early religion and philosophy to show him the direction he seeks. This is what Jung meant by man's preoccupation with himself and his modern trust in the "psychic life." There is no need here for a technical discussion of what psychology tells us. We would find confused and uncertain voices even among its disciplined practitioners. A good deal of psychology is, however, no more than tested common sense arrayed in uncommon names.

There are two focuses of man's concentrated attention upon life. By his very nature he is interested in himself. This may begin with a puzzled and awkward attention to his toe and end with a gracefully argued thesis about his immortality, but the interest in himself is there all the while. Whether externalized in a foot or internalized in an idea, it is always there. And he interprets his interests, whether in toe or heaven, in terms of what satisfies him. His satisfaction may demand a toe, or the adumbration of what later will come as his wish to be praised by his mother for his cute contortions, or it may be, in his argument about immortality, his desire to assure himself that he merits eternal life. There are all sorts of ego drives about which we have endlessly been told, but they all are alike in that they understand action as important primarily in relation to its contribution to the satisfactions of the actor.

The other focus of attention man finds outside himself. Beyond the foot at which he tugs looms his mother who, for reasons she does not explain, picks him up and thus interrupts his calisthenics. He may not be pleased with this interference, but when he finds substituted for his toe something that tastes better and makes him feel comfortable inside, he is vaguely aware of a good external to himself in the person who seems unaccountably to be sharing his life. This is a paradigm of man's gradual acceptance of society as something to which he must give attention. He will discover very soon that other people are both a nuisance and a help. He will also discover that since there is some good for him in these exterior contacts, he can use them, more or less, to his advantage.

It will not all be as easy as this, for he will soon realize that every other person he meets is also undertaking to derive from his own contacts the maximum amount of satisfaction he can get. It will be clear to him that every other ego is responding to its own ego drives, and this does not always issue in the happiness or the security that he wants above all else. So he will develop irritations, resentments, hostilities. It may be to his advantage—and he may learn this early—to dissemble a serenity he does not feel. Thus he will accumulate a hidden store of latent emotions that some day, to his surprise and that of others, will erupt in self-assertiveness for no apparent reason, or for a wholly mistaken one.

By the time he is independent of those individuals who can coerce the style of his behavior, he will have encountered the other external pressures that compel his conformity. Here is tension; it is felt in the mind, in the muscles, and in the arteries. How can he resolve it? He is an individual within a social complex: how can he be free and yet yield to order? His behavior is rationalized to his satisfaction but not to that of his fellows, so there will be argument and perhaps bitterness and estrangement. He must make adjustments. Ideals are shattered against the hard surface of real facts; dreams evanesce into

71

disappointment and disillusion. The shell about his ego hardens, and he becomes an egotistical fool in revolt against the world; or his ego, unprotected, softens to jelly, and the world makes him into a shapeless conformist to be squeezed into whatever pattern is currently popular. Around his inner self whirls the world. It is bright with good things he wants and reaches out for in order to satisfy himself, but it is also dark with sinister things that frighten him, and when he winces or recoils, he hates himself for not striking a defiant pose for the benefit of the world which he thinks is always looking at him.

The problem is not solved either by protection or by exposure of the ego. Man's self will not allow him is disfranchize himself. The effort to do so would be paradoxically, an assertion of its inviolability. Nor can man's self deny the world about him, for in so doing he would make another world of fantasy. He would fall again into the egocentric predicament. All the while he must be making an adjustment between egotism and selflessness within the anxious confusions of practical living.

5

I have commented on the problem of the ego as it appeared within the thought forms of early Hebrew experience and the way in which it lacked the precise outlines of later times. Today it is obvious that psychology has given sharpness to a good deal of religious as well as professional thinking about the self, and this is something for which we are properly grateful. But our concern here is with the way in which the ego has come to be man's other god, if not indeed his only god, and the way this affects his behavior. The philosophers have been plagued by this assertive deity, whether as an omnibus or as an imp; and modern psychology, which Jung says is man's scripture to guide him in his preoccupation with his inner self, has shown us how, try though we may, we cannot escape this thing that by turns charms and bedevils us.

It remains to say something about the moral consequences of all this. Here the problem seems fairly clear. In fact this is what gives importance to man's awareness of himself whether he is thinking in terms of eighth-century B.C. religion, eighteenth-century philosophy, or twentieth-century psychology. What happens to man when he gives rein to his ego? What happens to his family, his social group, his world, when he worships himself? This is a moral problem.

It may be stated thus: Man is confronted by God, who demands, for good reasons, that he shall have man's complete and sole loyalty. This is his demand of the living soul that he gave man as the most important part of his total equipment.

There are two ways man may meet this command. He may rebel against it. This will not necessarily be an angry or ill-mannered attitude. He may, as many moderns have done, decide that he can get along better alone, that he has established patterns of behavior that make it unnecessary for him to consult a vaguely apprehended monitor. If he should put his attitude into the language of the Decalogue, he would say: I shall have no other god beside me. This is self-worship, candidly confessed. And in so far as the object of his devotion provides the ground of moral conduct, he will organize his moral concepts and actions about the core of himself, about what he thinks is the good. He may turn out to be an exemplary man in terms of personal and social behavior. It is by no means true that all egotists are rascals. Nor is it necessarily true that they are all obnoxious. Indeed with the measurable relaxation of the moral pressures of the Hebrew-Christian religious tradition as we observe it today, the self-worshiper is as often as not the self-reliant man. He may be the pioneer who hazards most because he believes most in himself. He may be the genius who creates works of art in his own image or invents devices that capture in greater concentrations of manipulable power the energies of creation. To be sure, it is easy for us to say that much of modern art is the unhappy answer to man's urge to sculpture or paint his own image, and that man's ingenuity has made him afraid of the instruments he has made. Such observations, however, will not do very much to abate man's enthusiasm for himself, however they may explain the debauchery of art or the irresponsibility of some scientific research.

The other way man may meet the demand to make God his only God is to accept it. This is, of course, the worship of God and will result in the effort to make all behavior conform to what is regarded as God's will—that is, what is from the standpoint of God the good which man should pursue. It is the general renunciation of this as a religious and ethical norm that is the most arresting and significant fact of twentieth-century culture.

Man's worship of himself, what we have called "alterdeism" because it is not one God that distrubs his mind but another god that activates his behavior—this self-worship is plausibly rationalized. We have seen how in origin (living soul), in reflection (the egocentric predicament), and in modern psychology (man's preoccupation with the inner energies of life) the ego has always been known to have an important if not the determining place in man's thought and action. It is not without interest, though the significance may be questioned, that in the English tongue it is the first personal pronoun, "I" that is capitalized. This is a distinction that is shared only with the third personal pronoun, "he," as it is used in references to God. Does the tongue repeat more subtly than we sometimes suspect the pretensions of the ego?

Now man's claim to the right to self-worship is always stated in terms of the good. He will be warned that his ego will trick him into false ideas about the good, to the point sometimes of inverting values. This, however, will not deter his efforts. And more often than not good will be conceived in terms of power. Is not a weak ego a pitiful or contemptible thing? Does one not realize the eternal purpose for himself by becoming strong? How strong? Well, are there any limits one should put on strength? God is omnipotent; what then can be wrong in trying to be like God? The stronger, the godlier.

It is here that the danger begins to be exposed. Power, which is the aim of egoism, is not the end it sets for itself. There is no such thing as power in the abstract, and egoism becomes egotism when power becomes a means to self-satisfaction, a means to the gratification of the ego drive. Thus the more power the ego acquires, the greater devotion it has for itself. Because of a sense of power it is more reasonable to believe one's self a god and to palm one's self off on others as a god. This actually is done by those we deprecatingly call egomanics. From Augustus Caesar to Hitler the list is long and sobering. The master of the Kremlin today does not call himself a god, but he lacks nothing of the practical deification that is necessary to his ego satisfaction. And lest we think this usurpation of the divine status has been indulged only by secular rulers, we need only to be reminded

74

of the pretensions of the vicegerent in Rome and other self-styled spokesmen of the Eternal.

Such antic posturing would be absurd if it were not dangerous. But the self-acclaimed god, who in his exalted role is only more daring and more successful than those of us who decline the accolade, finds it necessary always to act in character. His egotism starves him and gluts him by turns. He must perform godlike prodigies of action or assign godlike dimensions to his puny efforts. How clearly Shakespeare saw this:

> Upon what meat doth this our Caesar feed,
> That he is grown so great? [3]

The answer was that he was feeding on himself.

Beyond this there is a final stage. The power-distended egotist cannot stop short of despising those whom he has overtopped, and to his contempt is added truculence.[4] Because he worships himself, all men should do the same; so he thunders: "Thou shalt have no other gods before me." And then, to follow through to the ultimate sacrilege, he has sometimes said to God: "You too! You shall have no other gods before me!" This is the nethermost level to which the pretentions of man can plunge. Call it original sin, not in the sense of being congenital but meaning possessing a novelty and recklessness of which only the ego worshiper can be guilty.

6

This is the moral consequence of egotism. Extreme perhaps in presentation, and we will be reminded that I have described it in its pathological form, that we rarely see egotists of this sort. Precisely so, but the extremity of philosophical nonsense was reached by those who claimed that only the ego is real. The very danger lies in the fact that it is the nature of the ego to reach for power and to pretend

---

[3] *Julius Caesar*, Act I, sc. 2.
[4] Cf. *ibid.*:

> "Why, man, he doth bestride the narrow world
> Like a Colossus; and we petty men
> Walk under his huge legs, and peep about
> To find ourselves dishonourable graves."

that it has grasped it, to the denial of every other claimant. This is as true of Caspar Milquetoast as of Machiavelli, of me as of Mussolini.

We should not be surprised then that in the growing ethico-religious consciousness of the children of Israel the radical demand of the First Commandment was a basic insight. And from our perspective we can see why this should have been: only by the worship of God can man be protected from the moral disasters of self-worship.

It has been customary in our times, when the decline of the worship of God has distressed us, to fulminate against the other gods man has set up before him. Things, we say, or materialism, are man's god. The sense of ownership is perhaps the earliest way in which the ego gratifies itself. But Wealth is not the god of our materialized, greedy society; it is the altar boy who burns fragrant incense before the grinning Ego god. Or we say Blood is our god. This is perhaps the second way by which the growing ego is nurtured, the sense of belonging that makes us feel we are wanted and loved. This may be aided by the fact that we were born with a good name, or a silver spoon in our mouth, or a pink skin on our body. But social prestige and racism and nationalism are not gods; they too are acolytes before the pedestal on which the ego is perched. Or we say Wisdom is our god. This comes along in proper sequence to flatter the expanding self. Wisdom is gentle and inclined to humility. And God is truth, and the more we have of truth, the more we have of him. Ultimate wisdom would make us God's equal and independent of him. But Wisdom is no god. It may be an angel hovering about the enthroned ego that strains to catch its chanted words of praise: "Holy, holy, holy, art thou; the whole earth is full of thy glory." Meaning me!

7

What has the worship of self done? What is the fruit of man's preoccupation with himself? It cannot be said that its result has been all, or mostly, evil. In such matters it is impossible even to draw up a trial balance. Certainly man's attempt to understand the ego by the means made available by modern psychology has achieved notable and wholly gratifying results. We would not return to the naïveté of earlier days. And, we think, the factor of understanding ourselves more accurately has not been unrelated to the levels of culture that we have achieved.

But this understanding has produced correlative dangers. Where understanding has resulted in self-satisfaction or self-worship—and this despite its palpable absurdity is what often happens—it has not enlarged our souls (and we deliberately use the common word of religion); it has shrunk them. We have become puny gods, puffed up to disguise our pigmy proportions. Selfishness (and this is another common word) has made us powerless to achieve largeness of soul. We remember that it is power that is the central concern of the ego. We must also be reminded of the irony in the circumstance that permits our urge to power to evacuate us of power. Are we not throughly sick in these times of the swollen egotists who still have not learned the folly of their pretentions?

Similarly, if we think in terms of group egotism—the pride of class, nation, race—it is manifest that we have not won the worship we think that we deserve; we have won the contempt that we fear.

8

I have not undertaken to find the solution to the dilemma into which our worship of the ego, man's other god, has thrust him. That must be reserved for the final chapter, within which the testimony of the whole of the divine directive, from Sinai to Calvary, is surveyed. For the moment we return to the foot of the desert volcano and hear again the word of the Lord: "Thou shalt have no other gods before me." Never more explicitly was an ancient admonition directed toward our modern century. Look at our world. We are afraid. Of what? Of a proud new culture which, after banishing the bourgeois God of the West, has created itself in the image of God. We, whose repudiation of God is not official, stand appalled by the conscienceless and ruthless egotism of the self-worship in the Kremlin. With what shall we oppose this faith and the tyrannies it inspires? Shall we huff and puff and blow ourselves up to such terrifying dimensions that it, by comparison, will assume the reduced proportions of a lesser deity? There are some who have no other resource. We must be so strong, we are told, that no power or aggregate of powers can successfully challenge us. This is the story we send across the air waves of the earth hoping to vault the protective curtains behind which frightened men crouch, that they may be reassured that there can be no danger to those who will come under our benevolent power or who will worship us.

What is their answer? It is not pleasant to hear. Should we attend to it? By all means, but for the moment there is the reverberation of an ancient sound above an ancient mountaintop we will do well to hear again. It is the word of One who wants for us only the good, as individuals struggling against ourselves and as groups in conflict across the world. It keeps saying: "Thou shalt have no other gods before me."

CHAPTER V

The Image Problem

I HAVE been arguing, in what I called a parenthesis, that the chief rival of God is and, for all we know, always has been the ego. Because this has important bearing on the judgment man passes on his behavior, it was thought advisable to indicate what has been happening to the ethical norms of the modern man who worships himself.

1

Getting on with the record of the commandments, we next encounter a proscription of images as an aid to monolatrous devotion. This is generally regarded as the Second Commandment, standing clear of the preceding one in its intention as well as in its position and for that reason it is to be understood independently. It is perhaps more useful, however, to regard it, along with the Third Commandment (about taking the name of God in vain), as integral to the first. I have called attention to the fact that the Decalogue has long been seen as a double exposure, the first bringing into focus man's relation to God, which is the essence of religion, the second pointing up man's relation to his fellows, which is the heart of the moral problem. Religion is not guaranteed solely by devotion to a deity. It inevitably seeks practical ways in which it can express or realize the idealization of the good it calls its god. For this reason the simple command to have done with all claimants for devotion except Yahweh was not enough. There had to be safeguards against the impulses that divert man's devotion. Man's enthusiasm and heedlessness both tend to betray him; the former dilutes religion by adding to it the figments of the lively imagination—the making of images—the latter by a careless use of the name of God—the creation of ritual.

I shall at the outset acknowledge a difficulty. There are attitudes attributed to Yahweh that later generations of worshipers either amended or allowed to fall out of sight altogether. This is another way of saying that as time moved on, the moral qualities of God were apprehended both on more elevated and on deeper levels. The dimensions of his character grew with the expansion of the experiences of those who knew him. The alternative to this view is unacceptable. It would affirm that the nature of the Divine was fully understood the moment he finished speaking to Moses, and thus would permit no growing revelation of his being. This from the corrected standpoint of later reflection would put God in dubious moral relations to those he claimed by right and covenant. We can escape making God out as palpably immoral only by making the early apprehension of him palpably incomplete.

2

This is pointed up clearly in what we know as the Second Commandment: "Thou shalt not make unto thee a graven image, nor any likeness of any thing that is in heaven above, or that is in the earth beneath, or that is in the water under the earth: thou shalt not bow down thyself unto them, nor serve them" (Exod. 20:4-5).

Here we are introduced to an interesting bit of moral confusion. We have no difficulty recognizing that the *worship* of an image, "graven" or "any likeness," which means sculptured, molded, or painted, is a dangerous perversion of the religious impulse. The results of this sort of abuse have been exposed and the reasons for them explained. But is there a correlative misuse of the religious impulse in the *making* of graven images? To be sure, the text may imply that these images in general were supposed to represent the Deity himself and that making them would afford opportunities to the stupid to misunderstand, the perverse to misrepresent, and the impious to caricature. And yet this is not what the command said. It did not say, "Do not make any images of me," but, "Do not make any images unto thee—not images of a god but of creatures above, upon, and beneath the earth." This is not to quibble about words; the point it suggests is important. Do we find Yahweh forbidding those activities that have always been the art function of the human mind just because some might—and would—set such artifacts up as gods and worship them? Here is a distinction so clear to us that it could not have been overlooked by the Lawgiver. We must account for it by the inability of the primitive religious mind to see its inconsistency. There is nothing wrong in making an image; if there were, the world's greatest artists have been the greatest sinners. There is something wrong in worshiping an image if in the act the reality back of all man's—and God's—images is lost sight of. Beyond that we cannot go.

Let us move back further into the dimness of the creation story to point this up. One of our proudest boasts—and it may be that by this boasting man shows himself to be a sinner—is that we were created in the image of God. Indeed we regard this as one of the profoundest of religious insights. More than that it is, a priori, the basis for the political thought of the democratic West. We will go to war to defend this dignity we indefeasibly own, even though defending it means the slaughter of millions to whom the same dignity must be allowed if we are faithful to this primary insight about ourselves.

There is no way of knowing why the Creator did this or, for that matter, how, or what present credentials man owns that prove it was done at all. The record states the fact: "And God created man in his own image, in the image of God created he him; male and female created he them. . . . And God saw everything that he had made, and, behold, it was very good." (Gen. 1:27, 31.) Insist though we may that this is the language of epic poetry, it must nevertheless stand as the most important metaphysical postulate of the early Hebrew mind concerning the nature of man. Moreover today, despite the ill use to which the idea has been put, we have no notion of giving it up. We are as ready as ever to decimate the populations of the earth to prove our faith in it. If it is a pitfall to the proud, it is firm ground to the forlorn.

I have said above that we do not know why the Creator did this,

81

but we have a notion on which we stand fairly well agreed. Discounting heavily man's desserts as we look at him today, we may assume that before he had learned how to shame himself and his Creator by sin, the image of God represented the highest good the Creator could imagine. Not only was this image the finest the creative Mind could conceive; the act of creating man was the highest creative act he could achieve. To be sure, this is insufferably boastful and deserves the rebuke that we lay against all such prideful talk. But in all candor can we assume any less? Was man as the image of God a shabby concept and man the creature a shoddy job? Was God going to turn over the created earth, freshly furnished with every living thing, to a poorly conceived and constructed creature? We may now say that God's optimism was not justified, but that is an oblique way of confessing that man is still a wretched sinner in God's sight. Still we must allow the highest understandings of this tremendous creative act to be the true explanation. Otherwise it doesn't make sense at any point.

Now if God created man in his own image—which certainly for us can have no reference to physical characteristics—why should not man make God in his own image? It has long been the favorite jibe of the flippant that this is exactly the way man got his God. God made man, and man returned the compliment. We doubt that this has ever been taken seriously. Obviously if that explains the origin of man's ideas about God, it leaves unexplained man's ideas about his own origin. Our concern here is not, however, a metaphysical but a moral one. There is nobility in man's thinking that he, in ways he cannot fully understand, bears in himself the divine likeness; and great comfort in feeling that God bears in himself our image. Do we not say that he suffers and grieves, that he rejoices and despairs, that he judges and forgives? The alternative to such comforting ideas is the disturbing one that he is wholly other, an idea currently popular in some circles, or the terrifying one that he is so different from us as to be the enemy of all that we are.

3

We see the common sense in the idea that God must be made real to us in fact rather than effigy, nor do we want to extenuate the idolatrous impulses in man's soul that find expression in various ways. We are concerned simply to point up the source of a moral difficulty that still bedevils us. Presently we shall have more to say about the image-making propensity of man, something we think is in itself a gracious gift of God. Later also something must be said about the relation of incarnation to the general matter of image making. Do we not speak of *Imago Dei?* At this point I want to indicate a practical consequence of our confusion, something that at this hour militates against man's complete self-giving of himself in devotion to God which is not only a reasonable service, to borrow the familiar Pauline phrase, but which is the heart of the religious experience.

Man's *alterdeus* is his ego. This is modern man's preoccupation according to Jung and the ground of his current moral behavior. We have seen that this has not produced altogether satisfactory results. Man was made in the image of God. Foolishly he thinks he can worship himself. This leads him ultimately to the ruin that awaits all self-aggrandizement.

The ego, being what it is, will not be able to assess moral failure in its correct perspective, but it will feel very clearly that something is wrong. It would seem to be the case that the person whose acquirement of power—which is the basic ego drive—is the most conspicuous is less satisfied than the entries in his ledgers should encourage him to be. The ego that can flatter itself can concurrently feel wretched. This in the forms of classical religious thought is what is calculated to bring man back to God. Sometimes it does; more often, perhaps, with proper ego perversity it sets him on a detour that bypasses God. Having failed to win repose for his soul by worshiping himself, and being yet unready to "rest in the Lord, and wait patiently for him," he worships man, not himself but humanity.

Humanism was not a religious deviation in the experience of Israel. This is a striking fact since the worship of humanity is of great age and has affected wide areas of the world's culture. One needs only to think what Confucianism has done for Asia as the cohesive social factor in a very old and wise culture. It is correctly pointed out that the wisdom of the sage never was meant to be and never was a religion. It was a system of ethical relationships that derived from an idealized man—the *chün tzu*—or Superior Person. He was possessed of six qualities: benevolence (*jen*), rectitude (*i*), courtesy (*li*),

83

understanding (*chih*), honesty (*hsin*), and filial piety (*hsiao*). These need considerable explaining to be satisfying to one who is looking for a perfectly orbed moral system, but the ideal of the Superior Person and devotion to it made a record of sizable proportions for twenty-five centuries.

The appeal of humanism derives largely from the fact that it reduces the esoteric factors in personality to the minimum. God is inscrutable; anybody can understand a man. Both of these generalizations are false, but the ideal human being is more easily conjured up than the ideal god. Furthermore man is momentarily ingratiated by the notion that he is the image of God, but his satisfaction with being simply a man is—as a practical matter—greater. Hence it is fairly simple for him to project his pride in his humanity to worship Mankind, however unformalized and vague it may be.

4

A little more than a century ago Auguste Comte gave currency to a system of philosophy he called Positivism. Its religious aspect was called the worship of humanity. In 1933 a group of Unitarian professors in New England issued a Humanist Manifesto which was in essence a restatement of the positivist religion of Comte. We have here not a substitute for the worship of the self, but a parallel to it. Man's worship of his ego is in a sense inevitable, since try as he may, he cannot escape himself. I have said that the validity of God's claim for man's sole loyalty stems from the fact that only thus can man be saved from the moral disasters of self-worship. Even so, man will hazard the risk; and one of the forms the risk takes is worshiping, not his own private ego, but the composite ego of humanity. This escapes the odium of selfishness, and man can point to the status and record of his kind with both proper pride and due modesty. Herein lies another threat to the First Commandment.

We repeat that it comes from the feeling supported by the biblical tradition, that man is made in the image of God. If man is true to himself, he will be true to God also; and being true to God he will be true to humanity. When Polonius offered a "few precepts" to Laertes, he summed up his advice in what may be the most often quoted of Shakespeare's lines.

84

> This above all: to thine own self be true,
> And it must follow, as the night the day,
> Thou canst not then be false to any man.[1]

Polonius, being a first-class humanist, might have added, "Nor to any god."

And for that matter, so far as we know, Polonius was talking good sense. There is a long and distinguished lineage that connects modern man's worship of humanity with its earliest manifestations in Greek thinking. I repeat that this was not a Hebrew heresy though the children of Israel came close to it in some of their later enthusiasm for their status as the chosen people. Such nationalism is a humanist heresy, even as humanism is a Christian heresy. Still and all, mankind has come a long way.

> There was an ape in the days that were earlier;
> Centuries passed, and his hair became curlier;
> Centuries more gave a thumb to his wrist—
> Then he was Man—and a Positivist.

That may be bad anthropology and indifferent verse, but it puts together after a fashion at least a part of the story. Curly hair and a thumb are not sufficient equipment to bring man to his present state of cultural development. He must have been endowed with subtler gifts. The Hebrew said he was the image of God; the positivist has been satisfied to say humanity is the image of man.

Now the danger in the positivistic humanist view is not different from that encountered by the frankly egotistical mind. It cannot eliminate the transhuman factor, try though it may. So it will deceive itself by sublimating humanity to the transhuman level. Thus when the individual ego, aware of its inner contradictions and failures, seeks something to take firm hold on, he projects the ideal man to humanity and makes humanity God. Thus all the values he knows are human values. Gone is the Eternal, and in his place it put a space-time continuum; gone for him is the transcendent judgment on man's behavior, and in its place is put the mutable consensus of the race.

[1] *Hamlet*, Act 1, sc. 3.

It is no disparagement of the excellence of character of many who call themselves humanists to point out that their positivist faith has worked out its cruel logic in the modern Marxist idea of the dehumanized man. That is not the way Marxism puts its idea of human nature; it is the logical result of what it says. A simple judgment on the worship of humanity can be put in three propositions: (1) It must flatter itself to live (this is the egocentric predicament again). (2) It must refuse all absolutes and follow the line of relativistic morals. (3) It cannot escape the fact that there is no such thing as humanity; there are only human beings, lonely amid hostile forces.[2]

5

I seem to have stepped back to the First Commandment in what has just been said, and the reason for it is that the question of images as a subject for divine prohibition seemed to introduce us to the dilemma of the pure humanist. Morally he may have much to say for himself, but there is one barrier he cannot pass: as to the egoist the ego is the norm for behavior, to the worshiper of humanity, humaneness is the ultimate of morality. The tendency to equate humane sentiments and action with godliness and goodness is very persuasive. Is it true that what is humane is good, what is inhumane is evil? This conceives of behavior in lofty terms, but the danger that lurks in it is that we can never be sure what humane means, since we can never be finally sure what the human being is. Is he a superanimal or a subgod? This is part of the problem of capital punishment and the nub of the argument about mercy killing. It is our contention that his nature, his conduct, and his destiny cannot be fully understood except within a context which is coextensive with a transcendent and eternal order. This means God.

Our difficulty with the idea of the relation of images to our loyalty

[2] No more eloquent statement is to be had of the spiritual death (pessimism) that befalls pure humanism than that of Bertrand Russell: "We see, surrounding the narrow raft illumined by the flickering light of human comradeship, the dark ocean on whose rolling waves we toss for a brief hour; from the great night without, a chill blast breaks in upon our refuge; all the loneliness of humanity amid the hostile forces is concentrated upon the individual soul, which must struggle alone, with what courage it can command, against the whole weight of a universe that cares nothing for its hopes and fears."—*Mysticism and Logic* (New York: W. W. Norton & Co., Inc., 1929), p. 54. Used by permission.

to God is seen in another connection. It raises the question of the relevance of image and symbol to the experience we are to have of God. Remember the Second Commandment does not say, "Make no graven image of me." It would be easy to accommodate ourselves to that. What it is less easy to do may be seen in four problems, each of which is a fragment of the larger one: the relation of image and symbol to our loyalty to God. In passing it may be pointed out that in our religious cultures we have avoided this problem by saying nothing about it. The world of our times is cluttered up with images of every living thing and of not a few abstractions. If the basic religious belief of our culture were to be judged solely in terms of our abstention from image making, we would be of all religious cultures the most disobedient to the Mandate to Humanity.

There is a literary problem here in the fact that twelve different Hebrew words and two Greek words are used in the Bible to convey the idea of "image." The Greek words we have transliterated into English: "icon" and "character." The Hebrew words express a variety of meanings all the way from anything set up—a pillar, for example—to an effigy that was worshiped or to a vision or a dream. In its verb form to use the imagination meant random meditation or careful rationalization. In Rom. 1:21 ("vain in their imaginations") the word is *dialogismos* rendered elsewhere as "reasoning." This leads us to conclude that there were numerous ways in which the active mind expressed itself in image making and that the images created were void of any moral quality as images.

But this leads us to a psychological problem. The mind has no option as to whether it will or will not create images since its activity has to do with little of anything else. It is impossible to think without images. Words are the visual images of ideas; sound and sight give communicability to words: no image, no word; no word, no communication; no communication, nothing at all. To forbid the making of images would be to forbid thinking. But, we are reminded, it is graven images that are forbidden. To be sure, but the graven aspect is altogether incidental to the image making in the mind. And does not the story of Sinai have it that Yahweh engraved the word-image of his moral ideas on tablets of stone with his finger?

To these considerations must be added those that concern image making and likeness making as a basic factor in the development of culture. It is the imagination that has created culture. The word is the image of the idea, the digit is the image of quantity, the sound is the audial image of melody, the house is the image of shelter, and so on and on. That these images all have utility and for this reason survive among us does not subtract from their primary identity as images. What is to be said for art, and architecture, and drama, and invention? These are the indications of the quality a civilization possesses, and all of them are the result of the image-making faculty of man without which he would live as unimaginatively as the animals.

What then can be wrong in image making? Nothing. The moment it is per se in a moral category it is meaningless. Even God was guilty, if there be guilt, of using his imagination and making an image of himself. It is this, we incline to think, that has made the Second Commandment as it might literally be applied to all the imaginative enterprises of men of no effect. We glory in our graven images and in our likenesses of all that is in heaven, on earth, and under the earth.

<h1 style="text-align:center">6</h1>

If this segment of the early formulation of man's proper relation to God is to have more than antiquarian meaning for our times, how is it to be understood? It must be taken as an effort to protect the undisciplined mind against its limitations. Since the untrained intellect cannot think in abstractions (and except for that esoteric cult of pure mathematicians that means all of us), it tends to reduce everything to image or symbol. So far no harm, but the undisciplined image maker tends to identify the image thus formed with the reality it represents. Uncle Sam is the image symbol of the United States, but he is not the United States. The flag is also an image symbol, and there are those who would do for the flag—die in battle or avenge an insult to it—who would not be interested in doing anything for the folk who are the United States. Thus the identification of image with reality can create the norms of individual and social behavior. He who refused to salute the flag in school (a case was litigated in the U. S. Supreme Court involving members of the Jehovah Witness sect) was regarded as unpatriotic or even subversive. This does not mean that the defendant had seen through the danger in allowing an image to determine his conduct. The fact is that other images, not generally shared by others, had determined his variant behavior and had put him in an invidious light. The danger is there, and it can become very threatening. Remember Hitler and the Swastika. Furthermore each mind tends to make its own images. Children make word images for their ideas and abandon them only when they find them useless outside the family that understands them. Their elders do the same thing. There is no simple norm for image making though there are patterns for its use that have evolved by the necessities of living together. For this reason temperament and circumstances and mental health affect the images we make. We may be morbid or depressed or afraid; we may be healthy, lighthearted, or confident. Whatever our state, the images we create to protect us from the world or to thrust us forward toward it will be conspicuously affected. This is partly why we have so many aberrant religious sects, for nowhere else does image-symbol making indulge itself quite so prodigally.

This proliferation of substitutes—father, mother, hero, devil— that go by the false name of God are the cause of no little spiritual wretchedness and perhaps of quite as much moral confusion. For all our religious sophistication we are confronted by the fact that the demand of the Second Commandment has by no means lost its relevance for our times.

We shall, however, still try to understand it properly. This word was dealing with a matter that no doubt had for a long time caused trouble. The Hebrew children in Egypt and in the other scattered areas where they had lived had long been surrounded by religious images and symbols. Isis, the symbol of fertility; Horus, the hawk-headed god of the sun; and Osiris, his father, the god of health— these and the lesser animal deities of Egypt were familiar to them. Astarte of Phoenicia, Ishtar of Assyria, Baal of Canaan—these were image-symbols of their powerful peoples. But they had their private protectors also. Rachel stole the teraphim (household gods) that belonged to her father when she was preparing to escape with Jacob, and she lied to Laban when he suspected she was concealing them by sitting on them. (Gen. 31:17-35.) The ark of the covenant once carried silver images of mice and emerods as protection against the plagues they were not sure Yahweh could handle alone. It is not surprising, therefore, that to those primitive folk it was necessary to enjoin the making and using of images of any sort lest even such good images as they might fashion would corrupt their loyalty to Yahweh. They must not be allowed to pattern their religious beliefs and practices after the crude manner of their neighbors and contemporaries.

We conclude then that this broad proscription of images and likenesses was an *ad hoc* directive to the primitive religious mind. The making of idols debases religion and keeps it primitive; the making of images on the contrary can be for the disciplined mind an aesthetic experience wholly free of any moral connotations and at the same time rich with religious inspiration. One must not discount the spiritual reward of a period of devotion in St. Patrick's Cathedral in New York simply because one may be disturbed at prayer by those who buy candles and set them before the image of a saint.

God seems to have been trying to make clear that he was to be not only the only God of their thoughts, but the only God of their worship and service. Why does man worship himself? We have had a good deal to say about that. How does he worship himself? Partly by creating images and symbols that prove his cleverness or his power. Having proved his handiwork, he admires the proofs of it; and then if he is not careful, he will fall down before the image he has made. It may be a dynamo, a book, a marble figure, a glowing canvas, a bomb, or a basilica. This takes his eye off God. He falls before his art or his ingenious device. He sticks in his thumb, as did the nursery-rhyme symbol of all such devotion, and pulls out a plum and remarks enthusiastically upon his greatness.

7

This, we say, was *ad hoc* legislation; but it can hardly be thought an *ad hoc* matter. The peril of image making is not in the image per se but in its power to deflect devotion and action from God to self or to the artifacts man has made.

Later the relation of this to the Christian doctrine of incarnation will be scrutinized. In Christ is the image of God made perfect. "He that hath seen me hath seen the Father." These are important words. For the moment, however, I may point out briefly certain practical results the Second Commandment seems to have had on the cultural development of Israel. This culture was basically religious, a religion that rested, as we are discovering, on profound moral and spiritual foundations that were early laid down. The incipient monotheism that was to flower in late centuries was evident in the explicit monolatry of the First Commandment and the proscriptions in the Second Commandment that helped to protect it. The subsequent history of the Jewish people has shown them more adept in the fields of thought than in the disciplines of art. This generalization will stand though there are notable exceptions of Jewish excellence in art, particularly in music. But before Phidias in the fifth century B.C. was building the incomparable Parthenon to house the gods of Greece, who by his time were accused of misbehaving in the houses of the people, Amos had been thundering his denunciations of the moral indifference and spiritual flabbiness of the priests and people of Bethel. Can it be that the ancient tradition barring image making tended to develop sensitivity to life in ethical and metaphysical rather than in aesthetic terms? Has not this been the art of the Jews? And one may ask whether the establishment of the new political state of Israel would ever have come about had there not been the uninterrupted current of ethico-political hope running deep beneath the century-old frustrations and sufferings of her people.

We conclude then that although there appears to us to be little moral reason for disallowing man's image-making capacity, there were practical *ad hoc* considerations that made it advisable. Today we can still feel the tug that would pull us away from the central religious devotion that constrains us. Because man is made in God's image, he thinks man as worthy of worship as God. This is image worship on its subtlest and, we are inclined to think, at its most disappointing level. There was wisdom then in the ancient insight caught in the Second Commandment, an insight that lay less within the area of moral idealism than in the practical area of religious devotion. Those to whom it was given observed it to such an extent that

91

certain aspects of their culture were shaped by it. The image symbols around which much of our private and corporate life is built today makes us wonder whether, sophisticated though our approach to this venerable maxim may be, we might profit by further study of the ageless wisdom found in it.

CHAPTER VI

The Jealousy of God

THE QUESTION raised about the matter of image making as related to the word image in the processes of thinking and the art image in the development of culture was softened by our recognition that it had practical importance to people who not only were erecting a structure of religion, but were organizing private and corporate life within it. Man's confrontation of God is the most fateful of all experiences if for no other reason than that God's demand for priority is unequivocal. Correlative to this demand is the promise that thus—and only thus—can man achieve the "measure of the stature of the fulness" which is the divine intention.

1

We have no difficulty, I have said, accommodating ourselves to the proscription of images as objects of worship. We are able to think up good reasons that would hardly have occurred to the primitives. Their worship of the golden calf was visited, so the story goes, with condign and merciless punishment; their fealty to Yahweh was rewarded by manna and quail when the commissariat failed. To discount this as *quid pro quo* morality may serve some academic need, but to the nomads in the wilderness it was altogether a matter of survival. In part of the Second Commandment we encounter two propositions that to modern inquiry present a more serious difficulty than the problem of image making. Let us remember that this study is an effort to discover the residuum of moral and religious idealism contained in the Decalogue, and to account for its persistence through nearly thirty centuries, and to ask whether in the face of general religious indifference and moral unconcern, coupled with the aggressive antihumanism of the Marxist philosophy, this ancient code can survive in our times.

It is too much to expect that the Hebrews could have fashioned a code that was free from what may be gingerly referred to as moral irregularities. The First Commandment was not predicated on a developed idea of monotheism; it represented a normal stage in the direction of the full development that came later. And the making of images was a practical and not a moral matter. A different mood confronts us, however, when we read what is set forth as the reason for God's claim to man's entire devotion. Speaking of the images man was forbidden to make, he appended an auxiliary order. It is curiously self-contradictory, for if man made no images, he would have none to bow down to or serve unless he borrowed from his neighbor, in which case he would not have technically violated the command against making them. Be this as it may, the stern words follow: "Thou shalt no bow down thyself unto them, nor serve them."

This, we say, strikes us as altogether reasonable in the light of the expectation Yahweh had of their solitary subjection to him as God. But the reasons given are disturbing. "For I Jehovah thy God am a jealous God, visiting the iniquity of the fathers upon the children, upon the third and fourth generation of them that hate me, and showing lovingkindness unto thousands of them that love me and keep my commandments." (Gen. 20:5-6.) If we were not accustomed to venerate these words, or if we were to hear them spoken by a contemporary who expected of us complete devotion, we would not like it. The brief preamble introducing the Decalogue identifies Yahweh as the one who saved the children of Israel from their slave status in Egypt. That was, as we would say, a matter of historical record. The qualities in himself that he posits as further claim on their continued loyalty to him are his jealousy and his vengefulness. The latter quality is softened but little by the more ingratiating promise of lovingkindness to the obedient.

2

We confess at once that the jealousy God here assigns to himself is one of the qualities least calculated to evoke loyalty. Jealousy, at least on the human level, which is the only level where we know it, as quickly disqualifies one as an object of devotion as almost any other mood. We do not like jealous people. We do not trust them. Could we love them on command or serve them except under duress?

This may be dismissed as indicating man's ability to think of God only in terms of experience that is real to himself. We are familiar with this difficulty, but it hardly gets down to the moral foundations on which these directives rest and which, we contend, are the reason both for their longevity and for their modern relevance. What is the moral problem of jealousy? Presently we shall consider the morality of vengeance and reward.

We can know jealousy only as a human experience, and as such it has an unsavory reputation. Not for nothing is it called a green-eyed monster. It is an emotion and like all emotions is connected with one or more of man's three primary instincts: the ego instinct, which is self-aggrandizement and preservation; the sex instinct, which is self-perpetuation and extension; and the social instinct, which is self-alignment and identification with others. There are other ways of putting this, but these three categories are easily recognized in ourselves and in others. By them man preserves his psyche, his species, and his community.

Now jealousy is related to these emotions only in a destructive way. Observe its development: it begins in a sense of inferiority, projects its sense of hurt to someone who appears to be superior, and ends by hating the superior individual and desiring his removal or even his destruction. Jealousy is dramatized most frequently in the turbulence of romantic love. The one in love discovers someone making overtures to her beloved. For a moment she is mildly amused at the futility of the foray, but the moment the beloved appears interested in her rival, she is chilled with a suspicion that perhaps her rival has more compelling charms than she. Her self-examination will be confused and most likely mistaken, but her feeling of inferiority will exaggerate the fear of superiority in the other. She will hate her rival and contrive her downfall. Her anxiety will perhaps betray her into injudicious advances calculated to take the rival's initiative from her. This may excite pity or disdain in the lover she fears to lose. The harder she tries, the more embittered she becomes; and if jealousy ever works itself out to its ultimate issue, it finally accomplishes the ruin of the happiness and hopes of the one upon whom it has seized. Green-eyed monster indeed!

3

This introduces our difficulty, and we must find a way out of it. In the first place we recognize that to hold on to this ascription of jealousy to God with the grim literalism some bring to the study of the record is to make an understanding impossible. Jealousy, I have said, is a compound of the sense of inferiority and fear and a desire to destroy one's rival. All three of these can have no meaning for God. Surely the sense of inferiority or fear have no place in our thought of him. To be sure, in a religious situation where there were thought to be rival deities, it would be easy for the votaries of each cult to cast suspicions on one another's gods. But the point of the loyalty of the Hebrew children to Yahweh was that he was more powerful than all other gods and had nothing to fear. And however limited may have been the early understandings of the prerogatives of the God of Abraham, we recall nothing in the Old Testament record of the sort of heavenly warfare between rival gods that characterized much of the mythology of the Greeks. If then God cannot feel inferior to and afraid of and belligerent toward a rival, how could God be jealous?

There is another approach; it moves under the direction of the idea of covenant. However vague this may seem to have been, the heart of the matter was clear: because of a certain compact entered into by Yahweh and the Hebrews, and symbolized in various ways, there could be no exit from its obligations for any reason. The covenant was in perpetuity though it was not proof against change; no backing out was to be allowed by either party. Jealousy for the maintenance of this eternal confederacy was necessary; God would be jealous; so would those who were his special agents among the people. It was jealousy of this sort that compelled Moses to order the slaughter of the worshipers of the bull god. Nevertheless though we grant the gravity with which the covenant was regarded, is "jealousy" the right word to describe the concern to protect it or the threat to avenge its breach? Furthermore, were we to agree that jealousy can convey the intended meaning, is the behavior of the aggrieved party—in this case the Almighty—such as commends him? Once, we are told, he deluged the earth because the covenant of Eden had been flouted; and he repented of that and promised it would never happen again.

No; jealousy, to cover such a circumstance, must be twisted into such meaning as would defy identification by those who know jealousy as a malady of the human spirit. Assuming the indulgence of such a mood were morally untainted, would not the act be better called nemesis, or the operation of an impersonal and invariable moral law? The nemesis of the Greeks or karma of the Hindus fit the situation better than the jealousy of the Old Testament.

There is still another approach by way of an altered rendering of the original text. Again this needs safeguard against trying to achieve a satisfactory explanation by means of a spurious literalism. At the same time there is an interesting fact that has not always been noticed by those who have puzzled with the problem. There are two words in the Bible translated "jealous": the Hebrew *qana* and the Greek *zelos*. Both words have another rendering: "zealous." Observe: "I the Lord thy God am a jealous God" (Exod. 20:5 K.J.V.); also, "The zeal [zealousness] of thy house hath eaten me up" (Ps. 69:9). Again: "Jehovah, whose name is Jealous" (Exod. 34:14); also, "Come . . . , and see my zeal for Jehovah" (II Kings 10:16). Again: "Jealousy is the rage of a man" (Prov. 6:34); and, "Jealousy is cruel as the grave" (Song of S. 8:6 K.J.V.); "A meal-offering of jealousy" (Num. 5:15); also, "He . . . was clad with zeal as a cloak" (Isa. 59:17 K.J.V.); "It is good to be zealously sought in a good matter" (Gal. 4:18). Now it is an interesting coincidence that in English the words "jealousy" and "zeal" look very much alike, but it is no more than an accident of language. On the contrary, it is significant that both the Hebrew word *qana* and the Greek word *zelos* may be interchangeably rendered as jealousy or zeal.[1]

[1] Note Robert Young, *Analytical Concordance to the Bible*. "Jealousy: to make jealous or zealous, *qana:* Deut. 32:21: They have moved me to jealousy, and so on." "Zeal: to be zealous, *qana:* II Sam. 21:2: " 'sought to slay them in his zeal.' " Also: "Jealousy, to make very zealous or jealous, *parazele:* Rom. 10:19: 'Moses saith, I will provoke you to jealousy,' " and so on.

This is not to say that the meanings are identical but that in the original they are so similar as often to have been interchanged.

There is, however, what we think is an important distinction. Zeal, whether *qana* or *zelos*, is morally neutral. In the Greek it derives from the verb *zeo*, which means "to boil" and is descriptive of a degree of intensity, ardor, warmth—in a word enthusiasm. Jealousy, on the contrary, whether *qana* or *zelos*, is an emotional and moral response to a situation, not a measure of intensity. The man who is zealous about golf is simply an enthusiast, but his wife, who is jealous of his golf, is so because it is a rival for her attention. It will not occur to him that his golfer's zeal is a moral matter, but her wifely jealousy can easily create a moral issue between them.

There is ground, then, for a question as to whether the rendering of *qana* as jealousy in our passage has not been a translator's error. To have it say: "I Jehovah thy God am a zealous God," is to say something about God untinctured by the invidious moral connotations of jealousy. When Phinehas transfixed with a spear an adulterous pair in their clandestine alcove, it was said of him that he exhibited godlike jealousy. (Num. 25:6-13.) It was not the first time, nor will it be the last, that such casual love-making has excited jealousy. We do not impugn the priest's son, but his jealousy may have been less godlike than reported. If, however, it was zeal, zeal for the purification of the camp of the harlotry that was thought to be the cause of an epidemic, he stands in a much less ambiguous position. Whatever we may think of the relation of zeal and jealousy, it is clear that the former is as free from moral taint as the latter is smirched by it. We may at least be allowed to ask the lexicographers whether in the case under discussion "jealousy" might not be more accurately rendered "zeal."

Without waiting for their answer we can deal with the situation in a way that should be considerably more satisfying than the ways offered by psychology, the covenant, and lexicography. It is found on the level where all of our study has rested. We need only to be reminded of the over-all intention of the Mandate in order to see where the reference to the divine jealousy fits. Was this not an effort to help the people understand what we have come to call the absolute sovereignty of God? Such language is too high for us, but it would have been higher for them had it been used. At this hour it is harder than it has ever been to speak in absolute terms of the nature of God. How can the emotions that stir the Eternal yield to the scratching analysis of our psychology or be brought to judgment by our puny moral sense? We look at Christ and see him free of the moods that torture us. Was he jealous ever? It was zeal, not jealousy, that prompted his only recorded act of violence. "His disciples remembered that it was written, Zeal for thy house shall eat me up." (John 2:17.) Deep in the heart of all God's revelation of himself, limited as it was by human stupidity and indifference, was the concept that was someday to emerge with the fullness of the sun over the shadowed landscape of man's groping mind. It was the idea that God alone was the ground and support of their being; it was with him alone that they finally had to do. There was no way in which the limited primitive intellect could apprehend this. But jealousy, a fierce, uncompromising, and destructive human passion, it could know. Nothing could stand before *that*. Maybe Yahweh was that way too. It is we of a later time who see that where there is no sense of inadequacy, there can be no fear and where there is no fear, no impulse to destroy. So it is we who say God cannot be jealous. Do we readily consent that there can be no other God before him?

4

Zeal, I have been saying, is morally neutral; but jealousy exposes one to dangerous moral actions. We feel that a case can be made for rendering *qana* zealous and thus can protect both the text and the moral reputation of Yahweh.

We find ourselves right back to the same difficulty with the words that follow—words that describe how a jealous God would act. "Visiting the iniquity of the fathers upon the children, upon the third and upon the fourth generation of them that hate me, and showing lovingkindness unto thousands of them that love me and keep my commandments." (Exod. 20:5b-6.) Is this not the way jealousy acts? Does not this enlargement by way of threat cast doubt on a softening of jealousy into zeal, no matter what allowances the lexicographers may make? If God is jealous, he would behave as jealous individuals do. "[There is no] fury like a woman scorned." "Jealousy is the rage of a man." "Jealousy," said Dryden, "the jaundice of the soul." We would expect, therefore, a jealous God to be vengeful rather than just. Vengeance is retaliation in terms of one's sense of personal injury; justice is recompense in terms of an objective code. We are told here that God is not penalizing a breach of the code; he is paying off hatred. It has been noted elsewhere that the absence of fixed penalties alongside the specific items of the directive is a unique feature of it. What we are looking at now is classifiable not as penalty, but as the divine resentment of a personally suffered indignity.

We have never been comfortable about this. One of the assumptions of justice is that only the guilty shall suffer penalty, and by no just reckoning can a child removed 4 generations from an offender be regarded as an accomplice to a sin 120 years past. That would be vengeance with a vengeance. Of course it was repudiated by later thinkers. Ezekiel furnishes us with its most quaint denial.

The word of Jehovah came unto me again, saying, What mean ye, that ye use this proverb concerning the land of Israel, saying, The fathers have eaten sour grapes, and the children's teeth are set on edge? As I live, saith the Lord Jehovah, ye shall not have occasion any more to use this proverb in Israel. Behold, all souls are mine; as the soul of the father, so also the soul of the son is mine; the soul that sinneth, *it* shall die. (18:1-4.)

Here vengeance has given place to justice, and anger has forfeited to tenderness.

It would appear that there were only two likely reactions to God's claim of absolute sovereignty or, more correctly, toward the God who made the claim: love and hate. The assumpton is that those who loved him would keep his commandments, those who hated him would not. His answer was iniquity to the latter, lovingkindness to the former. Nowadays we would perhaps call this an oversimplification of the matter of crime and punishment, of probity and reward. We would also say that there is danger in allowing settlement in each case to rest on such obviously subjective grounds. This is apparent in the language used: hate is avenged for four generations; love is rewarded unto a thousand generations. This invites interesting speculations. Does hate reach the state of exhaustion after four generations so that its vengefulness thins out and finally disappears? Who knows? Does love have the quality of indestructibility that can outlast a thousand generations?

There is no answer to these questions and we doubt whether an answer would, in any case, touch the moral problem. But these opposites—love and hate—do have moral relevance that is wholly independent of their longevity. Love, we have come to believe, is the fulfilling of the law. It precedes justice since where there is no love, there is likely to be no desire to see justice done; it follows justice since the divisions that are the result of justice can only be repaired by something that can transcend division. It is therefore altogether to be expected that love of God should be rewarded extravagantly and that the credential of human love would be keeping the commandments.

5

Hate poses a more difficult problem. It is a destructive mood; its inner fires burn up the sensitive tissues of the soul and leave it gutted. It cares nothing for justice, and if it did, it would be totally blind to the scales on which it was balanced. It is therefore an interesting question as to whether men can or do hate God. The phrase is rarely used. Certainly those who deny God may be as free from overt hostility to him as those who love him. To be sure, there are cases when life has been so intolerable that blame for its wretchedness must be assigned to some cause outside one's self. But even then is hatred the mood evoked? Is it not more often bewilderment or bitterness? There may be little to choose between these shaded and melancholy states of mind, but we doubt that the incandescent temper we call hate really describes the defrauded or defeated spirit.

The absence of hate toward God may be accounted for in another way. Even those who possess a tepid religious faith will say they love God, but the most obdurate sinner will rarely say he hates him. Why? Because our love of God, however feeble or fervent, can express itself only in constructive action. By our attitudes toward our fellows we evince our love of God. "If a man say, I love God, and hateth his brother, he is a liar: for he that loveth not his brother whom he hath seen, cannot love God whom he hath not seen." (I John 4:20.) That is good sense by any standard.

Conversely then if men were conceivably able to hate God, they would have to exhibit it in destructive action. Their hostility would not be directed at the sky but at their neighbors. And society would step in at that point and put the offenders under restraint. To paraphrase the language of John—and to invert its meaning—it is true also to say: "If a man say, I hate God, and loveth his brother, he is a liar: for he that hateth not his brother whom he hath seen, cannot hate God whom he hath not seen." That also is common sense by any standard.

Thus we observe that the nature of hate in the human spirit and the behavior of hate in human society serve effectively to limit its activity. This does not say that there are none whose attitudes are not hateful, venomous, destroying. Of them the world has always had too many. But haters of God? The roster must be very short.

Nevertheless, even though we can discount the fact of hate as a religious mood—for it could be correctly called that if its object were God—we are not rid of the moral problem involved in its punishment as specified in the passage we are studying. If there is one thing that the sensitized moral conscience has discovered, it is that vengeance is not an effective antidote for hate. "Visiting iniquity" might conceivably be regarded as a just requital for an evil act by reason of the law that like produces like. Visiting iniquity upon those who have no personal connection with the evil act except as descendants of the evildoer cannot be regarded as a just requital. It is malicious spite. This much at least we have learned from human experience. But even were it posited of the behavior of Yahweh, was it calculated to produce the desired results? God's intention, I have been saying, was to create a situation within which the human family as individuals and as a group could achieve the highest level of godlikeness. This calls not only for law and justice, but for mercy and redemption; and vengeance, a dubious ally of law, is the saboteur of redemption.

6

Thus far I have dealt with the negative or penal aspect of the problem and decided that vengeance is ultimately futile. That it found its way into this early description of the pattern of God's behavior toward the hostile indicates that moral understanding was at that point immature. But what of the aspect of reward? Loving-kindness for a thousand generations toward those that loved him and kept his commandments strikes us as a much more pleasing prospect. Is it for that reason any less suspect?

If we mean that there is no more justice in rewarding the unloving because their fathers loved than in punishing the unhating because their fathers hated, the answer is Yes. There may be an accrual of advantage that is left on deposit for coming generations because of the fact that love is creative and does store up good will. But that is something apart from the operations of justice. This is, however, not what the passage says. In the former case it was the iniquity of the fathers that was to be visited on the children; in the latter case lovingkindness was promised to "them that love me and keep my commandments." In the former the fathers' sin blighted their descendants; in the latter everyone was on his own.

This strikes a congenial response and makes it possible for us to see the dilemma that faced these early moralists. Let us assume that experience had taught them that there are two basic human reactions toward one's fellows: hate and love. Hate is met with hate—not with a simple smoldering resentment but with a consuming flame. Thus the blood feud prolonged its inconclusive vendetta, hate exciting revenge and revenge creating hate, unto the third and fourth generations or longer if necessary; and it became a part of the code of primitive honor for the head of the clan to keep the quarrel going. Love was as different in its results as it was opposite in character. It could be evoked only on a person-to-person basis and corroborated only by acts of devotion and service. Families could be divided by hate; community was possible only by love.

We see here then the pattern of moral concern that is observed everywhere. There is no problem with people who love each other; the problem is with those who hate. A religion that expresses itself in love and obedience to God is no problem; the difficulty comes when rebellion makes redemption necessary. Projecting their own experience onto the experiences of God, they made him reward love handsomely, but deal with the contumacious cruelly. It did not take long, as ideas develop, to discover that they were right in the first instance and wrong in the second.

Of course all this has been said as if it were felt necessary to protect the literary integrity of the biblical record even if it involved questioning the moral integrity of Yahweh. We do not accept the alter-

103

natives since our concern has rested on deeper levels. The First Commandment demanded for Yahweh the primary loyalty of the people. No other gods were to share their fealty. The Second Commandment undertook to protect the fickle affections of the people against the seductions of images, images or likenesses that were not to be made or if made—a curious concession, if that is what it means— were not to be served or worshiped. Now because human rivalries and the hates and loves they engender are often deep and enduring, it was natural that there should be attributed to the God that rumbled and flashed above them in the portents of Sinai the same sort of rivalries and the same ways of settling them. Upon those who allowed themselves to be corrupted by the idols or the rituals of other gods, iniquity in the form of compounded sin or natural calamity was to be visited. This would teach the apostate a lesson and warn his children who, whether innocent or guilty, shared the penalty. To those who loved Yahweh there was the promise of endless felicity.

We must not lose sight of the fact that the Hebrew mind was morally sensitive in a way unobserved in its contemporary cultures. It was to be expected then that the moral problem posed by the alleged jealousy of Yahweh and the clear injustice of making innocent generations suffer for the sins of their forebears would sooner or later be corrected. We have seen that this was the case. And if the lexicographers allow the rendition of *qana* as "zeal" in this instance as it is in many others, we see an aspect of the confrontation of man and God that is highly significant. What about a zealous God?

Were it not better—and this is the primitive mind putting a question—for God to be overzealous in punishment than underzealous in reward? If hating God had to be punished, would the faithful quibble about the injustice suffered by three or four innocent generations if they themselves were guaranteed lovingkindness for a thousand? Here was a zeal to which they could respond; here was a God who demanded of them absolute allegiance but who recompensed it well. To the realistically-minded it was a guarantee of individual and social security that a fickle god could not give. Only, that is to say—and this is the mature mind speaking—a God who is absolute sovereign can be trusted absolutely.

When it comes down to cases, it is our trust in the zeal of God that sustains us when the designs of God are inscrutable. Zeal, as we have said, is a quality of spirit, a measure of intensity, a gauge of patience, a proof of invincibility. It is this, as much as anything else, that all the generations of men have needed, and our own, we sometimes think, more than any other. It comes down to the oft-repeated question: Does God care? Each generation repeats for itself the struggle at Mount Carmel. "Call ye on the name of your god, and I will call on the name of Jehovah: and the God that answereth by fire, let him be God. And all the people answered and said, It is well spoken." When Elijah was taunting the prophets of Baal, the fire of God was the consuming flame of jealousy that was presently to consume the altar. "And when all the people saw it, they fell on their faces: and they said, Jehovah, he is God; Jehovah, he is God." (I Kings 18:24, 39.)

Perhaps we will not ask for such demonstrations of God's power or for such proofs of his absolute sovereignty. And we shall certainly not taunt the worshipers of the rival gods—the ego and humanity—in the language that Elijah used: "Cry aloud; for he is a god: either he is musing, or he is gone aside, or he is on a journey, or peradventure he sleepeth and must be awaked" (I Kings 18:27).

But we do need constantly to be reminded that our God is a flame of fire, not of jealousy setting the torch to hate, but of zeal endlessly brooding in concern over the generations of the earth.

CHAPTER VII

The Name of God

IT IS not easy for us, to whom names and the process of naming are so commonplace a matter, to realize how complex it really is. Not that naming of a child today involves anything much more than taste or lineage or family pride. This is simple except for the possible differences of opinion often involved. What I mean is that the business of identification, both historically and in practice, is not simple. The first thing we see about a name is that it is used to separate the object named from all others. Actually this tends to reduce the object since to limit means to subtract certain relations from it that help give it significance. The whole, we are fond of saying, is greater than the sum of its parts. It is quite as true to say that the part is greater than a fraction of the whole.

Personal names perhaps had their origin in groups that conceived themselves to be originally descended from the same source, animate or inanimate, a god or an animal. This parental source is known to anthropologists as the totem. The wolf, eagle, sun, moon, or what not, was part of the name of each member of the group and was conveyed perhaps by a simple gesture or a crude yet easily recognizable symbol worn or traced on the body. Child (or son) of the wolf, the bear, the sun, the god—this identified the individual to others in his totem. It was perhaps a long time before he needed any other tag. The Anakim of Deut. 2:21 were sons of the giant. Zamzummim is obviously a nickname. It meant "the powerful." Today we playfully call our sons of Anak, "Big Boy" or "Muscles."

In addition to totem names that indicated blood kindred there were aggregates of people who had local names. In Josh. 13:6 we read about "the inhabitants of the hill-country." This was name enough to identify them. We still speak of hillbillies and know pretty well who they are. Similarly people of the plain, the bush, the cave, got their names from their habitats or from some peculiar characteristic their locality imposed. Eskimos, for example, means "raw-eaters."

Personal names first came about by an incident or object connected with the birth of the child.[1] The practice among the early Semitic peoples followed the custom of identifying a child simply by calling him the son of his father: Simon Bar-Jonah. The Romans appropriated nicknames and gave them respectability. Plautus means Flat Foot, and the Flacci, famed family to which Horace belonged, were the Flop-Eared.

1

We have come a long way since the primitive mother fondled her baby and called him "wolf child" or the angel appeared to Mary and told her she should call her son Jesus "for it is he that shall save his people from their sins." Now we have birth certificates and laws to protect us against aliases. But this long journey has not taken us one step away from the fact that to give a name to anything is to separate it and to take from it some of the subtle quality it has by identification with the group. It is further evidence, if any is needed, that civilization takes away from the individual some qualities he can never recover. Perhaps this is the hidden reason why men organize themselves into moose, elks, eagles, owls, red men, and so on; and students in educational institutions are known as bulldogs, wolves, wildcats, tigers, and other fauna. It is a harmless and amusing revolt against being prosaically ticketed as John Henry Doe.

How did the name "God" come about? A name, the gram-

---

[1] A boy born in China on the seventieth birthday of his grandmother might be known as "seventy" until his milk name was abandoned for a school name, which in turn was selected because of some good omen.

marians say, is a noun; and a noun is a word used to denote a
thing, a quality, or action existing or conceived by the mind;
it is a substantive referring to one who, or that which, is independent. There are common nouns, collective nouns, abstract
nouns, and proper nouns. Proper nouns are the names of persons
or places.

God spelled with a small *g* is a common noun, the name an individual object has in common with others of its class, as man, city,
mountain. It is a simple matter to change this common noun to a
proper one. We dilate the small initial letter into a large one. Thus
a baker becomes Baker, and a god becomes God. So accustomed to
this have we become that to write a proper name without capitalization may be regarded as a veiled insult to its owner, as writing God
with a small *g* is a sign of ignorance or impiety.

Time was when it was not so easy. Grammar is an afterthought
of words as theology is an afterthought of religion, and it is easier
to talk than to parse. The naming of God has been a problem of
theology and not of religion, and for that reason it has not been a
simple thing to settle. We cannot be sure that the process by which
anthropologists describe the evolution of names can be accepted by
theologians in the effort to understand how God got his name.
There is, nevertheless, what appears to be an interesting, even if it is an
unimportant parallel. It has always been easy for men to think of
"gods" as the designation of a group of beings. What their totem
would have been if they had been spoken of in those terms, we can
guess. Flame, sun, moon, wind, thunder, flood, almost any prodigious
portent of nature could have stood for those who embodied a particular manifestation of power. Again, as in personal names, it was
common in earlier times to conceive of a god or gods as inhabitants of a
special area. The hillmen and the men of the caves who were known
by those designations prostrated themselves before the skymen or
the men-of-the-sun. Or, and this was true in making personal names,
some unique quality gave the name to the god. He was the god of
harvest of war, of fertility, of art, of wine, of melody. He was the
God of Battles, God Most High, the Lord God of Sabaoth (meaning
the Lord as ruler over all: note how naturally we fall into the device
of capitalization). He was not in the earthquake, the wind, the fire;
he was in the still, small voice. El, Adonai, *El Shaddai*, Elohim, Yah-

weh—these names of God are familiar to students of the Old Testament, and each of them carries its own distinctive meaning.

I have commented elsewhere on the important fact that polytheism to the primitive mind and to the primitive residuum, even in the sophisticated mind, is the easiest settlement of the problem of God. Let every man have the god he wants or as many as he thinks he needs.

What man has always wanted and still insists on having, is a god to meet his immediate needs, a god near at hand, a local god. When a Muslim finds himself in very great trouble, it is not to almighty Allah that he appeals, but to the local Weli, even as the Catholic in similar circumstances prays to his patron saint or the Virgin Mary.... With all peoples everywhere it has been to the friendly little spirits near at hand and approachable that man has looked for protection, and not to the great gods of the Pantheon or to the great High God when there was one.[2]

Thus the names given to the gods by persons who selected them by locality, group, quality, or personal utility could not escape being many.

2

But what is the name of God? We give god a capital letter and make him God. We give him a title, Lord, which means Master; and Master is corrupted to Mister. Thus the Lord God is in effect Mr. God. This is so unsatisfactory as to be little short of incivility.

Now there is clear evidence that this problem was apparent to the probing mind of the early Hebrew cult of Yahweh. The ancient record represents God as identifying himself: "I am thy shield, and thy exceeding great reward" (Gen. 15:1). Abram could understand that. Similarly could Isaac, digging wells for his flocks in the neighborhood of hostile Philistines, understand. "I am the God of Abraham thy father: fear not." (Gen. 26:24.) But this is a long way from the vision of the seer of Patmos, who reports God as saying of himself: "I am Alpha and Omega" (Rev. 1:8 K.J.V.). This is an abstraction that is still beyond the reach of most minds.

We must not overlook the fact that such high theistic idealism is found also in the earlier record. When we learn of the effort of

[2] Theophile J. Meek, *The Review of Religion*, IV (1940), 288f.

Moses to get a name that would impress the unhappy slaves by the Nile, "God said unto Moses, I AM THAT I AM: . . . Thus shalt thou say . . . , I AM hath sent me" (Exod. 3:14). There is some disagreement among scholars as to what this means. Unsearchableness, say some; essence or existence, say others. But if theologians differ, what were the slaves expected to think? There is little to choose between unsearchableness and essence since the essence of God is to say the least unsearchable, but between Moses and the toilers he was to save there could have been little common understanding of so austere, not to say, obscure, a word.

Whatever this may have meant to those who wrote the story, for us it comes as close as we need to get to a statement of the absoluteness of God. We must take care not to put into it what it may mean to us but what it could hardly have meant to them, but a minimum understanding allows us to see that the Hebrew mind was reaching for concepts that were to take them far beyond the simplicities of the god-man relations of those early times. Of one thing we may be certain: We observe here an effort to escape the limitation that the giving of a name always imposes. "I AM THAT I AM" describes God without limit; it deals with the ultimate; he is the origin, the essence, the terminus of being. One stands in wonder that so tremendous an idea could have suggested itself so early.

And yet it is not a name, even though it is the answer Moses got when he asked who owned the voice that was speaking from the burning bush. "Behold, when I come unto the children of Israel, and shall say unto them, The God of your fathers hath sent me unto you; and they shall say to me, What is his name? what shall I say unto them?" (Exod. 3:13.) What Moses got was not a name but a description he could hardly understand. When he and Aaron finally confronted the stubborn monarch with their demand for the freedom of the children of Israel, he said: "Who is Jehovah . . . ? I know not Jehovah, and moreover I will not let Israel go" (Exod. 5:2). To which Moses and Aaron did not reply in terms of Yahweh's description of himself in absolutistic terms. "The God of the Hebrews," was all they could say. This was centuries away from "I AM THAT I AM" in general understanding.

Since giving a name is setting a limit, can God have a name? If he is All, however difficult this is to understand and relate to the less-than-all, there is no name by which he can be known except perhaps "The All." This is not only intellectually difficult; it is emotionally frustrating. The All that spreads itself wide in pantheism shrivels up, inevitably, into the private deities of polytheism. This is why God has been given countless names and has been incarnate in endless shapes to suit individual tastes. We call him Creator, Sustainer, Father, Friend, Judge, Lord, Redeemer. And they are all good names. But which is the name of God?

3

The bearing of this on the Third Commandment should be apparent: "Thou shalt not take the name of Jehovah thy God in vain; for Jehovah will not hold him guiltless that taketh his name in vain." If God has no name but only a variety of descriptions of himself, how can this commandment have any meaning?

It will be obvious at first that the point of this commandment is a practical one, having to do with an attitude of man rather than the nature of the Divine. It is unlikely that it dealt specifically with one name, though Yahweh is used. There is too wide a diffusion of the names of God in the Old Testament and too great difference within critical scholarship as to the preferability of one name to another to make us think that Yahweh was peculiarly sacred and therefore to be protected against misuse. The emphasis falls, we are confident, on that aspect of the religious experience to which all the thinking of the Hebrews pointed: the moral meaning of their relation to the Eternal. To them it seemed important that as men addressed him, by whatever title, they must maintain an inner attitude worthy of him. Man confronts God; this, I have said repeatedly, is the most fateful fact of human experience. When he meets God, how shall he speak to him? If on the human level this is important enough to demand certain amenities of respect, and deference, and restraint, or even of silence, how much more important is our address to I AM?

4

It is our attitude that counts. What does it mean to take the name of the Lord in vain? The word "vain" itself is imprecise and allows a variety of renderings. *Shav*, the root form, is most simply translated as "false"; and yet there are many places where the meaning

111

seems inaccurate when thus rendered. Job 11:11-12 is an interesting case in point. Taunting Job for what he thinks is dishonesty ("Oh that God would speak, and open his lips against thee"), Zophar reminds Job that "he [God] knoweth *vain* men: he seeth iniquity also even though he consider it not. But [*vain*] man is void of understanding, yea, man is born as a wild ass's colt." Here the word is used twice, first as cognate to dishonesty and second as synonymous with stupidity. The whole book indicates clearly that no such identification is held by the author. Indeed part of the emphasis of the drama is that evil and ignorance are not the same thing.

Vanity as "futility" is familiar in the Old Testament. The summary of Ecclesiastes that dismisses life as emptiness, as striving after the wind, is perhaps as cynical and as inaccurate a summary of life as we will encounter anywhere. The creation of man as a futile enterprise is querulously implied in Ps. 89:47: "Oh remember how short my time is: for what vanity [futility] hast thou created all the children of men!" The ideas of hopelessness and emptiness are indicated in Ps. 127:1: "Except Jehovah build the house, they labor in vain that build it," and in Mal. 3:14: "Ye have said, It is vain to serve God; and what profit is it that we have kept his charge, and that we have walked mournfully before Jehovah of hosts?" One is constrained to observe that religion conceived in terms of walking mournfully before God is in the nature of the case a vain performance.

The point to be emphasized here is that all these shadings of meaning are given to one word *shav* though there are numerous other words also translated "vain" or "vanity." More interesting, however, is the discovery that the chief emphasis of this word seems to fall on two aspects of man's experience—work and worship. It is easy to understand how no little of the labor of a man's life can be thought empty of satisfaction or permanent value. All may not be striving after the wind, but a good deal of human effort leaves the hands as empty as grasping at the air. It is also easy to understand how, because of the vagueness and wandering of mind that distracts worship from its purpose of communion with God, men have said it was vain (empty) to worship. And when one's worship was concentrated in a selfish desire that was unrealized, it became vain in terms of uselessness.

If, then, we confine our understanding to the proscription of the vain use of the name of God to the single word used in the text, we seem to see it bringing into focus the twin aspects of the religious concern—worship and work. It needs to be asked, then, what a vain use of the divine Name in worship and work is.

We ought to have left behind us long ago the notion that the Third Commandment is a prohibition against swearing. Certainly no encouragement is given the impulse to use "cuss words" by pointing this out. How easy would be its observance if we needed only to be careful of our vocabulary. How widespread is its breach as we listen to the inelegances of modern talk. The matter goes deeper than that. Whether it is immoral to say "God damn you" depends on factors beneath the tongue level. It might be a prayer, albeit a savage one. It appears that an early saint had a hand in such a commitment: "Hymenaeus and Alexander; whom I delivered unto Satan" (I Tim. 1:20), though he does not record the language by which the transfer was ordered. The awesome fact is that he did not take the name of the Lord in vain.

No; taking the name of God in vain was a matter of moral concern, a matter of morality, that had its center in an attitude of heart, not a use of the tongue. This is what is meant by saying that worship and work are twin focuses of this commandment. In a general way worship is the reverence paid by special acts of devotion to God, to the gods, or to holy persons or images. It is a basic spiritual response to beauty, to power, or to mystery, sometimes in fear, wonder, gratitude, surprise, or a solemn mixture of all four. The imagination can be engagingly exercised in visualizing the first act of worship by the first adoring creature. Its simple, primeval honesty stands in contrast to the highly formalized ceremony that captures and directs much worship today, not only within the Hebrew-Christian community but wherever men worship the world over.

The earliest act of worship was no doubt a spontaneous reaction to a portent of nature. It was followed by a posture, then by a word, and later by a votive offering. This was the line along which liturgy developed, and today the most highly elaborate ritual practices are simply the development of the original mood, posture, word, and gift to more pretentions forms. It is epitomized in the experience of Moses before the burning bush. The portent surprised him, and he stood still; the sense of holiness overwhelmed him, and he took off his shoes as a votive offering; and we may assume that he took a posture of reverence while the voice spoke from the midst of the fire.

The liturgical guide to worship among the Hebrews was not put together until the Tabernacle was built, and it became necessary to provide a corporate expression of their devotion ever so often. By the time of David the priestly caste was very numerous and highly specialized. It is interesting to recall that the last act of David, after he had abandoned the throne to Solomon, was to organize the Levites for the continuation and enrichment of the temple ritual. Some idea of the extent of the undertaking is indicated by the statement (I Chron. 23:3-5) that there were 38,000 priests of whom 24,000 were to "oversee the work of the house of Jehovah," 6,000 were officers and judges, 4,000 were doorkeepers, 4,000 "praised Jehovah with the instruments which I made, said David, to praise therewith." Allow as we may for possible exaggeration, the fact remains that the impulse to worship had developed phenomenally in Israel. The Temple did duty both as the court of justice and as the court of song. One wonders how, if the musicians and celebrants ever all got together in the Temple, the congregation was accommodated.

5

Now if the impulse to worship is awe and gratitude, the defeat of worship is stertotype. For this reason the conflict goes on endlessly between the spontaneity and formalism, between the liturgical and nonliturgical worship experience. The free service can be debauched by boredom on the one hand and by hysteria on the other; the formal service can be deadened by inattention or overpretentiousness. Any worship experience that takes the mind and heart away from God, the center of devotion, ceases to be worship and becomes, no matter how simple or how ostentatious, cant.

It is at this point that the relation of the votive offering to worship becomes important. Sacrifice occurs in both primitive and highly sophisticated religions for the reason that the impulse to give a visible demonstration is integral to the experience of reverence or fear, and a gift supplies the best medium. Thus every religion has developed its ritual of sacrifice. Beginning apparently as a gift to assure the favor or to avert the hostility of the god, it moved from pious bargaining to an act of homage, the symbol of allegiance. This by no means accounts for all the types sacrificial systems that exist, it is enough for the point that we think necessary to make, which is that so innocent a motive as presenting a gift in supplication, expiation, or homage lends itself to easy corrupting. Not only does the act become an end in itself, but the priestly caste, that has a vested interest in the proper functioning of the sacerdotal scheme, is subject to the temptations to exploit the worship impulse or to contain it within the deadly routines of stereotyped practice. The result is the venal priest or the stupid one, and the superstitious worshiper or the sleepy one. In either case worship degenerates into sacrilege. This is not to say that because of the abuse of the votive impulse it should be discouraged. It is to be protected from misuse by relating it to life in ways that lie outside the strictly liturgical area.

This means making common experience sacramental. We have said that worship and work are two rudiments of the religious experience. The former subsumes to itself all men's rational and emotional processes, the latter what is called, not too exactly, the practical. There can be no separation between them; this was the insight of the prophetic protest against "thousands of rams, or with ten thousands of rivers of oil" or "the fruit of my body for the sin of my soul" (Mic. 6:7). This, Micah said, was the word of the Lord against those who were prodigal in their sacrifices but niggardly in justice, mercy, and humility.

It by no means follows that the sanctification of the common task is immune to the evils that beset ritualism. Once again it will be observed that where there may be one saint who can invest simple toil with the grandeur of service to God, there will be a hundred who will make work an escape from the specific religious obligation. So the prophet will complain about the priest, and the priest will disdain the prophet, and true worship both of ritual and of toil will languish. It is true to say *laborare est orare*, but those who say it will often make labor a pious escape from praying.

6

It is my contention that what has been said is directly related to the Third Commandment. Unless we are to regard the caution about vain use of the divine name as an early effort to purge speech of profane idiom, we must see it as a concern that the moral atmosphere in which man confronts God shall be kept free of flippancy, false-hood, and evasion. This is what vanity is in worship and work. We are not allowed to bow down and serve images; no more are we allowed to bow down and serve God with spurious substitutes for true worship, whether they be priceless gifts or pageantry.

At this point an interesting conjunction of ideas comes into view. I am far from saying it is contrived, and yet because all moral idealism rests on the same deep level, it may be more than coincidence. We have asked the lexicographers whether we may say that our God is a zealous God without distorting the intention of an ancient word. Whether or not they concede this point, we can go on without their indulgence and say that if he is not a zealous God, he is no God at all. This is not a matter of semantics; it is a matter of common sense. It is the language of human experience that states that God is tireless and invincible, but no less plausible for its mortal taint. "He that keepeth Israel will neither slumber nor sleep." (Ps. 121:4.) That too is earthy talk. Because God is committed to an eternal purpose, his attention to it must be invariable and measureless. To borrow the language of the commandment, God does not take the cosmos in vain. His interest is not casual or contingent. Man would not hold him guiltless if he were flippant, or insincere, or evasive.

This means that man, as he confronts God, enjoys—or accepts—a reciprocal relation with him. God's zeal must be matched with man's devotion. Again we point out that it was an absolute devotion that was demanded. Aside from the theoretical support of this there were the practical considerations that compelled it. There were in the minds of these wilderness children other gods and other cultists who worship them. Sometimes their ritual and their service were seductive; sometimes they were simply more convenient. But toward them there must always be a sort of intolerance that would save their protested devotion to Yahweh from insincerity. "Take heed lest your heart be deceived [literally, lest your mind become so open], and you turn aside and serve other gods and worship them." (Deut. 11:16, R.S.V.) This was not a common attitude in the ancient world. The early Hebrew protagonists of their faith preached vigorously against the neighbor cults who threatened their religio-political integrity. Indeed the whole prophetic movement is a double-pronged protest: against the evils of alien cults with which the Hebrews were

116

always in dangerous proximity, and against the desultory and debilitated religious devotion they found within Israel. This protestant quality was unique in its time, and it accounts in large measure for the perpetuation of the moral and spiritual idealism of which we are the cultural beneficiaries. God had insisted that their devotion was to be given only to him, but it was not to be a vain devotion; it was to be honest, constant, and unpretentious. If God's choice of Israel was a serious matter, their choice of him must be no less so.

This put their relation on a high level or, as I have been saying, on a deep foundation. The wonder is that at such an ancient time in the formation of the religious consciousness so deep a foundation could have been touched. And yet this is a part of the explanation for the perpetuation of the ideals that have given shape to the ethical component of our culture. Religion, we are told, is a factor in every human life. Because of this it can easily be taken for granted or treated casually. Against this tendency the spiritually sensitive of every generation have raised their voices. Is this not because they have seen that the insincerity that destroys both personal and group security is the same thing that degrades the religious experience?

7

This commandment therefore may be seen to have two intentions: It asks of man a zeal for God similar to God's zeal for man. It will, of course, be sullied by the weakness and the folly of man; but if the intent is there, man will always be able to turn again in confession and renewal. The second intention then is that the zeal be honest. This is the point at which man's difficulty in worship and work occurs. Not that he is consciously dissembling attitudes he does not feel, but that his powers of concentration are weak. There is no solution for his dilemma; he must recognize it and struggle with it. There is no guarantee that the monastery full of segregated saints will provide escape from the errant mind. No more can he who loses himself in dedicated service be sure that his labor is not in "vain." Thus the language of a worshiper may be as chaste as a nun's at vespers and his attitude withal, as flippant as an adolescent's. If there is no heart in prayer, why not repeat the multiplication table? This sort of thing is, we believe, taking the name of the Lord in vain; and it is done every day by many of us who would choke on an oath.

117

"Jehovah will not hold him guiltless that taketh his name in vain." This is a mood very different, we think, from the vengefulness of the Second Commandment. Perhaps it seems softened only because it is negatively stated. Would it sound more threatening if it said: "He will hold him guilty"? Perhaps. In any case we feel that the weight of these words does not come from the heavy hand of an angry or petulant deity. It is basically a simple statement of the observed consequences of insincerity. Within the orbit of human relations the insincere attitude cannot escape the stigma of guilt, for at the base of every immoral act there is a lie. How then within the orbit of divine-human relations can insincerity expect impunity? Honesty is the best policy, we say. Dishonesty brews its own inner poison. An insincere religious act or profession is an affront to man. It is intolerable to God. It was said a long time ago, but nothing we have encountered between then and now encourages us to think that the guilt laid against taking the name of the Lord in vain has ever been lifted.

CHAPTER VIII

The Sabbath Day

UP TO this point our studies have covered the first three commandments, which, we observed, are perhaps more profitably understood as three parts of the one great command that demanded of the wilderness nomads absolute allegiance to Yahweh as their only God. From here on the emphasis lies within a different arc of the circumference of divine-human relations, an emphasis so striking that a brief summary of what has so far been said should set the difference in its proper perspective.

The biblical record we are studying appears to the uncritical reader as a straight narrative of the epic events that began with the creation and ended with the pleadings of the prophet Malachi. That this is not the intention, and therefore cannot be the correct understanding, has long been clear to careful students. The editorial collaboration during and after the tragic period of exile sought to preserve the ancient lore and give it a measure of consistency. But the historic sense of these men was not guided by the canons of historical study as we know them. It seems that their pilot concern was to authenticate the basic fact of Hebrew history: in some unique and changeless way Yahweh had entered into a covenant with Israel in order to achieve his eternal purposes among men. Their written history was for this reason both tendentious and polemical. The success of the editorial enterprise is proved by the way their apologetic was accepted for centuries as a chronicle. That the new perspectives established by modern scholarship made possible a much more satisfactory understanding is obvious to those who have become habituated to their use. It is equally obvious, we think, that the relation of the religio-ethical insights of the Hebrews to our Western moral culture can be apprehended only within this framework. If we are concerned to reassess and reassert the ethical base upon which our culture rests, we shall be disappointed if we understand the record in any other terms. Religious indifferentism and the aggressive ir-religion of the new colossus of the East should make us careful to keep our expository tools sharp. We still believe that in some unique and changeless way God has a covenant with humanity in order to achieve his purposes among men. Our method of study has not abated our faith in that.

The Ten Commandments, set within an episode of high dramatic intensity, are the formalization of a long period of practical living. It is more important for us to see them as an epitome of experience than as a series of ten simple maxims graven on flat stones by the sharp finger of God. Elements in the long contact Israel had with Yahweh gave a unique moral quality to this brief ten-lined compendium of wisdom, but it was the quality of moral elevation, not of moral perfection. So long as the Hebrew people maintained their loyalty to Yahweh, their moral sensitivities were made more and more acute. Ultimately within the Hebrew tradition there would come that refinement of moral idealism which was to set the pattern for the ethical culture of the West. This means, therefore, that it is not surprising to find peaks and valleys in the code. The profound base upon which all human experience rests—man's relation to God—has not been dislocated. We still believe that only as man confronts God does he discover the directions in which he must travel, whether alone or in company with his fellows, toward the fulfillment of his own destiny.

The first part of the Mandate deals with this relation to God and man. It is so important and so fundamental that in order to establish it, attitudes are ascribed to Yahweh that seem to us to be morally questionable. Seen against the then current idea that Yahweh had to maintain his preferred position among other gods that were constantly subverting his claims and seducing his chosen people, his alleged tactics of threat and reward are understandable. The editors must have struggled with this, for we know that later writings exhibited attitudes that had sloughed off his putative jealousy and vengeance. By the time the New Testament was written, these had disappeared except in those passages where the rabbinical and nostalgic mind expressed itself in ancient terms.

With all the allowances that we feel must be made if we are to understand fully the great Mandate and protect it in these days when it is threatened, we still cannot expunge the deeply laid feeling that in its approach to the human problem the first proposition is set where it belongs. Man is powerless to overcome the difficulties of individual and corporate living without acknowledging both the fact of God and man's primary loyalty to him. It is this that gives meaning to life and that opens the door to the supplies by which the spirit of man must endlessly be replenished. Lest man in his pride think he can dissemble a loyalty he does not truly feel, worship and serve a God he does not sincerely adore, we are warned that such flippancy will not escape the blight of guilt. God will have no frivolous followers who take his name in vain.

1

The Fourth Commandment moves us into another area altogether. Taken as a single command it occupies more space than any other and only a little less than all of the three that precede it. It goes into great and perhaps unnecessary detail. It gives a reason for itself that clearly stems from an ancient tradition but which could hardly have been entertained as fact by those who put it into the record. "And on the seventh day God finished his work which he had made; and he rested on the seventh day from all his work which he had made. And God blessed the seventh day, and hallowed it; because that in it he rested from all his work which God had created and made." (Gen. 2:2-3.) This is the Creator of whom Isaiah was to say in a later age: "God . . . fainteth not, neither is weary" (40:28). Obviously the later seer was convinced that God never got tired.

But let us hear the full text:

Remember the sabbath day, to keep it holy. Six days shalt thou labor, and do all thy work; but the seventh day is a sabbath unto Jehovah thy God: in it thou shalt not do any work, thou, nor thy son, nor thy daughter, thy man-servant, nor thy maid-servant, nor thy cattle, nor thy stranger that is within thy gates: for in six days Jehovah made heaven and earth, the sea, and all that in them is, and rested the seventh day: wherefore Jehovah blessed the sabbath day, and hallowed it. (Exod. 20:8-11.)

There is one understanding of this that derives from a literal acceptance of the chronicle of the Exodus. In the sixteenth chapter of the book of that name we come upon the children of Israel forty-five days after the night of their escape. The abortive effort of their Egyptian pursuers to overtake them had allowed them time to make temporary bivouac, but it had also given them time to think over their predicament and to decide that liberty was not a universal blessing. Their discouragement was deep; hunger had dampened their enthusiasm for freedom. Death at the hand of Yahweh in Egypt was preferable to life under the guidance of Moses in the wilderness. Water was scarce and brackish; food was meager, and foraging was hard. It was Moses' fault, and there was no lack of voices to tell him so. The murmuring of the people frightened him, and he called on Yahweh to protect him. Yahweh showed him a tree, which he cast into the bitter water and it was sweetened. Bread and meat in the form of manna and quail were promised, and when they miraculously appeared, "they gathered . . . every man according to his eating" (Exod. 16:21). This sort of thing deserved a celebration, so Moses told them: "This is that which Jehovah hath spoken, Tomorrow is a solemn rest, a holy sabbath unto Jehovah. . . . See, for that Jehovah hath given you the sabbath, therefore he giveth you on the sixth day the bread of two days; abide ye every man in his place, let no man go out of his place on the seventh day. So the people rested on the seventh day." (16:23, 29-30.) It is interesting to observe that this time it was not Yahweh who needed rest but the people.

It is hardly likely that this was the origin of the Sabbath. A seventh day for the cessation of certain secular acts has been found in Babylonian and Assyrian calendars. That it was even more widely customary is indicated by a Babylonian fragment that says: "The shepherd of the great nations shall eat no roast flesh, . . . the king shall not mount the chariot, . . . the physician shall not lay his hand upon the sick," and so on. This referred to the seventh, fourteenth, twenty-first, and twenty-eighth days of the intercalary Elul, which conformed closely to Jewish Sabbath rites. Furthermore the frequent occurrence of the phrase "new moons and sabbaths" in the Old Testament indicates that there was a lunar significance to the days as divisions in calendar time that had no direct reference to the completion of the creation episode and the rest day that followed for the Creator.

2

We are on surer ground when we assume that instead of the observance of a seventh day, for whatever purpose, being an institution uniquely Hebrew in origin, we see it as a fairly general practice in neighbor cultures that acquired features of a distinguishing kind as the Children of Israel used it. It is difficult to find anything other than a sentimental connection between the Sabbath as a memorial to the completion of the work of creation and its later observance. The sentimental interest was there and served, as we shall see, the important purpose of relating the Sabbath to Yahweh. Otherwise it could have been thought of simply as a social law made solely in the interests of man's secular activities. One of the creation accounts (Gen. 2:4f.) makes no reference to the distribution of the creative operation over six days, and it is unlikely that the form of the Decalogue that was in the hands of the editors contained a reference to the six-day activity of Yahweh. Inclusion of it in the body of the commandment was a reflection of the fact so often alluded to here: namely, the insistence of the Hebrew mind that God was the ground of all being and the explanation of all experience. If this is sentiment, we could use more of it, so long as it is not substituted for the facts as it is possible for us to ascertain them.

Astronomy was no doubt the primary cause. The phases of the moon since the most primitive period have helped man keep account of the time. The moon is as reliable a timepiece as men have had, and something in its invariability gave it sanctions needed for both social and religious practices. The moon was as obvious and as dependable to the Hebrews as to their neighbor people, yet they never worshiped it as a deity. Rather—and this we think is significant—Yahweh, they said, used it as a monitor. It was to be expected that this twenty-eight-day cycle with its seven-day phases should have been thought of in terms of religious symbolism and have given to the people whose God-awareness was so acute reasons for many things they did. The origin of the Sabbath must therefore be found within a lunar measurement that provided a seven-day week as an interval of time.

Beyond this it is difficult to go. There is a striking absence of reference to the occult science of astrology in the Old Testament though neighbor lore abounds with it. In a somewhat obscure reference Amos, that fiery prophet, after denouncing the excessive liturgicalism of his day and pleading for the exercise of justice and righteousness, accuses the house of Israel thus: "Ye have borne the tabernacle of your king and the shrine of your images, the star of your god, which ye made to yourselves. Therefore will I cause you to go into captivity beyond Damascus, saith Jehovah, whose name is the God of hosts." (5:26-27.) If the reference to the "star of your god" means Saturn, there is ground for believing the Sabbath might have had its origin in an astrological week, the first day of which was sacred to that planet. This is, however, unsupported by further references. The week of seven days is found, even in antiquity, among several cultures; and this suggests that it was arrived at independently and for natural reasons for convenience. The four quarters of the moon are the most obvious division of the month. New moon and full moon are almost everywhere occasions of delight; worshipers respond to them no less than lovers. It was an easy step to divide between them, in both their waxing and their waning periods, and designate a day that had particular interest and eventually was set aside for special uses. The use of new moon and Sabbath together suggests that the one gave rise to the other. Hear Amos again: "Hear this, O ye that would swallow up the needy, and cause the poor of the land to fail, saying, When will the new moon be gone, that we may sell grain? and the sabbath, that we may set forth wheat, making the ephah small, and the shekel great, and dealing falsely with balances of deceit?" (8:4-5.) He was upbraiding those whose villainies were interdicted by the Sabbath and the new moon, whether or not they were observed with any great show of piety.

3

In times later than those that are presented as the period of the giving of the law, the Jewish Sabbath had become a unique institution. That it was singularly important in the Jews' civil and religious life is indicated by the fact that the Romans found it necessary to exempt them from all military service since they would not make war on the Sabbath day. "When they would not comply with their persuasions, but continued to be of a different mind, they fought against them on the Sabbath-day, and they burnt them as they were in the caves. . . . And they avoided to defend themselves on that day, because they were not willing to break in upon the honour they owed the Sabbath, even in such distress; for the law requires that we rest upon that day." [1] There is evidence of subtleties that arose to protect the holy day more and more from misuse and to segregate it for special exercises or none. If Amos in the seventh century B.C. saw its abuse, not by simple violation but by excessive and insincere observance, there is little wonder that Jesus should have swept through its cluttered detail with the famous principle that man is more important than the amenities, social or religious, by which his life is directed.

Nevertheless the Sabbath was even at an early date important as a sign of Jewish particularism. It was a curtain drawn between the world and the exclusive confederacy of the people of Yahweh. One may imagine the sense of awe or uneasiness an alien would feel among these determined folk who every seventh day ceased from everything that could be called work. Even acts of humane solicitude for man or animal were disallowed. The ox stayed in the ditch; the sick man lay untended. Indeed worship—which to some no doubt has always been the Sabbath day's most onerous toil—was not allowed in the Temple. "Sabbath [meaning worship] was not kept in the sanctuary." Strictly speaking, this special day was appointed not so much to worship as to gaiety. Isaiah 58:13 describes the holiday mood that was expected. The negative duty was to cease all work; the positive obligation was to wear one's best attire, eat convivially, and relax.

Obviously this sort of thing did not come about by a command at Sinai. Laws are the coded experience of the race; they are built up out of natural and agreed-upon conventions that need the sanction of statute and penalty. The legal passages in the Old Testament that treat the Sabbath as an arbitrary and fiat sign between Yahweh and Israel come to us from postexilic times. The older laws seem to demand little except adjournment of daily toil. It was a holiday for those whose daily labors from dawn to dark were exhausting. It is,

---

[1] Josephus *Antiquities*, Bk. XII. Ch. VI.

however, not easy for persons habituated to grinding and routine chores to do nothing. The development of rituals of play and worship, there being in many cases very little difference, was natural. Festivals were evolved by the imaginative, the focuses of interest being various. Strabo, a Greek historian and geographer and contemporary of Christ, wrote that he had observed, as he surveyed the history of his own people, that they and the barbarians, among whom he would have included the Jews, had one thing in common: they accompanied their festal rites by a remission of labor. A Hebrew scribe would have probably reversed it and said they accompanied their remission of labor by festal rites. This would give to the Hebrew Sabbath the religious and moral character it had long exhibited.

Thus the Sabbath had become a prescribed religious feast day, like the new moon and the regular seasonal celebrations. It was at its best a beautiful and moving expression of genuine piety and loyalty to Yahweh. When after the exile it became the concern of the secular arm of the community and its breach was punished by death, it had already lost its spontaneity and become the target of man's evasion and subterfuge. Sabbaths and new moons were odious to the later prophets, and it was the casuistry of the later Pharisees that evoked the stern word of Jesus about the punctilio by which they had subverted the day.

Nevertheless it is not difficult to see the reasons for identifying the observance of the day as a memorial to the completion of Yahweh's creative activities. It gave man a sense of sharing in the creative process as he toiled in the fields to subdue the earth over which he had been given dominion. If, following the moon's cycle, he kept the seventh day for rest, how better justify it than by seeing his recess as a parallel to the great day when the whir of creative activity was hushed in the limitless silences of the inactivity of the Almighty?

Therefore when we encounter the Fourth Commandment, we meet a mandate that was the result of much experience. The Sabbath had already been established; from now on it was to be remembered. It may have been sporadically observed; from now on it was to be kept holy. This meant inviolate. The demand that man labor "and do all [his] work" was as much a part of the commandment as that he should cease all toil on the seventh day. This is a positive aspect that has generally been overlooked. The ecstatic vision of an eternity of

126

Sabbath rest, which is the notion some have of heaven, rules out the element of labor without which the respite would of itself become insufferable. It was a Sabbath unto Jehovah. Here we see the authentic and unique religious note that sounds through all Hebrew thinking. No matter what advantage was to accrue to man by a day of relaxation, he was not to forget that his rest was in itself a form of worship, aside from the opportunity it afforded him for more formal devotion. Some have captiously observed that each member of the menage was put under this proscription except the materfamilias. Son, daughter, servant, and cattle were to rest. Even the stranger, unused to such disciplined indolence, was to conform. Was wife alone to be a perpetual drudge? We doubt it. The silence of the record is hardly significant. We have never heard of its being literally accepted even by the most literal-minded of housewives.

It was because Yahweh had blessed and hallowed (sequestered) it that they must obey. But surely this did not mean that rest was more blessed than toil. The Creator did not set greater store by his day of relaxation than by the six days of his prodigious work. It is, we believe, within the area thus suggested that our understanding of the relation of the Sabbath to contemporary culture is to be had.

4

We have seen how the Sabbath idea has passed from observing a moon phase to a holiday, and from a holiday to worship, and from worship to law, and from law to casuistry, and from casuistry to a flouting of the whole business. We do not need to be reminded that within our culture the observance of the Sabbath has changed radically. From its literal following by the Puritans, to name only one group, to complete indifference to it by modern law and practice there is a wide gulf. It would almost appear that even what could be called the religious mind of our times has repudiated Sabbath observance except for an hour or two, grudgingly—or perhaps willingly—allocated to the formalities of religious service. There once were days, and not too long ago, when travel, for example, was avoided by the devout as scrupulously as profanity. Now there are some who would say that Sunday is, of all days, reserved for riding about and perhaps for swearing. Is there any point then at which the Fourth Commandment can touch us and our times realistically.

We are no longer under the spell of the moon except during our romantic years. Our calendar does not obey the phases of lunar change. They are not accurate enough for us. At last we know that from full moon to full moon the elapsed interval is not four weeks of seven days but 29.5305884 days. Not that this astronomical refinement of man's early calculations has disillusioned him with the inconstant moon and turned him to the surer fidelity of the sun, but that he does not think of life as ordered by any astral arbiter whatever, however unerring its motions through the sky.

This is one way of saying that Sabbaths and new moons as such rest lightly on the modern mind. Our laws have taken shape from our habits or inclinations, and the disposition to honor the Creator, who by now should have had a sufficient accumulation of memorial days, is as remote from us as creation itself. This is true in spite of the fact that never before has man been so well equipped to learn about the outer worlds and to adjust to certain aspects of his life to them.

We have no doubt, however, that the intention of the Fourth Commandment was never primarily a matter of the moon. Man was its basic concern. The Sabbath was made for man and not for the moon, or for that matter, for Yahweh. Why then for man?

There are two explanations for this. The first goes back to certain references that seem to indicate that while teaching of the law was a part of family discipline, the Sabbath was also set aside for instruction of both young and old by the scribes. Josephus says: "And the seventh day we set apart from labour; and it is dedicated to the learning of our customs and laws, we think it proper to reflect on them, as well as on any [good] thing else, in order to our avoiding of sin." [2] The second assumes that it was a day set apart primarily for worship. It is probable, however, that not only was worship not prescribed; it was not allowed. When finally the Sabbath became the day of worship, it was by default. The complexities that developed in the growing community of Israel had the effect on religion that is generally observed: it became specialized, the professional activities of priests carried out on special days, days that originally had been cleared of other responsibilities and were therefore easily converted to the use of those with a vested interest in worship. Thus also came

[2] *Ibid.* Bk. XVI. Ch. II.

about the development of ritualism and the correlative multiplication of sumptuary legal regulations designed to protect the day.

This, as the prophets came to see, was a profanation of the Sabbath. It destroyed what the day was ordained to preserve. Thus Sabbaths and new moons became hateful and despicable, to use words cognate to the more familiar. "I hate, I despise your feasts, and I will take no delight in your solemn assemblies. . . . Take thou away from me the noise of thy songs; for I will not hear the melody of thy viols." (Amos 5:21, 23.) This is strong language and certainly not merely peevish. Amos was a profoundly religious man, who was troubled always by the Almighty, who confronted him and demanded of him that sincerity of devotion that the ancient Mandate had thundered was every man's chief duty.

What then was the basic element in man that called for setting up the Sabbath within his regimen? One thing we confidently know. The word meant the *cessation of work*. Such accretions of meaning as it picked up tended to obscure the importance of mere rest. Perhaps it is at that point that we can return to it with suggestions for our times.

5

There is no necessity here for lamenting the modern misuse of the Sabbath or, as we more conventionally call it, Sunday; nor do we propose to rescue the values of the ancient day by abandoning all the practices that are identified with the modern day. That is as impossible as it is unwise. But there are others who have no technical Sabbatarian interest who are directing attention to the price that is being paid for the frenzy in which much of the life of most of us goes on. They do not tell us to go to church; they tell us to go to sleep. They are less interested in religion than in relaxation. They do not say to us: "Take life seriously"; they say: "Take it easy."

Now before one can come into the presence of God in worship, he must have stood a moment in the vestibule of quietness. Worship may be conflict, man wrestling with himself and with God; it may be rapture, reaching for ecstasy; but it must begin with the cessation of all those routine practices which up to that moment have drained his strength. But the worship the holy day provides was not, and we say is not, the end for which the day was designated. It *was* a day for rest. It *is* a day of rest. It has more meaning as a time of re-creation than as a memorial to creation.

We have learned a good deal about the physiology and psychology of rest that the ancients could not have put in the forms familiar to us: the alternations of excitement and calm, of action and repose, of systole and diastole, of anabolism and catabolism, of appropriation and assimilation. As man does not live by bread alone but by word also, so he does not live by motion alone but by pause also. After the day the night; after toil rest; after exhaustion repletion; after weariness sleep. These are the measured cadences of living.

There was a time when greater leisure—it was hardly simple piety though we sometimes say it was—allowed man to pause during the day before a shrine. It was by the roadside, or in his house, or by a spring. His brief moment before it was not very profound religion perhaps, but it was a symbol of something profound—the therapy of relaxation. We must not romanticize the past just because we scold the present, but the simple fact is that we do not have the shrine habit any more. The places of rest to which we flock are places of diversion; we try to relax by getting excited. To be sure, much of the labor of the average man is dull and dispiriting and invites reckless compensations. An investigator in a great automobile factory reported that after a week on the assembly line the average worker knew no way of breaking its tedium except liquor, women, and religion. Each produced a quick euphoria followed by prostration. Then Monday and the assembly line again.

This is not an altogether complete picture of life, but it is not for that reason an altogether inaccurate one. We do not run with the phases of the moon but by the fine print of timetables; the relentless entries on appointment books, the noisy ringing of the telephone, and the tireless and silent turning of the hands on our electric clocks—these give us little respite. Doing nothing, says a modern wit, is a lost art. It has become the unpardonable sin. The modern logic goes: To do nothing is to loaf; to loaf is to be a bum.

6

I have pointed out that the specifically moral quality of the Fourth Commandment is less explicit than in the other maxims. I do not for that reason think it is lacking. In very truth to keep inviolate a day of rest may actually be the surest safeguard of moral sensitivity. Certainly the multiplication of activity, even of a specifically religious nature, can demoralize life. This poses a serious problem to those who have a genuine concern for the maintenance of the institutions within which modern religion operates. An occasional prophet raises his voice to shout like a latter-day Amos that the noise of our solemn assemblies is obnoxious to the living God. For the most part he is regarded as a neurotic or just a plain nuisance. But if we fairly faced up to what he says, would we not have to ask ourselves whether our Sundays are not perverting into worship a period that was meant originally for rest? The idea that man must worship on a special day is wholly alien to our religion. It is a corruption either picked up from other religions or festered by our own spiritual laziness. This is dangerous talk, but if coming together in our solemn assemblies does not provide rest unto our souls, it may well be possible that the net result, to an honest observer, may be a violation of the Sabbath. That may not come within the preview of what is conventionally called morals, but it comes very close to the intention that was at the heart of an ancient and much misunderstood word: Remember the sabbath day; keep it inviolate. "Be still and know," or as the Vulgate puts it: *Vacate et videte*.

CHAPTER IX

Honor to Parents

HONOR to parents would appear to be such a natural attitude that the necessity for demanding it might be reduced to the vanishing point. Such is the normal reaction, though we may at the same time suit our own inclinations as to how we confer honor and how long. This is to say that the Fifth Commandment seems superfluous. Or, put otherwise, the impulse for it is supplied in psychological, biological, and social factors that are universal and have universal meaning and result. Being the kind of animal man is, he will behave toward his parents as he should if he is to survive. This is an easy and withal a quite mistaken idea. It says the blood bond between human parent and child keeps them together quite apart from the need for moral pressures.

1

It is not denied that this commandment, which touches us as intimately as any, seems not at all to touch the moral and religious depths that underlie the other relations we have discussed. What is it in our contact with our parents that is specifically religious? We may exhibit attitudes toward them that are quasi-religious: adoration, dependence, obedience, service, and so on; but these can also be manifest toward others who are neither our parents nor parent substitutes. When the Confucian code demands of the son filial piety, which means that so long as his father lives, he is to be completely subservient to his wishes, it seems to be saying what our commandment says. Certainly until very recent times this was enforced more rigidly within the Chinese culture pattern than our commandment has been in ours. Yet there is no suggestion of religion in the Confucian order unless the necessity for worshiping the father after he is dead be so regarded.

Nor is this command clearly related to man's necessary loyalty to God. This is important though easily overlooked. It could very easily have been made to serve a double purpose by saying that honor to one's earthly parents was the symbol of the honor one must pay to one's divine parent. Thus by filial devotion to father and mother devotion to God could be assured. But this is not what was said, and there may be a profound reason for it. Is there not a real danger to the devotion we render God if it is nothing more than an extension of the loyalty we show to our parents? God, we are told by some psychologists, is merely a father substitute. Some fathers may regard themselves as God substitutes. This ready confusion promises no good from either end. Perhaps, after all, there is wisdom in putting this mandate on a purely practical basis.

It is apparent that there is where it rests. Its practicality is so plain that advantages are promised although they are for the filial child alone. The parents, aside from such satisfaction as honor naturally gives, are in line for little more. To the children, however, are extended the rewards of long life. There surely is no impropriety in wishing that the parents also might have shared more tangible advantage. Why should not the incentive for our honoring them be that *they* also, or even primarily, would live long in the land which the Lord had given them. There is an unpleasant hint of selfishness in the honor motive as it stands. If there is not honor for honor's sake, is honor for the sake of the years it promises honor worth accepting or worth giving? An earlier command warned that the consequences of the fathers' sins were to be visited on the children even unto the third and fourth generation. Did such parental misbehavior cancel the children's duty to honor them? Is not honor to be bestowed, even on parents, only when it is deserved? Or is there something in the nature of the parent-child relation that is different from all other human relationships and which *ipso facto* puts it in a moral category all its own?

133

2

It is unlikely that there is very much puzzlement about such questions today. We have our parents: if we are fond of them, well and good; if not, we are stuck with them anyway. To be sure, we like them, more or less, even when they irritate or bore us. The civil law provides that if they are in need, we must provide for them. If we cannot afford this, the county home will take over. When they are the secure wards of society, we will perhaps find it easier to honor them than when they lived with us or puttered helplessly about the old place or lived in our spare room. This sounds cold-blooded to the point of being repugnant to those of us who really love our folks, and yet it sets forth something of the way in which the modern generation responds to the command to honor parents. Honor—that's easy; it is the matter of a regular letter and an occasional memento. But honor that involves taking care of them—well, that's one good way of shortening of our days in the land the Lord is giving us, not them. The last ten years have conspicuously increased life expectancy, and there is a rising ratio of old folks to the total population. They have to be cared for. Instead of honor they should be content with social-security credentials. Thus we seem in a fair way at last toward solving the problem the Fifth Commandment was framed to handle. It ought to follow that we will soon be able to dispense with it altogether. This, we think, comes pretty close to describing the mind of the average member of middle-class society. Do not the social psychologists tell us not to live with our parents when we have families of our own, and to exhaust every possible expedient before we let them live with us? No matter if there's a housing shortage! This is not a reassuring picture. And yet, though the modern may raise questions about it, comes the familiar and awesome word, venerable with wisdom: "Honor thy father and thy mother, that thy days may be long in the land which Jehovah thy God giveth thee."

There is doubtless some strong pull of retrospect in this mandate. It is the sort of thing that could not be promised in advance—long life to the filial—since life's longevity or brevity is actually determined by many contingent factors. Looking back, as the compilers of the ancient lore did in putting together the Sinai story, it was easy for them to see that the explanation of the long life of Israel within the narrow margin of their Palestinian homestead was not unconnected with the relation that had long existed between faithful children and honored parents. This would today be called a datum of social history. To them it was something that was related to, if not indeed resting on, the basic fact of God as the determiner of destiny. This calls for further comment.

3

The place of the family, the construction of the family, and the values of the family in the development of human society are the stock in trade of the sociologist and his anthropologist colleague. Man as an animal must live in a group. He is protected and taught by the group. Within the larger group the smaller family exercises peculiar influence. It is the nucleus within which the rudiments of living are learned which enable the individual to make his way within larger groups and thus transfer his acquired wit and skill to the groups that will succeed him. But why the human family comes about is a matter of debate. Is it dictated by the instinct and indulgence of sex? The world has seen many kinds of families: patriarchal, matriarchal, monogamous, polygamous, polyandrous, polygynous, communal, and authoritarian. In so rife an area of study speculation is rife and no united opinion is yet available.

One generalization, however, is possible; and it is pertinent to my discussion as other aspects of the matter are not. The dominant figure in the family, as it is regarded purely as a social phenomenon, is either one or the other of the parents. The claim of the mother rests in the importance of the maternal functions of bearing, nursing, and weaning the young. She is the initial source of fertility and the primary source of food. The claim of the father rests on his superior physical powers. He fells the forests, slays the wild beasts, builds the hut, and puts marauders to flight. Thus he is the source of security.

Now every organization is a way that has been devised to get something done, and a social institution is therefore to be understood as a way of satisfying and extending human needs. A society dominated by the mother is likely to be more closely knit, self-conscious, and vegetative; while that dominated by the father will be more restless, predatory, and belligerent. Thus two types of family unit have developed, sometimes in complete isolation from each other, but more often in such proximity that they have cross-fertilized each other.

It is impossible to secure data to support the proposition herewith advanced, but the operation of psychological factors lends support to it. Is it not true that a mother-dominated group would draw more males to the leader and the father-dominated group more females? The conscious need of the matriarch for the physical qualities she lacked would be paralleled by the patriarch's wish to draw to himself qualities in which he was deficient. Thus came about the polyandrous family in the former case and the polygynous family in the latter. This puts the origin of the type of family back beyond the type that has fully emerged.

No culture has ever existed without the family institution. Its utility arises specifically from the nature of the human animal. For its life it must have physical attachment to others, as a child, as a mate, and as a parent. It must have material equipment, land, and shelter; utensils, tools, and weapons. Beyond these it must have nonphysical possessions—name, status, regulations, and rituals. The family is a fixed institution no matter how multiplied its varied types, and the preponderant factor in determining its type is the mother or father dominance.

4

The family is more than this, however. In a unique way it appropriates a nuclear responsibility for the human needs that are met in other institutions that function independent of the family group. These are the school, the court, and the market—more technically known as education, law, and economics. There is no need for describing the ways in which these functions emerge in the family. It is obvious that they have developed institutions of their own, each highly rationalized, self-conscious, and, when necessary, arbitrary. At the same time these organized patterns of group living could hardly have come into being had their germ not been planted and cultivated in the family. Furthermore it can be stated that the day in which the family, the pattern of which is shaped largely by matriarchal or patriarchal dominance, cultivates learning, discipline, and ownership and exchange, referred to above as education, law, and economics, determines ultimately the over-all type of the mature culture built around them.

This is easily illustrated. The infant child learns early to distinguish between hostile and friendly influences around him. Thus he will be schooled in those two giant impulses of love and hate, attraction and revulsion, which so significantly determine the way he will react toward others as an adult. The creativity of love and the destructibility of hate are his earliest tutors, and they teach their lessons well. Beyond this, and quite as important, is his learning to talk. Words are the symbols of ideas: the more words, the more ideas; the more facility in the exchange of ideas, the greater the measure of communication; the more communication, the greater the extension of culture. If the child never learned to talk, he would have to converse in buzz, grunt, bark, or chirp. The resulting culture would reach no higher than the hive, the sty, the pack, or the flock.

The elementary fact that every group must be organized in order to achieve its ends means that the family must experience and inculcate order. How far the behavior of animals is due to training, we do not know. That there is discipline, we can easily see. But is the robin's low-level flying taught, or is it in its chromosomes as certainly as its ruddy breast? Order within the family is not mainly in response to genetic factors. The variety of family habits, from jungle pigmies to Park Avenue patricians, is proof enough of that. Each individual learns what his family wants him to know in order that the group can get on together with a minimum of friction. This is the origin of the sense of law and the realization that transgression brings penalty and that conformity brings reward. This sense of family order and law and consequence is the base upon which the larger community erects its structure of civil law and social practice.

Similarly also the family provides the foundation for the initial operation of the dynamic of an economic system. The child reaches for the bright object and holds it in momentary delight. Later he will possess it and defend it against his marauding playmates. Later he will learn to exchange it for something he likes better, and finally, with the precocious acquisitiveness of some brats, he may possess and keep more of what his fellows once owned. Through all this, however, there runs a sort of natural discipline which he will observe. It is only when as a mature monopolist his desire to possess is insatiable that he

137

rigs an economic order to suit him and his class and sets at naught economic laws that do not suit his whim.

5

The importance of the family is clear, and the pattern of the family, I have said, is determined by which of the dominant influences of matriarch or patriarch prevails. The latter assumption may be no more than speculation about factors beyond the reach of research; the former is definitive fact. And it is at this point that my discussion relates itself to the Fifth Commandment.

The Genesis mythos represents the family in its primitive and elemental form: father, mother, and offspring. Not all the components of the family had reached a very high level of organization in Israel by the time its chronicles were set down. The idyl of the Garden was a romanticized story of the first family, to the literalist the most ravishing of all tales, but to our study a phase in the thinking of the Hebrew peoples, not only about their origin but about the importance of the family group as they had learned to think of its place in the unfolding of their destiny. The primeval pair were set in a new world which they were to subdue, dominate, and replenish.

It could not be done by man alone; certain aspects of his threefold commission needed qualities he did not have, so he was given a helpmeet. But they could not do it alone; they needed children. These came after the expulsion from Eden and no doubt for the good reason that work turned out to be harder outside the Garden than inside. Thus we have the charming picture of the first pair, our primordial parents.

The character of the idyl makes it of little use to the sociologist. Even the reference to the sin of the woman and the easy complicity of her spouse confuses instead of guides us. It was for her ready yielding to the serpent, that most subtle of all the beasts of the field, that the physical pains of parturition were to be greatly multiplied. The man, as part of the settlement, fared better: he was given rule over his wife. Such pain as he was to suffer was to be from the grudging earth, the thorns, the thistles, and the grievous toil with which he was to win the family's bread.

Now we do not rest too great weight on the exact wording of this story, but we think it is arresting that man's authority over his wife, because of her attention to the serpent's voice, did not extend to the family. If the ancient family of the Hebrews was patriarchal, it was due, not to fiat but to social pressures. We see the man as I have already described him, restless, predatory, belligerent. But the dominance he was given over his mate was qualified by a subtle advantage she held. "Thy [desirability (giving the word its full meaning)] shall be to thy husband." This equalized authority in a very practical way, for while the male is still the dominant creature with big muscles, the female is prepared to checkmate his dominance her own sweet way.

What this adds up to is that at the period of the promulgation of the great Mandate the family pattern was fixed: father and mother, and children, who were to honor them. And we think it is significant that honor is asked for both father and mother. There were some cultures in which such a command would have ignored the mother altogether. She was the unrelieved drudge. If she failed in her primary function of presenting her spouse with male offspring, she could be discarded or supplemented. This was what Abraham did and recalls, as did his effort to sacrifice his son, a primitivism long since left behind. Mother, as I have pointed out, seems to have been omitted from the recess allowed everybody else on the Sabbath, but we think that is an oversight. By the time custom was coded, the woman stood on equal footing with the man.

6

The significance of this for Western culture can already be anticipated. We find here evidence of an established monogamous ideal for the family and the intimation of equality between husband and wife. How much weight we can put on this is a question. Moses was a polygamist, and there was a long tradition of the husband's superiority over his wife. At the same time this proposition cannot exclude these two features that have been powerful in shaping the quality of our culture. It has, therefore, importance beyond the recital of an observed fact. It makes necessary at this point a more specific treatment of the parent-child relation as we know it and its relation to the prescribed attitude of the children toward their elders.

The growing development of this relationship is one of the fascinating facts of family making. For quite some time our children are unaware of us in any except physical relations. When the capacity and inclination to be free of these physical ties become active, two things happen to the child: he wants to be free of his parents; he wants to be like them. Here the tension between independence and imitation is created. At this point, or in this area, the relation between parents and children changes. As physical dependence diminishes, another begins to take its place. Call it broadly psychological or spiritual; it is a substitution that it seems very important for the human species to make, even though making it almost invariably creates tension.

It is at this point of tension that the Fifth Commandment becomes explicit and direct. Its focus is not the family per se, though the family is there. It does not redefine the relation between father and mother; it specifically demands that the children honor them.

What does honor mean? We must be careful that we do not translate a Hebrew word as we have appropriated a Latin word. Honor, fetched from the Latin without alterations, has meanings all the way from simple respects to grandiose display. This, however, is not the meaning of the word that is sparingly used in the Old Testament. The king who wanted to lift an alien to a position occupied by a traitor asked the latter what should be done to a man the king delighted to honor. (Esth. 6:6.) This is a rare use of the word and is not within hailing distance of its significance in the Mandate.

The word is *kabed* and simply means "heavy." It applies equally to a situation that is critical or to a grief that is prostrating. No gala overtones accompany it. Our word "gravity" comes nearer to its correct sense than "honor." Now this does not mean parents are to be regarded as burdensome. Unhappily we need no commandment to make us feel that way. It does mean, in the very direct language of common speech: take your parents seriously. The prediction follows: you may live a long time that way.

I have pointed out that this admonition seems tenuously tied to moral considerations, if at all; but it is bound by stout fetters to common sense. It is conceivable that a man could scorn his father's wisdom without being a scoundrel, but he will not scorn it very long without being a fool.

There is limited biological reason for this. The elders have learned to take care of themselves and can teach their young elemental animal prudence. In primitive life this makes the difference between living and dying. Kipling's story of the elephant child tells how he

140

was warned about drinking from the river where the crocodile lived. He did not honor his father and mother. One day the crocodile snapped his jaws shut on the little beast's soft snout, and when he tried to pull away, it was stretched a dozen times its normal length. Thus the elephant got his long nose; his long life was, we assume, attributable to his subsequent amenability to parental advice.

It is equally true that biological factors work in the opposite direction. There is an instinctive compulsion that makes the parent, particularly the mother, take the child seriously. She will savagely protect with her life the little creature that is threatened. But aside from the instinctive need for food that draws the child to the warm and ample source of it, the instincts in the young tend in the direction of individuation and independence. It is exactly this that makes important the hoary warning about giving gravity to what our elders say. It may have what instinct can lose. It interposes its influence at the point where the rational directive begins to take over from the instinctive compulsion.

This is no effort to inculcate a sentimental regard for our elders who, as their age advances, become less and less able to take care of themselves. The word is "honor" not "provide for." Nor is it a contingent duty. One might self-righteously say that honor goes to those to whom honor is due, and therefore only as parents deserve honor should they have it. This is to confuse the meaning of the word. One must take one's father and mother seriously even if they are altogether dishonorable. It is quite possible that the most valuable lessons for our mature guidance are to be found as much in the failures and vices of our parents as in their successes and virtues.

If it is not a sentimental attachment we must maintain, how is it to be understood realistically? At once we see that our parents are the cultural nexus between the past and ourselves. Biologically no parents mean no children and the end of the species; culturally no parents mean the end of culture. Imagine that all the inhabitants of the globe today were magically reduced in age to two years or less. This would mean mental as well as physical age. In eight or ten years those who had been able to survive would have become juvenile savages. It would make no difference whether all the lore of science, government, religion, and art had been preserved in libraries, laboratories, museums, and churches. All the external aspects of culture would be

141

meaningless to those who had not learned within the family and at the hands of their fathers and mothers the rudiments of experience that make these things meaningful and useful. The stories of packs of wild children in Europe living like beasts after the ravages of war had destroyed homes and parents is still too fresh in our recollection to doubt the possibility of this.

If this is true in general, it is more obviously true in particular experience. One who takes his parents seriously becomes in himself a cultural nexus with the next generation. He will be able to appropriate at great saving all the funded experience of living that his elders have made secure and handy for his use.

<h1 style="text-align:center">7</h1>

I have already commented on the consequence that is to follow this correct attitude. Its result is length of days. It has seemed a bit unfair for the children to be rewarded for honor they pay. Is it not a duty? Why did not the command say that by taking one's parents seriously they—the old folks—would be spared to serene old age? The reason seems simple: Longevity is not a reward of virture; it is the result of wisdom. Nothing can be more palpably true than that those who correctly and consistently appropriate the wisdom that comes from taking their fathers and mothers seriously really do live longer, other factors being equal. This, we say, is clear, though we are unaware of any studies of the operation of this law in the experience of individuals. In the experience of cultures, however, the evidence is in. The two oldest contemporary cultures, those of the Chinese and the Jews, have respect for parents as the center of social experience and obligation.

It is easy to misuse or distort this commandment. Reference has been made to the way social-security cards and county homes have supplemented if not taken over our care of the aged. This, I have said, has nothing to do with the basic intention of the Fifth Commandment. But there are other ways by which it is bypassed or misused. Honor, I repeat, does not mean the cheap flattery or the often grudging attentions we pay. Nor does it mean a slavish attachment to them. The past, as it is represented by our parents, can never be represented by us. A recent novelist observed that the past is something for the young to dip into, not to drown in. There is a danger

142

that our affection of our parents—if our attitude is no more than that
—may be maudlin or escapist. We have been warned of the perils
that await children who have developed father or mother fixations
which if unbroken can do endless damage to personality. The tension
that exists between taking one's parents seriously and ordering one's
own life independently is a powerful one, but not for that reason un-
wholesome. Those who try to abate it either by staying tied to apron
strings or by a radical cutting of all ties are sure to get into trouble.
It is by maintaining the tension at the proper tautness that it can
become the source of both wisdom and happiness.

Above all things, however, this proper relation between child and
parents should not be allowed to make the parents smug, demanding,
or sensitive. There is such a thing as parents taking their children
seriously in ways beyond those that are distinctly biological. The
animal protectiveness of the mother must give place to the respect she
can have for her maturing daughter; the flexed muscles of the father,
who wants his boy to be tough and rugged, should be relaxed in the
presence of his son's first serious questions about the deeper meanings
of life. There is, therefore, a reciprocal obligation that rests also on
parents: Parents take your children seriously that their days may be
long in the land. When Paul wrote his friends in Ephesus, he thought
it necessary to remind them of the two sides to the proposition:
"Children, obey your parents in the Lord: for this is right. Honor
thy father and mother (which is the first commandment with
promise), that it may be well with thee, and thou mayest live long on
the earth. And, ye fathers, provoke not your children to wrath: but
nurture them in the chastening and admonition of the Lord." (Eph.
6:1-4.)

8

So practical a matter as this, as it touches alike both individual and
culture, has a place, we are persuaded, in any orderly society. It
touches the family without which no society has ever been possible;
it touches culture without which the achievements of society cannot
be preserved.

Its moral character, therefore, seems to rest on the plain fact of its
utility. And yet we are not altogether satisfied to leave it there. Seen
within the context of the development of the Hebrew moral and

religious culture, it appears to have a basis that is deeper than its simple utility. We do not forget that the relation of Yahweh to the Hebrews was that of parent to children. This relation, lacking the blood tie that united them on the human level, had to be guaranteed first by a covenant and then by the legal bond. The natural affiliation with its parents felt by the child was changed into a moral relation that God demanded of his children. Honor to him was indeed a matter of taking him seriously. That is what the first three commandments are all about. It was inescapable, therefore, that this should have found its place solidly within the code that was to control their behavior.

The remaining part of my inquiry will deal with man in specific relations to his fellows. They are properly called social relations, but for reasons that will become apparent they are also profoundly moral. There might be reason for including the admonition about parents within this group of social obligations that follow in the next four commandments. I have not done this because the relation of the God-parent to his children gives, I believe, a somewhat different coloring to the parent-child relation in the human family.

9

It remains to relate this whole question to contemporary culture. Where does the Fifth Commandment touch us? This has been suggested in the discussion about the relation of sex to family pattern, of family to society, and of the child-parent affiliation as the nexus of civilization. There is nothing of which we are aware in our times that will cancel or falsify these general relationships.

There is concern, however, over the threat to our ethical culture posed by the Marxist philosophy. In a sense the Soviet state has become the parent. It has arbitrary powers over its children, powers the parents of blood cannot challenge. And it demands honor—in terms of being taken seriously—as no earthly parent would dare. One remembers a remark in an address made by Lenin in 1923 before the Commissars of Education in Moscow. "We must hate," said he; "hatred is the basis of communism. Children must be taught to hate their parents if they are not communists." There is a good deal that might be said about this. The Commissars of Education were given a sizable job. They must have known that hate is not a reliable educational devise. But what is most striking is what Lenin seems to have forgotten—that if one learns to hate one's parents because they are not Communists, one will not be able to love them when they become party members. One will perhaps go on hating them for other reasons —perhaps because they had ever been non-Communists. And not to love one's parents is to fray the bond that keeps culture held together. How, one may ask, can Communist culture expect to survive if it inculcates the opposite of the only mood that makes cultural continuity possible? Hate will have to present more impressive credentials than honor has before we agree to its superior cultural utility.

To be sure, the hatred of the past is one of the qualities of the true Marxist. History, we are told, has never been; it is only now on the point of being made. Therefore all those things that have been called the value and the wisdom of the past are errors or illusions. They must be destroyed. Take them seriously? How be serious about what never was? But this is the way to lose the capacity to take anything seriously. There is still wisdom in the ancient word, and it is just possible that it contains the surety for survival for which the world so anxiously looks today.

CHAPTER X

Our Moral Bill of Rights

IT SEEMS advisable, in order that my inquiry maintain its proper proportions, that a second parenthesis be inserted at this point. It fits easily between the two halves of the Decalogue, the first of which deals with religious attitudes and the second with moral behavior. The cleavage is not absolute. We have noted that the command to honor our parents fits as well, if not better, the category of moral behavior. I did not put it there for the reasons stated in the foregoing chapter.

1

From here on we move into a different area of interest. Our attitudes toward God cannot accurately be called moral though they will indubitably involve moral consequences in almost everything we do. Attitudes toward God are religious, and to reduce them to the status of controlled behavior, which is the essence of morality, is to alter them. God demands that we acknowledge him as absolute sovereign of all life. To deny this to him is not immoral; it is irreligious, since religion is that which unites us to the God who is the uniting energy of all phenomena.

For the same reason attitudes toward our fellow men are not religious. It is as much a heresy to worship man as it is man's supreme duty to worship God. Man is irreligious when he refuses to worship anything; man is immoral when his controlled behavior—whether the control is himself or another or a group—violates what have come to be accepted as necessary norms by which the life of the group is organized. His immorality will tend to break down the organization and frustrate its efforts to achieve the ends for which it came into being. It will also break down his own inner organization of ideal and action, and defeat his efforts at self-realization.

Commandments Six through Nine expose the problem of morality in its simple essence. The Tenth Commandment falls back to an attitude of mind and for that reason does not belong naturally with group Six to Nine. These four maxims in the great Mandate are predicated on certain presuppositions as to what man is. Its simplest statement is that which regards him as the created image of God endowed with a living soul. What engages us as we study Commandments Six through Nine will therefore fall within the context of the Hebrew-Christian understanding of what man is. It is important not to lose sight of this because there are other formulations of a doctrine of man, and we shall not avoid confusion unless we stay within our own tradition. It would make a great deal of difference, for example, if we studied Six through Nine within the framework of the Polynesian idea of what man is and the moral order that has been built up around it.

God is sovereign; this is the base upon which our studies rest. His sovereignty rests on his priority of existence—he was before time—his creative activity—he created time—and his sustaining relation to creation, both as administrator and judge. He will, in other words, outlast time and pass the ultimate judgment on the creative enterprise, which is history. Man stands in relation to this sovereign God. Take this away from him, and his religion is forfeit.

The reason man is confronted by God is that he is a part of the created scheme, but within it he occupies a unique position. He is endowed by the spirit of God in a way that cannot be affirmed of any other thing. If he cultivates this endowment, he advances toward what for lack of a more precise name is called divine sonship. If he prostitutes or debases this endowment, he declines toward animality. All the while, no matter what he does, he is under the transcendent judgment of God, who alone and finally can decide whether he has achieved one or the other status, or how far he has approached them. God may judge man's animal (physical) reactions, but he certainly judges him in terms of his use of his divine powers. The development of godlike power is righteousness; the degradation of godlike power is sin.

For what was man created? The late G. K. Chesterton said it was not good for God to be alone. This may be more than whimsey since man has always seen himself as a companion of God when he was good and as a fugitive from God when he was bad. But we assume that man was created not simply to become a splendid animal, a sort of pet of the Eternal, or to win for himself only the creature comforts of security and what we call a high standard of living. The end for which man was created will be discussed in some detail later; for the present I can say he was created in order that he might achieve divine sonship and thus become the true companion of his Father. He cannot do this alone though he will make heroic, and sometimes comic, efforts to do so and will often claim noisily that he has achieved success. This is the problem of ego worship we have already encountered. Frustration attends much of his enterprise. At times, then, he will reach up that his hand may touch the hand of God. God, always aloof, always brooding, always anxious to help, always wise to refrain, will respond. This is the grace of God in redemption.

2

When man deals with man, the situation is different, though it is set within the general frame of reference thus outlined. Man is what he is, and there are other men who are what they are. They will not worship one another. What will they do? This the moral problem, and it is exposed the moment man confronts his fellows. He soon discovers that if he is to deal with each of his fellows in terms of caprice, or the need or whim of the moment, he will be unable to develop any integrated pattern for himself or with them. He decides, then, that the experience of the ages of human contact have turned up certain ways of getting on with his brothers. These seem to have survived because they have rugged power or flexibility. They have proved practically useful in helping him become a good human animal and a good man.

In these studies I refer to commandments Six through Nine as a moral bill of rights. This is, of course, borrowing from the more customary usage familiar to us as the Bill of (civil) Rights. This latter lies within the context of man's agreed-upon political structure, but a moral bill of rights derives from presuppositions that have less to do with a political order than the order of his own nature. So when we talk in the language of our common legal heritage, we say man has "certain inalienable Rights, that among these are Life, Liberty and the pursuit of Happiness." These, Thomas Jefferson said, were endowed by his creator. It is a moot point whether he was talking as a democrat or a deist. But when we look at commandments Six through Nine, we put it thus: Man has certain inalienable moral rights. They are life, integrity, property, and justice. Thou shalt not kill, commit adultery, steal, or bear false witness against him. These four sins are violations of man's inherent moral rights.

3

John Macmurray has said something to the effect that the moment a man is aware of having a religion he has lost the awareness of being religious; because religion is an all-embracing experience, and a religion is a formalized and fragmented aspect of experience. It may be argued that an individual in isolation may sustain an informal relation to God correctly described as religious, but in company with his fellows he must have some sort of formalized order of behavior. It is not true, then, to say that the moment a man becomes aware of a moral code, he has lost the awareness of being moral. Furthermore it is for this reason likely that the rudimentary distinction between religion and morals is apparent at this point. A corollary is interesting: religion is an absolute experience; morality is contingent. Here the contingency derives from man's ideas with respect to God and man.

There have been those who complained that the Mandate is put in negative terms. This is a derivative of the never-say-don't school of child training and rests on the spurious notion that a proposition negatively stated is less effective than when positively put because something in the psyche resents being forbidden. To tell a child not to touch a hot stove will induce him perversely to do so. Therefore tell him to touch something cool and thus deflect his interest and intercept the danger. All the facts do not support this. If a man is about to drink poison, he will not be deterred by the suggestion that he try a glass of milk. No less will he be likely to agree to the greater felicities of brotherhood if he is determined on homicide. It is necessary to say both "do not" and "do." Very often the former is more direct and for that reason more easily understood.

As a matter of fact the Mandate uses both forms: thou shalt not make any graven images; thou shalt honor thy father and thy mother. There is, we think, nothing in the human psyche that revolts more against one than against the other. The revolt is not against the form but against the fact of imposed restraints. He who digs his heels in when he is told he must not will not noticeably relax when told that he must. It is exactly the resentment against being told what we can and cannot do that constitutes the problem of controlled behavior within the group, or more simply of morality. We doubt seriously that a series of moral maxims scrupulously phrased in positive terms would turn out a fellowship of saints. No more is the negative statement of commandments Six through Nine responsible for their light pressure on our behavior.

At the same time we agree that consideration of these four propositions as a statement of a moral bill of rights may have some value for this study. It converts them from negative to positive orders. This we do not think very important, though the fastidious may be better satisfied. What is important is that it tends to sharpen the outline of the doctrine of man that incubates the commands. If we have no clear idea of what man is, we shall not know whether to kill him or let him suffer. Similarly if we do not understand man's capacity for virtue, how shall we estimate the moral quality of his behavior except in terms of slavish conformity to code. If we do not correctly comprehend what property is in its relation to human personality and action, how shall we know whether he should be assured or dispossessed of it? And finally if the nature of justice and man's reasons for accepting and exercising it are unknown, how shall we know whether the witness we present is, in the last analysis, true or false?

It is immediately apparent that this invites certain important considerations. The doctrine of man implicit in the commands was of course not formalized in them. It could not have been given orderly presentation, either at the alleged time of the Sinai revelation or when the editors were compiling the record in the seventh century B.C. Doctrines of man, in fact, did not begin to take formal shape until the seventeenth century, when the importance of man, as a result of the Renaissance, assumed unthought-of dimensions and when, partly for the same reason, the dimensions of God were reduced. We must be careful, therefore, not to read back into the ancient record ideas and ways of thinking that are congenial and cultivated among us today. At the same time without the granite base the eroding friction of the human struggle would never have exposed the peaks of idealism and understanding which, as I have so often said, mark the moral and spiritual eminences of the religious topography of Israel. We cannot easily assign any other reason for their having remained normative for so many centuries. It is in this profound, and for a long time inarticulate, understanding of human nature that they seem to have the stamina for survival.

CHAPTER XI

The Right to Life

WHY NOT KILL? Perhaps because it is improvident, or untidy, or inelegant—or because we have been told not to. It is a shocking fact that today it is easier to give reasons for killing than for not killing. The cause of this must lie in the fact that we have lost one doctrine of man and found another, or are trying to get along without one, improvising as the occasion demands.

1

Our concern here is less with what is called a theological doctrine of man than with a series of moral propositions. Man is made in the image of God; that is a theological doctrine. Man should not kill his brother; that is a moral doctrine. The two cannot be kept separate at all points, but there is a line that can be drawn with more or less clarity between them.

The story of the killing of Abel by his brother Cain is an attempt to deal with the basic problem of human relations: What can a man do with someone so like and yet seemingly so different from himself? This epic is not so old as it seems to be because it's found in the fourth chapter of Genesis. It exhibits a sensitivity to certain components in the human dilemma that must represent a much later time than that which witnessed the first primitive homicide. That it is set in a quasi-religious context is also important. It was Yahweh's displeasure with Cain's offering that activated Cain's fratricidal anger at Abel. It was the voice of Yahweh that startled him with a question when

Yahweh saw the trickle of blood across the troubled ground. And the ending of the story finds Cain banished from the face of the Eternal. Nevertheless the important factors are moral. It was a conflict between two men.

It is too bad that the fashioner of the ancient tale left untold what might have been one of the most interesting of all conversations. After Cain's offering had been refused for reasons that are not given—except that he "did not well"—Cain went and talked with Abel. What did he say? He had been very wroth and his countenance was fallen and his mood was not conducive to friendly talk, but the fact that he went to him may give us a clue. Something in his relationship to his brother was tied into his having been repudiated by Yahweh. Did he justify himself before the more favored man? Little point in this. Perhaps, as an angry man might, he spoke disparagingly of the offering Abel had made. Or maybe he told Abel that if they were to get along, Abel would have to become like him. He would have to give up herding sheep and help him raise "fruit of the ground." This is one way we try to come to terms with the differences that irritate us. Change our annoying brothers into a likeness to ourselves.

Or he might have said that their relations, badly damaged by Yahweh's invidious choice of Abel's sacrifice, could be repaired if Abel agreed to keep himself and his flocks off Cain's property. The sheep had spoiled some of his crop. Pen them up or fence them off. This is another way we deal with our odd brethren: keep them in their place with a warning that they will get into trouble if they trespass in our territory. Thus the ghetto, the other side of the tracks.

This lost conversation intrigues the would-be interpreter, but he must come back at last to the inference that what Cain told his brother amounted to his decision that they could not get on at all and the solution to their problem lay in the elimination of one of them. Perhaps because Cain was already angry and therefore the aggressor, he was able to take his adversary by surprise. "When they were in the field, . . . Cain rose up . . . and slew him." (Gen. 4:8.)

2

The consequences of this hideous act are interesting. Cain, having discovered that his brother was both like and unlike him, decided that he was an enemy. By ever so little he might have been led to

153

regard him as a comrade. But that would have both spoiled the story and falsified the long record of man's bitter struggle with his brother. What followed was a repudiation by nature of this unnatural deed. Not only was the voice of Abel's blood articulate with an anguished cry; the ground that received the warm, ruddy flood cried out its curse on the murderer. Never was he to see again the soil respond with fruit to his plowing and sowing. Worse than this he was an outcast. Not only would nature withhold her fruitage; she would watch his vagabond and fugitive wanderings until he could flee no more.

Cain protested to Yahweh that his punishment was too great. Not only was he outlawed by the earth; he was banished by God. Alien in a vengeful cosmos, he would see in every hand a weapon sharpened against him; hagridden by fear, he would flee only to find himself ambushed by unseen enemies. Yahweh, so the story goes, mitigated somewhat the severity of nature's ban. He set a mark upon him that warned others to let him alone. This was poor comfort; to know that one will not be slain by angry men because they fear retaliation is scant recompense for losing the companionship of one's fellows. Better be dead at their hands than to live under their scorn. The story's end shows us the first fratricide departing from the presence of God to dwell in the land of Nod—the land of the forever wandering.

3

Our point is that most of these relations are moral. His quarrel with his brother, the heavy blow that felled him, the many-tongued voice of the blood, the curse of the ground, the promise of thriveless toil, the fugitive flight, the chilling inner fear, and the enmity of all men—these are moral relationships; they have to do with man's response to the world of nature within which he is set. We are provided, therefore, with a hint as to what an ancient editor thought a storyteller thought about man. He is the work of the Creator, set within a plexus of relationships with which he must deal. All men are alike; all are different. Differences may be composed or exaggerated. In the former case community is possible; in the latter fratricide is sooner or later inescapable. It is a painful dilemma, and man, caught in it, excites our pity. Being what he is, he likes himself and believes in what he does. But this brings him into conflict with his brother, who is caught in the same kind of egoism. His efforts to make his brother like himself are not thought to be generous; they are prideful and blind. No more will he make himself like his brother for the very reason that he cannot do it. At the same time nature is a panorama of endless variety. How dull life would be if identity were its only pattern! What a stupid world if every person were like every other! Man sees this, but within him is that impulse he cannot somehow deny or resist. He must be himself. So if he cannot find a level of life above differences that composes a new synthesis without canceling differences, he must regard difference as danger and those who are not like him as interlopers. He must kill them to save himself.

4

This story, we say, is freighted with ageless insight. It had no doubt been passed from mouth to mouth for untold generations, its point being grasped by some, missed by most. When the time came for the wisdom it contained to be co-ordinated into an order by which men were to live, the Mandate said: "Thou shalt not kill." It was clear, unambiguous, terrifyingly uncomplicated.

We may ask, however, why it was included. Moses, the putative giver of the law, was a murderer. We are told that when Aaron and the bull worshipers danced about the golden calf, Moses ordered their butchery; and brother fell on brother in grisly slaughter. These calf worshipers were different; they would not be persuaded that Yahweh was the god to worship. Therefore they should die. Was the earth silent after that orgy of blood? We have heard of wars of religion and how those who waged them called on their gods to bless their arms. And in wars of conquest and subjugation and revenge the same thing has been done. It is somewhat puzzling how this bit of moral admonition got into the code. To be sure, the critical problem is simple: the editors of later centuries put it back into a context out of which it most likely could not have emerged. But the moral problem is not so easy. Israel possessed by killing the homestead offered her. It was the divine purpose that Canaan should be the land of promise where the great saga of God's revelation was to be enacted and told. Could it not have been won from its tribal owners by persuasion or bought on a long-term basis? Did not the intentions of Yahweh make necessary killing the aliens who possessed by squatter's rights the land they were to lose in bloody warfare? No matter what theological overtones we allow ourselves to hear, this is distinctly a moral question.

5

The inquiry, however, must go back beyond the ancient lore and ask why it was finally agreed that to take the life of another human being was to be prohibited. To be sure, there is no specific statement that it is human life that is to be protected; but to assume otherwise is obviously unsupportable. The commission with which the newly created lord of the earth began operation indicated that he was to "be fruitful, and multiply, and replenish the earth, and subdue it; and have dominion over the fish of the sea, and over the birds of the heavens, and over every living thing that creepeth upon the earth" (Gen. 1:28). To this was added the right of man to eat herbs and fruits. To birds and beasts and creeping things green herbs were provided for food. This would, if literally observed, have made man as completely vegetarian as his humble herb-eating cogeners. The likelihood is, however, that man was carnivorous before he learned to eat raw fruits and cereal grasses.

What is of interest to our study is that he was not given the same sort of dominion over his fellow man that he was allowed over his brute companions. It took skills that were a long time developing to subdue the animal he needed for food, and greater skill for its domestication. To get along with his human correlate required skills of a wholly different sort. This is part of the meaning of the story of Cain and Abel. When the older man dimly realized that he could not get on with his younger brother, he dealt with him as a marauding beast. That he was by the penalties on this act reduced to the status of a marauder is in a subtle way an intimation of what becomes of men whose only resource for dealing with intractable humans is a club.

In other words life per se is not inviolate. The right of the human to kill seems basic to his capacity to live. Schweitzer has built a philosophy of civilization on an a priori reverence for life. The will to live is universal and absolute in every organism. That it must be assisted in the struggle for life becomes the primary moral obligation. This is an extension of the right to life and the command against killing to everything that lives. He concedes that this must be qualified since to eat means to destroy, and when a venomous snake or a leopard threatens life on the hospital compound, he is handy with a gun. But he will not needlessly crush an ant.[1]

Life, the biochemist tells us, is a dynamic molecular organization kept going by oxygen and oxidation. Death is the natural irreversible breakdown of this structure, always present and only warded off by the structure-preserving action of oxidation. Life needs no commandment to protect it; it has no moral rights. All it needs is an element of which there seems to be limitless supply and a process that is fairly automatic.

By the same token if this is all there is to life, we can find plenty of reasons for destroying it. Certainly in its unpleasant, and therefore for us unnecessary, forms we come close to feeling a moral obligation to exterminate it. Many a farmer feels a sense of pious satisfaction after a day of dusting his cotton patch against the boll weevil, and in earlier days some of us counted the dead potato bugs that had succumbed to an affusion of Paris green with a sense of statistical participation in the divine plans for man's dinner table.

We are not dealing with a biochemical problem, however. Life, as we are concerned with it, is set primarily within a moral context. Boll weevil and potato bug are as exempt from moral obligations as we are spared moral compunction in their destruction. It is only as life is seen upon a higher level that it becomes morally important. This level, as best we can understand it, is concerned with the divine intention. Life in all its forms is the result of the creative act of God. This puts in the language of religion what science also says in other terms. Despite a prediction recently made that the chemical origin of life will be discovered within the next half century and will be biochemistry's crowning achievement, we are still little nearer than Archbishop Ussher was four hundred years ago. Furthermore when the chemical origin of life is finally ferreted out, we shall still have to know the origin of the chemical elements that combine to "create" it. Even then the problem of ends will not have been resolved. Why life at all?

[1] This recalls a verse of Cowper:
"I would not enter on my list of friends
(Though graced with polished manners and fine sense,
Yet wanting sensibility) the man
Who needlessly sets foot upon a worm."

From our perspective life is the result, as I have said, of divine creativity. Its meaning is found in the creative intention. It follows that the reason for its protection or destruction must also be found there, and this is what the Genesis mythos is concerned about. The creation, as surveyed at the close of the sixth day, inspired in the Creator high enthusiasm. "Everything that he had made . . . was very good." Was it good simply in its created state, or was it good in terms of the end it was designed to serve?

It is no simple matter for us to say what that end was, though this does not seem to keep us from saying so with great confidence. The biblical tradition, however, is clear. Man stood in a unique relation to the rest of the shiny new cosmos: he was to subdue and dominate it. This required of him certain qualities of mind with which he was uniquely equipped. More than this, however, it required of him a spiritual quality which is known as moral sensitivity. It was the sense that he must do certain things in the light of a responsibility that was superior to subjugation and domination on the physical level. This was the best he knew about pursuing the divine intention. This is what we call doing the will of God.

It is clear to us who are human beings that life as it is observed in us is different from any other manifestation of it. This natural pride is easily deflated by much that we do, and if the animals and flowers ever ruminate—as poets say they do—on man's stupidity, they have less exalted opinions than we. Still and all, we can do no other. The check on our pride comes when we realize that given this superior status, we come under severer constraints. Because we are what we are, and never mind how we got that way, we must feel and respond to impulses that never activate the lower orders. These are moral obligations. They may at times be felt with respect to the lesser creatures, though these are less moral than sentimental. We can never react toward a fellow human creature except in moral terms. If this gratifies a sense of importance, it also oppresses us with its sense of duty.

Duty, then, is understood in terms of what end man as a creature is intended to serve. We must look at human life in its origin, meaning, and value through the spectrum of what God expects of us. Oxygen and oxidation are as necessary for human life as for the unicellular organisms, but they cannot supply man with what makes

158

him tick. These two aids serve for us a purpose far beyond keeping a physical process going.

6

Thus we see that killing or protecting human life is a moral matter determined by the ends for which we believe it to exist. If human life has no meaning beyond itself and its processes, we may argue that its premature termination in some cases is the best thing that can happen to it. With equal plausibility it can be maintained that all our efforts should combine to extend it. If physical life is an end in itself, it may be difficult to decide what should be done about it. Is the end served by longevity even unto painful and impotent years? Or is the end served by heightened vitality assisted by synthetic hormones? When vitality declines, life should end. This has been the practical solution of the problem of infirmity in some societies. Plato is said to have approved the exposure of ill-begotten infants, and in Tahiti time was when the duty of the eldest son demanded that he dispatch his father with a surreptitious blow on the head when he reached his sixtieth birthday. Each of these was given moral sanction of a sort, since each was thought to be serving the proper end for which life was designed. In Plato's case the end was conceived partially at least in terms of infantile robustness; in the case of the South Sea islander it was conceived in terms of a guarantee against final senility and indigence. Were they not morally justified?

Out of this idea of the end for which man was created stems the impulse toward self-preservation, claimed by some to be his primary instinct. Whether this is so or not, self-preservation is blessed by dubious moral support. Obviously the end of my life is the end that I set for it. I shall not therefore encourage my son to slay me at sixty; nor would I, had I been born a monster and able to consult my disappointed parents, have consented to my delivery to the wild beasts. Therefore, if I am to decide what my life is for and if you thwart my efforts to realize it, I shall get rid of you and regard it as a moral achievement. Otherwise how shall I reach my morally determined end? I shall have no difficulty persuading myself that this works out to my advantage and perhaps to yours. It reduces itself to the simple matter of getting rid of the less viable or less worthy organism in order that a more deserving and more promising organism shall live. You will not agree, and the argument will be transferred to the lists where we can fight it out. The better man will win, even though he may be the worse.

7

This is the practical solution that Cain reached, subject of course to certain refinements of thought that he doubtless did not indulge himself. And it is the practical solution of all those whose idea of the end of life as it is sought by man has no transcendent referent. We have long been familiar with the dictum of Kant which he regarded as basic to all moral action: Never treat a person as a means to an end but as an end in himself. Kant arrived at this judgment by way of his analysis of the ego and his belief in teleology in nature. The ego, which enters into the synthesis of cognition, is distinct from it and is always conscious of its own unity and identity, a self-consciousness not derived, but given. The teleology in nature rests on a transcendental theology which makes perfection the principle of systematic unity, connecting all things according to universal and necessary laws, the chief of which is the existence of the supreme good.

It is somewhat strange that Kant, holding as strongly as he did to what he called a physicotheology, which was a synthesis of the human and transcendent, should have posited for man a teleology within himself. Only thus could he have made right moral action determined by regarding every man an end in himself. This is not the biblical tradition, nor is it the end that was formulated by the Westminster divines in the familiar statement to the effect that the chief end of man is to glorify God and enjoy him forever. Here clearly man is not regarded as an end in himself; he is regarded as a being that has his end in God.

When this is the case, our attitudes toward man and his life purposes are conspicuously changed. Physical life is hardly an end, else eat, drink, and be merry would be the correct formula for living. We would add to it a provision that any man who deterred our pursuit of this tripartite end would be, if necessary, summarily disposed of, accompanied by a display of moral self-satisfaction. Is life on

160

the level above the physical, whatever we may call it, an end in itself? If it is, then the sheer contemplation of the hermit or the raptures of the saint are the essence of morality. Whether the effort to achieve such a level of vitality carries with it the moral right to remove those who, pursuing baser ends, interrupt our elevated thoughts is another matter. In any case there is a strong temptation to invest such an end with the highest moral approbation, whether it be claimed by the saint himself or offered by his envious brother.

Not all those who refuse to accept the Kantian wisdom agree precisely on what the supreme end of man is, and herein lies the cause of certain moral confusions in our times. Some claim that society, its security and well-being, is the end of man. Here the state assumes to itself transcendent values and rights. In order to be secure it has the moral right to forfeit the life of the individual who menaces it. He may be a physical danger—hence capital punishment. He may harbor dangerous thoughts—therefore deny him his liberty or if he persists, kill him. Or it may be that the social order is secure in its physical aspects, so sure indeed that it has grown proud of its self-sufficiency. In this case the honor of society becomes the end of the individual. He must contribute to the distension of the collective ego. And if, perchance, the alien in the midst, or in the neighborhood, smirches our social pride—it is generally our national honor—we must go to war and kill him and the society which he represents. The limitless folly and futility of this is perhaps history's most peremptory judgment.

Indeed it would appear that the conflict between a truly transcendent and social end of man constitutes the major moral and spiritual struggle of our times. If the end of man is found, not in himself but in God, all his moral ideas and practices will be designed to achieve it. The individual in such circumstances will often count not his life as dear unto himself.[2] That is the heroism of martyrdom. It is, as I shall point out in detail later, the meaning of the Cross as a moral principle. If, on the contrary, the end of man is found in society— whether it be the state or a social stratum—the life of the individual will be lightly regarded; and if he opposes the designs of the state, his moral right to life will be canceled.

[2] Acts 20:22-25 gives the magnificent testimony of Paul on this point.

8

It would seem to follow from what has been said that the only moral reason for the right to life lies in a concept of man that begins with the belief that he by his nature is related to purposes beyond himself. In other words, man is not an end in himself. This is a tremendous faith, for such it is; and it involves, whenever it is accepted, moral attitudes that are monumental.

For all this is a lunge of faith, it is not any less susceptible to the support that can be brought it from so-called practical considerations. It may have already been obvious to the wilderness primitives that killing people had limited utility as an established social practice. We have no reason for thinking that they had reflected on such matters except for the folk tale of Cain and Abel. The purpose of folklore being the dual one of preserving a tradition and inculcating a moral, we may assume that those who heard the ancient story told in the dancing light of the campfire did not lose its point. Abel is ever the innocent victim of jealous spite; Cain is, to the end of time, the vagabond who carries with him the execrations of the soil, the scorn of his fellows, and the rejection of God. That he went to the land of the ever-wandering and took wives and begat sons is another story altogether. It may have been an addendum by a tale-teller who felt sorry for the misfortunes that dogged the footsteps of earth's first fratricide.

It may be asked today what practical values killing has confirmed. Being human and therefore in dominion over all living things, we can say that without the taking of the life of the lower orders man's commission to subdue and rule could not have been executed. The beasts he slew gave him skins and meat, the trees he felled gave him a hut, and a feather from the wing of a bird gave his spouse a bauble for her hair. These things were given him that he might become more than the creatures he was to tame. There is, indeed, an understanding of the whole growth of culture that rests upon man's skill in killing. Toynbee calls it challenge and response. The challenge of the creature called for the response of the subjugator.

But killing his own kind does something different. Allowing as we must for a lower sensitivity in the primitive man who first slew his fellow, we are nevertheless led to believe that the reaction he felt was not like his pride in knocking down a wild ox with a club. Nature prompts us at this point. Except at certain seasons there are no intramural battles within species. "Red in tooth and claw with ravine" nature may be, but she sees to it that each species protects itself and for very practical reasons. Our Genesis story prompts us also here. Cain, made aware of the enormity of his act, cried out that he feared for his own life now that it was known that he had taken the life of another. This was the early intimation of conscience which always begins in fear and moves on to self-rebuke.

If the purposes of natural survival and the importance of conscience are served by guaranteeing the right to life, what purposes are served by its denial? The many-voiced reply of the world returns its various answers. We live in a generation that has seen two great organized butcheries called world wars. The total killings are beyond precise computing, but were we able to give the statistics to the last fatality, our realization of the emptiness of war would be more acute. We have explained that these wars were necessary for the preservation of ideals—moral, spiritual, political, economic—that were threatened by modern sons of Cain. These ideals have not been preserved; they have been debauched.

And if this is not enough indictment, consider the circumstance that has made it necessary for governments to pass laws making genocide, the killing of a whole people, a crime. This would have seemed to an earlier age the ultimate in absurdity. There were reasons for legislating against isolated killings because men in passion or fear occasionally killed their fellows. Never before, however, have whole peoples or races been the victims of exterminators. And to what purpose, good or otherwise? The effort to justify this sort of thing in any terms invites contempt.

And what of the calloused conscience of the world that feels less and less the enormity of the sin of war? We are profoundly afraid of global destruction, but is our contrition as deep? War, always evil, is now, we are told, a necessary evil. Thus our consciences feel less acutely the prick that once sent us to our knees. The stupefying fact is that we are used to killing as no other generation since Cain. If the ground curses us, our ears are deaf; if the blood of the slain cries out, we wince ever so slightly and shrug in mild disdain.

Pacts against war are the modern expedient to stop the periodic bloodlettings that foul the earth. They have our support since they seem at the moment our only hope. But in the long run they, like every moral evasion, will not save us. We dare not pass laws to sanctify violent death; we pass laws to extenuate, to explain, or to call it by another name. And still our hearts are frozen with fear of the next mad shambles for which our ingenuity and our wealth are getting us ready. All man's civil rights bow out as carnage marches in, and man calls his brother an evil name to make killing him take on the aspect of nobility. And at the last the nation's highest award of honor will go to those who have killed most men under conditions of greatest difficulty.

We are still in the land of forever-wandering, still vagabond and fugitive from the face of God, still afraid of our fellows, still digging the grudging ground. Some say the doom of the race is upon us, and in hopelessness many await the day. The tragedy of it is less in the fact of multitudinous killing than in the fact that it does not need to be. God has not abandoned his purposes for humankind, even though man is debauched by his folly, his terror, and his sin. It is a long way back to the plain at the foot of Sinai, but the thunder of an ancient word still sounds like wind across the earth's moral wastelands. Only God can say it and not weary of repeating it, for only God has made man for himself and has never forgotten that man cannot find rest until he be found in him. This is his moral right to life, the talisman of his peace. It is a simple idea in four one-syllable words: Thou shalt not kill. But what a freight of destiny they carry on their backs!

CHAPTER XII

The Right to Integrity

THIS, THE SECOND in the moral bill of rights, logically follows the first. Man, I have pointed out, is thought in the biblical tradition to have his origin in a creative act and his destiny in the Creator's will. Neither his beginning nor his end is his own doing, nor is the meaning that attaches to life to be found within the space-time continuum within which his mortal days are passed. Between the termini of the divine will in creation and the divine purpose in completion stretches the long line of human experience out of which his moral successes or failures are made. The quality of experience is determined by what he is and what he does, but at no point does he transfer to another line, though the byways of folly and sin misdirect him and he gets lost in transit. These moral relations with his human brothers are as important for him as the religious connections that tie him to God, though they are not ultimate. He never escapes either the dilemma or the discipline of living within time under the aspect of eternity.

His right to life derives from his creation and his end, for without them he not only does not exist, but if life is taken from him, the purpose of his existence is frustrated. It is this that puts the moral ban on killing; it defeats everything for which man, within time, is endowed. To kill a man is a confession (remember Cain's experience) that nothing else can be done with him. The differences between individuals which make life both beautiful and exasperating, can be composed, if they serve the proper ends of life, in a higher synthesis. If this is difficult or impossible, they will be resolved by elimination of the weak by the strong. The strong are likely to be impatient with the weak, and this, compounded with the disinclination to use more subtle methods of getting on, is to them reason enough for eliminating the moral or intellectual sluggard. But killing, in war under quasi-legal sanction or in the execution chamber under highly respectable laws, is futile even though it appears for the moment to protect the group from the marauder and the criminal. Not all the gala trappings of military parade or the pious farewells to prison chaplains can cover up the stupid uselessness of taking away a man's right to live.

This is the rejection of an answer to the problem of getting along with those who differ from us rather than a solution to it. It sees killing, not as the exercise of justice, but as an unwarranted assumption of the prerogative that belongs only to God. It is proper to make allowances for the right of God, as he was conceived in earlier ages, to condemn to death those who incurred his wrath. That he was thought to use human agency to get the distasteful job done is also familiar to the pages of history. That he ever gave man the right to take life is questionable in the light of later insights. In a bitter passage (Deut. 32:1-52) the seventh-century editors put the great valedictory on the lips of Moses and had him say: "To me [Yahweh] belongeth vengeance, and recompence" (v. 35 K.J.V.); and in another famous passage we hear a man who could claim both physical and moral lineage within the ancient tradition say: "Recompense to no man evil for evil. . . . Avenge not yourselves. . . . Vengeance is mine; I will repay, saith the Lord" (Rom. 12:17, 19 K.J.V.). To be sure, he was talking specifically about dealing with enemies; but we have seen that an awareness of difference is the origin of the sense of enmity that in one way or another flares into direct action. No; when we decide that our final expedient is to kill a man, we confess thereby either our failure to devise a better method or our inability to redeem him. These may be honest confessions and good for our souls, but they still leave our enemy in a precarious position. The chances are that he will die disagreeing with us.

1

This summary gives us the continuity we need as we attempt to understand the second moral right. It was stated earlier as the right to integrity. On the face of it this looks like quite a distance from its familiar rendering: "Thou shalt not commit adultery."

This is not merely an attempt to state in positive terms what is in negative terms so easily understood. There is no virtue in putting it thus if it does not actually bring us nearer to the intention it contains. With us the act of adultery is extramarital coitus. The Seventh Commandment specifically proscribes this. Neither man nor woman can without moral turpitude indulge sexual intimacy outside the bonds of wedlock. This is so simple that it ought long since to have put an end to the venery that to the common mind is synonymous with immorality. Either it has been misunderstood, or the impulse to promiscuous sexuality is so powerful as to be irresistible, or so delightful as to be the apex of felicity that man has treated its prohibition as meddling with his private affairs or as insisting on the impossible. It may do some good to deny it to some people, but to others it is a waste of breath. We do not need the Kinsey report to prove that. Nor do we think that celibacy or sterilization or even marriage laws will solve this problem in human relations. Here we deal, not with one who repels us, but with one who attracts us. So long as there are hormones, there will likely be the clandestine bower. Unless—

2

Let us look at the matter historically. There is no story in biblical folklore dealing with the adulterous contact as there is with the man to man contact of Cain and Abel. Of a later date and of a more legendary than folklore character is the story of the virtuous Joseph and the seductress in Potiphar's house. This is magnificently told in the fictionized Joseph saga by Thomas Mann. Its intention seems to have been to present in the hero of the story what is in effect the Hebrew counterpart of Parsifal or Galahad in other lore. He is the man who uncorrupted by the allurements of flesh becomes the savior of his people. There is a correlation between austerity and moral leadership that seems to appear in all cultures. The self-indulgent can never indulge others; he who is ruled by his appetites cannot rule others by his laws. Thus, though Joseph languished for a while in prison because the siren whose love was spurned would have her vengeance satisfied, he finally emerged to become the favorite of the

Pharaoh. Everybody with the exception of Potiphar's wife lived happily ever afterward, though she, we assume, got over her pique and tried her charms on more susceptible members of the palace guard.

This was not a typical story, nor was it necessarily early. There was no adultery in Eden or outside it, we presume, and for a very good reason. And yet nothing is more constantly revealed in the ancient record than the concern of the morally sensitive over the aberrance of sex. In great detail the laws of Israel sought to catch every possible variation of this irregularity and to fix penalties thought sufficiently heavy to discourage it. While the woman involved seems to be held in greater guilt than her paramour, there is a surprising level of impartiality reached in dealing with the transgressors. By no means was the man, though less likely to suffer social scorn than the woman, allowed to regard his share as an escapade and hers as a sin. The moral (or is it merely sentimental) attitude of our times toward the "victim" of lust has greatly softened. We know how to take care of ourselves. If we get into trouble, it is the reward of clumsiness, not of retribution.

Now it is important to observe that the word *naaph*, translated "adultery," had no original reference to sex. It meant what adulterate still means: to mix a pure substance with a base substance. A Chinese student, struggling with an English idiom with which he was not familiar, once said that when U. S. Marines landed in a troubled area in China, they adulterated the girls in the neighborhood. It was in a way quite as accurate a use of the word as he could have given it, though it doubtless caused his missionary friend to smile when he should have registered shock. It was this meaning that the word originally had and it was first employed to describe the adulteration of religious practices by idolatry. Adultery was the worship of false gods.

It so happened that the neighbor deities to whom the early Hebrews were drawn were gods and goddesses of fertility. The connection between fertility and sex, between the potency of the creative process in begetting and bearing young and the Creator of all life, is easy to see. Not for nothing is God called Father or the mother of Jesus venerated with the hyperdulia of the faithful. Thus the Babylonian Astarte and the Assyrian Ishtar were a response to the deeply laid inclination to deify the desirability of fertility and the mechanisms of reproduction. It is an easy inference from the idea of deity, and the fact that it was debauched then—and still is—by a worship of sex per se does not subtract from it its profound meaning. The groves and the high altars which the corrupt kings of Israel built up and the prophets tore down were the rendezvous of sex worshipers. There is little wonder then that idolatry—the corruption of religion—became synonymous with sex worship, which was the chief feature of idolatrous practice. It was a depraved and demoralizing thing, but it won converts easily and held them with a devotion that was a frenzy in comparison with the ascetic austerities invited by the worship of Yahweh. What was to prevent the people in general from appropriating for conventional use the feature of religion that appealed most to them? This they have always done. Promiscuity in sex relations became, therefore, less a sin than an informal religious ritual which needed no temple for its performance. From that it was hardly a step to the realization that the ritual was more delightful in secret. At times we are led to believe that it pre-empted all other concerns. Hear Jeremiah: "How can I pardon thee? thy children have forsaken me, and sworn by them that are no gods. When I had fed them to the full, they committed adultery, and assembled themselves in troops at the harlots' houses; they were as fed horses roaming at large; every one neighed after his neighbor's wife." (Jer. 5:7-8.) This may be an overdrawn picture and is a libel, we think, on a noble and virtuous beast; but even so its ugliness cannot be hidden. That laws multiplied to intercept such evil doings and penalties were made more and more severe to discourage them is to be expected in a community that identified in a profound way man's relation to God with his behavior toward his fellows.

3

This identification of idolatry with sexuality meant that worship of the true God involved abstention from sex relations except under certain regulations. How early the family of the forebears of the Hebrews became monogamous we do not know; nor is it particularly important. Perhaps the primeval pair in the Eden idyl were an answer to those who would have preferred a multiple female menage. It is amply clear, however, that while there were polygamous practices

169

in Israel, this did not allow promiscuity outside marriage. It may indeed have been a way of discouraging it, though one, we rather think, not likely to be successful.

There were, moreover, reasons other than the identification of idolatry and disorderly sexuality that gave practical value to the commandment. These take us in the direction of a discussion of the nature of the family which has already been considered. It needs only to be said here that as the human family needs a type of solidarity that the lower animals get along very well without, that solidarity is very difficult to secure and maintain if there is irresponsible sex behavior in the parents. The protection of sex had, primarily, social utility before chastity as such became a virtue. There is a further fact which interests us but which must not be allowed to become the determining factor. Sexuality is a moral relation between human beings, and its regulation must therefore be in moral terms. It is arresting, however, to note that of all the larger animals only the human animal seems to maintain a practical balance between the two sexes. Normally there are just enough men to go around, and vice versa. Does this mean that there is a natural provision that makes promiscuity or multiple matings deviations from an order designed for certain needs the human must fulfill in ways different from his lesser kin? We warn against moralizing on such a point since we do not get our moral mandate from nature, and yet the fact is there, however mistaken we may be in our use of it.

Not only was it necessary for the protection of the family that illegitimate sex indulgence should be proscribed; it was necessary for the protection also of the individual. Just how much moral habit has to do with this, we do not know. It is certain that in other cultures the sense of corruption by promiscuous sex practices is less felt—if felt at all—than with us. The corresponding sense of guilt is thought to be less within such mores. We are told that until the coming of Christian missionaries to the Pacific islands, sex was indiscriminate and unincriminating. Not until the moralists of the West confronted them were they able to feel guilty about what to them had been as natural as plucking ripe fruit when they were hungry. This has raised very practical problems in so-called mission lands. But they are not relevant to my discussion. I am dealing with the basic moral structure of our culture. What is important for us is how we feel about the matter in hand. The Polynesians have another problem which may be discussed in other connections.

What we see clearly is that given our moral inheritance, deviation from the mandate results in a sense of spiritual corruption and moral guilt. Whether this is as superficial as culture is in some of its other aspects, or whether it rests on something innate in human personality and is involved in every human contact, is outside the range of this inquiry. The fact remains that there is this sense of corruption and guilt, each of which is a powerful factor in the moral situation.

It is our judgment that the guilt feeling that follows illicit sex behavior cannot be dissociated from something deep in the psyche. It is not caused merely by social mores which we have been taught to respect. For there is a real sense in which the sex act is related to creativity. How this was first found out has puzzled the anthropologists no end. He was something of a genius who discovered that the birth of a baby was related to love play indulged nine months earlier, but the real genius was the man who identified sex with creativity in a larger context. To create a child is creation par excellence. To the sex act was imparted a sacredness unattached to anything else except life itself. To misuse it was to adulterate it, to corrupt the highest human function. Fornication was an irresponsible use of the mechanisms of creation. In the realization of this sex became associated with moral norms.

4

Yet we still must ask why this should be. Is the answer to be found in the almost frightening intimacy it involves, in the utter self-giving of the psyche? In no other way is the soul shared. For this reason sexuality has been easily associated with religion. The two factors of creativity and complete self-giving are components of any real religious experience. Where else are they experienced in such complete and exquisite intimacy as in the sex relation? If this is true, then does it not follow that a misuse of the experience exacts penalties more subtle than law can prescribe? Is this not the reason that profligacy, whoredom, or even casualness leads to a sort of moral degeneracy that is loathsome? Much of modern fiction is testimony enough here. Is it not also the reason that because of the physical commitment of the sex act it easily becomes obsessive, a tyrant with a flaming brand that is put to all the delicate tinder of personal and group relations until they are consumed in its lovely ruddy fire?

This is true, we believe, no matter how the factor of mutual agreement enters into the experience. At the time of indulgence one will seek to persuade the other and both will try to agree that this is a matter wholly between them, that they two stand alone above the moral order, transcending all the commandments that have bedeviled all other transgressors. This is a pose, albeit an honest one, that is part of the blindness that the momentary obsession induces. How many times, countless beyond number, has the aftermath been a sense of bitter or angry self-reproach and a hatred of the partner? This is not altered by the fact that there have been great lovers whose love was illicit. They are the pet darlings of romantic fiction, the dramatis personae in the great tragic tradition, the better to warn us than to ask our emulation. Remember the story of Medea.

5

I have given this discussion up to this point wholly to the derived meaning of adultery for the reason that in our thought it has almost no other connotation. But earlier I said that a positive statement of the Seventh Commandment had much more spacious reference. It provides man the right to be uncorrupted, to be unadulterated, to have and to keep his integrity, to be good, or—to make it even broader—the right to be himself. This is warranted, we believe, by our understanding that the word *naaph* originally meant the degradation of all the qualities implicit in the second item in the moral bill of rights.

This brings us back again to the first tenet of the doctrine of man that we are seeking to trace out: man is God's creation; the end and meaning of his life is found within the purposes of his creator. When we read, "Thou shalt not corrupt," we are hearing an affirmation of man's right to be his uncorrupted self.

All this was lost—his ability, inclination, and right to be the created and uncorrupted son—by his contretemps in Eden. Once, before the Fall, he knew innocence; afterward he was never to know it again. This is a theological doctrine of great importance and is not to be lightly set aside. But I am trying to discuss the problem in moral rather than theological categories, and thus conceived, it is some-

172

what different in emphasis. Essentially it is this: What is the moral meaning of freedom?

I have commented at some length on this already, but an advance on what has been said is necessary. Man misconceives freedom in terms of independence and autonomy and thus exchanges true freedom, which is the voluntary commitment of himself to God, for the spurious freedoms of detachment and self-rule. Was the state of innocence in Eden incorruptible? No; the serpent corrupted it. Was man after his adulteration a different creature? No; he was still the created one destined at last to serve the Creator's ends for him. What then took place according to the ancient legend of the meeting of Eve, the serpent, the forbidden fruit, and Adam? Man, whose right to be himself had not been violated, corrupted himself in the exercise of that right. In being himself he sinned. Man, created and destined by God, has the right to subvert the whole cosmic process in so far as he can. Man sinned, but this was in the exercise of his right as a created son. The serpent sinned by violating the Seventh Commandment. It should not have committed the act of adultery.

We must not bog down in an argument as to which is the more culpable in a moral act. There are two parties involved; their guilt may be mutual or correlative, or one may be the victim of the other. But this does not touch the deeper aspect of each man's right to be himself—sinner if he will, saint if he can. The alternative to this says that man is not free; he only has a long tether. The Creator has contrived to give him a sense of freedom he does not have. Therefore he can never stray beyond the purposes of the Creator who made him. There is something very appealing in this. How reassuring to know man can never be lost. But if this is true, is not what we call salvation evacuated of all moral meaning? All those who corrupt or adulterate us cannot really destroy us; we are by our very nature immune to the ultimate dissolution, to the final death. This is as real a denial of freedom as that which would allow man no choice at all in the way he lives, in a withdrawal altogether of the right to be himself.

6

There emerges the paradox that is at the heart of all moral experience. It is the insight of the ancient sages of Israel that man was

173

created in God's image. Thus a splendor ineffable rested upon him. God's intention was for him to grow by the disciplines of mortal existence into a sonship that was achieved, not created. In order to win this status, he had to be free, free to debauch himself and the society within which he had to live, free also to become more and more like his Creator-Father and to build a society of the sons of God wherein God himself could dwell. The most important factor in his make-up was his freedom. In that he revealed most certainly the image of God. And that freedom was unqualified by anything except himself. He could sell himself in bondage to sin or to saintliness. He could adulterate himself; that was his right. *But no man had a right to corrupt him.* This reaches profound deeps of insight. I repeat that herein lies part of the explanation of the inerosible monolith of ethical idealism on which our culture rests. It may raise more questions than it answers, but it puts sharply up to us the question that is the heart of the moral problem of the Seventh Commandment.

This was part of the difficulty of Cain, whose intention toward his brother was to limit his freedom because he thought it jeopardized his own. Being unable to let him alone, he killed him. Having violated the Seventh Commandment, he violated the Sixth; having corrupted his brother, he slew him. There was bitter logic in the process.

This is not careless use of words though it is puzzling. Jesus in a familiar comment put the matter sharply: "It is impossible but that occasions of stumbling should come; but woe unto him, through whom they come! It were well for him if a millstone were hanged about his neck, and he were thrown into the sea, rather than that he should cause one of these little ones to stumble." And because the positive aspect of the warning introduces the creative energy of forgiveness, he goes on to say: "Take heed to yourselves: if thy brother sin, rebuke him; and if he repent, forgive him. And if he sin against thee seven times in the day, and seven times turn again to thee, saying, I repent; thou shalt forgive him. And the apostles said unto the Lord, Increase our faith." (Luke 17:1-5.) Little wonder, for a puny faith could not support it.

7

It is not difficult to trace the efforts of cultures to control promiscuity in sex relations. Because sex is so vital an endowment, it has not been easy to regulate. Among primitives, where it serves only the purposes of procreation, sex activity is relatively weak and periodic; it is as society becomes sophisticated and the secondary sex factors take on the aspect of art and grace that it tends to be an end in itself. Hence the Greek took a rather dim view of chastity. Their gods were beautiful and lewd, and among the four cardinal virtues of Plato—wisdom, courage, temperance, justice—there is a conspicuous blank. Rome struggled between the patrician extreme of a new husband every year and the pious extreme of Vesta and her virgins as the highest form of ethical religion. In much earlier times the ritual prostitution among Semitic peoples and the disinclination of Egyptian cultism to deal with such human foibles created a moral vacuum with respect to sex into which the idealism of the Hebrews moved. It was they who did more than any other people to abate the horrors of sexual promiscuity and to establish the family secure from philandering and infidelity. Marriage was a matter of course, childlessness a reproach; the family was a holy unit under the special seal of the divine approval. Only the Moslem civilization has maintained a comparable strictness in the matter of sex, and it derives, of course, from the same early source.

The story of Israel's difficulties in this area is familiar. The appeal of phallic and fertility cults was always close by and powerful, and manifold were the transgressions among kings, commoners, and priests. At the same time a new ideal was being slowly built and solidified into a type of behavior that is unique in the history of world cultures.

There are those who argue that the early Christian attitude toward sex degraded it into an evil thing. Bishop Ambrose, spiritual father of Augustine, spoke of chastity in three modes—virginity, marriage, widowhood. This was more of a concession than Origen made, who emasculated himself as an act of piety. In our times there may be a disposition to look back with supercilious tolerance on the prudery and prurience of Victorianism and to be satisfied with the way we treat this adolescent excitement with adult sophistication. These are matters for the social analysts and historians. The modern novelist will settle the problem with four-letter words, and we will have more and more information and gayer and gayer entertainment.

There is little room for complacency, however. As far as the

175

license

Seventh Commandment is made to deal specifically with the matter of chastity, it seems to become less and less a barrier to ~~freedom~~ in sex relationships today. Are we not free to be ourselves? And being endowed with this primordial glow, shall we not nurture its flame and dance about its bright altar? Perhaps, but not without cost. <u>The place of lewdness in the inner rot that has disintegrated civilizations is set in clear perspectives for those who have eyes to see.</u> No subject has more engaged the professional and legal interest in our times. We view with alarm rising divorce rates and point with pride to supercolossal technicolor portrayals of bed and bawd. But there is deep anxiety in homes and wild perplexity in young hearts that provide nothing of the relaxation that is healing or the prerequisite of moral well-being.

This is the problem of the Seventh Commandment in its acute and generally accepted form. There is, however, more than the matter of preserving a virtue, one of the cardinal virtues of Western culture. The assault against it is formidable. In the mid-thirties the <u>Soviets</u> promulgated regulations that appeared to end the family as a social unit. The falderal of marriage was to be abandoned as a bourgeois frill the "people" could get on without. Children were to be bred as cattle under the watchful eye of geneticists in order that the state would gain most and lose least in the production of the individuals that were to serve it. It sounded cold-blooded to sentimental Americans, a ruthlessness that played recklessly with man's most precious associations. Then within little more than a decade the system was changed, and the family was restored and chaste relations were encouraged. They were not at this point bourgeois nonsense; they were stark necessities and something the "people" needed in supporting a growing state.

We do not want to moralize about this, for a realistic understanding of it will be had only within the perspectives of the new Stalinist culture. We do not think that social exigency has persuaded them of the wisdom of returning to the moral wisdom of the West. Remember that it is a cardinal point in Marxism that there never has been history; the past is illusion and fraud, and history is only now on the point of being made. Thus, a priori, the laws and moral attitudes of our past are to them as decadent as our art and statescraft, if indeed they are not as dead. If, therefore, sex is to be regulated by

176

the state, it will be for the state's purposes alone. There will be no toleration of the foolishness about man's being created by God and directed toward divine ends. And there will be no Seventh Commandment; it is already discarded with the other items in the moral bill of rights.

Still and all there is reason for us to believe that the Seventh Commandment, as it deals with the towering concept of man's right to be himself, to be uncorrupted, to be unadulterated, in other words to be free, will not be discarded quite so easily. This has always been the center of the moral problem with us. Can we say it is the center of the moral problem in all cultures? Until we are sure on this point, we will kill our brother who has a right to be different from us if by being so he is inviolably himself. Or we will dispossess him of his property, or we will deny him the justice which his integrity as a created soul demands.

These are the matters that are immediately at hand. Our reflection upon them ought to cast further illumination upon the deeper meanings of the age-old word: "Thou shalt not commit adultery."

CHAPTER XIII

The Right to Property

IN OUR EFFORT to dissect out the skeletal doctrine of
man around which the body of our ethical culture has grown, we
have found two important components: man because of the nature
of his origin and destiny has, vis-à-vis his neighbor, a moral right to
life; and significance is given to life by his moral right to be himself.
The first of these presents the moral problem of existence, the second
the moral problem of freedom. To sharpen our approach I allowed the
Sixth Commandment to read: "Thou shalt allow a man to live."
Within the context of human relations this right is absolute. If it is
canceled by God, that is a religious rather than a moral matter.
Similarly we read the Seventh Commandment in positive terms:
"Thou shalt allow a man his own uncorrupted integrity." It is not
so simple a matter to claim an absolute status for this mandate for the
reasons that the extent to which a man is corrupted by himself and
not by the human plexus within which he lives, it is impossible to
say. Nevertheless we think it is entitled to a larger measure of autonomy than we are willing, most of the time, to give it.

This is a broad base on which to erect a doctrine of man dealing
as it does first with his origin and second with his essential nature.
Man is *of* God and *for God*, and man is free to be *himself*. This is
firm but not smooth. Ages of thought have not leveled off the para-
doxes and dilemmas that transect its surface. It has endured, we
believe, because it is solidity that the spirit of man desires. Given

that he can survive the rough spots and cogitate about them in his leisure moments.

There were two stories that pointed up the early thinking of the Hebrews about the integrity of life and freedom. The myth of Cain and Abel and the legend of Joseph and Potiphar's wife have narrative overtones it is important for us to hear. In the experience outside Eden the right of a man to live was disqualified by an angry brother; in the experience inside the room of the seductress the right of a man to be uncorrupted was asserted by himself. Cain is forever the villain as Joseph is forever the hero.

1

The Eighth Commandment is perhaps the simplest of all the ten. Taking what does not belong to one seems so clear-cut a misdeed as to need no subtleties of argument to prove it. And yet is it? What is it that makes mine what is not yours or his? Granted that social order would be impossible without a recognition of established property rights, how are these rights established? Does not the problem go deeper than possession to the reasons for possessing? Surely no one applauds a thief unless he is especially cunning, or bold, or powerful, or like Robin Hood poaches on the king's preserves to furnish venison to the hungry foresters, or like Lord Clive carves out a piece of India and presents it to the Crown, or like George III levies taxes without representation, or like the Guaranty Trust Company tells a plaintiff named Rogers he was wrong when he objected to a certain board of directors dividing a five-million-dollar surplus that belonged to the stockholders. Rogers said he had been robbed. No, replied the company; and the Supreme Court of the United States ruled that what Rogers had said was theft was honest business. After all it may not be so simple. "Thou shalt not steal" has been winked at so often that eyes have fallen asleep in weariness. Will a positive statement in terms of man's moral right to property help to keep us awake?

2

Here again, in a matter that so constantly concerned the Hebrew mind, there is no myth to set the problem forth. No Prometheus strives against the miserly gods and steals fire to warm the frosty night air at the mouth of the caves where mortals had shivered for eons. Was the forbidden fruit in Eden stolen? It is sometimes so described, but there was nothing surreptitious in Eve's gentle touch. The serpent had emboldened her by saying the fruit was hers and no evil would befall her tasting it. In any event her sin was hardly thievery so much as disbelief and disobedience.

There is a story, however, that deals with theft in a way that is as massive as it is dramatic—massive because the theft of one man brought a curse on all the people, dramatic because from the moment one soldier's lust for loot was gratified to the death of him and his family by stoning and burning the tale is told with movement and suspense. It is known as the sin of Achan. (Josh. 7:18-26.) No doubt it has been treated as all legendary records with appropriate embellishments, but it is the sort of tale that would have been endlessly told and its moral assiduously inculcated.

We must remember that this was no ordinary theft, no petty pilfering by nimble fingers. There was not always clear word as to what was to be done with the loot of battle. It was not always taken; sometimes it was refused when offered as reparations; sometimes, as in the present case, it was forbidden. At other times it was allowed as the reward for valor, divided equally among the warriors or between the Lord and the victor nation. In the case of Achan the issue was clear. Jericho had been reduced with great slaughter, and the morale of the Israelites was high. A foray to the east was necessary to clear the flank deployed near Ai. About three thousand men were dispatched and were soundly beaten by the defenders of Ai. Their loss of thirty-six men was negligible; their loss of face was frightful. They realized they were not as invincible as Jericho made them appear, and when they returned in panic to the camp at Shebarim, "the hearts of the people melted, and became as water."

Joshua, looking for an alibi, found it in Yahweh; but the Lord would not accept the blame. "Get thee up," he commanded Joshua; "wherefore art thou thus fallen upon thy face? Israel hath sinned; . . . they have even taken of the devoted thing, and have also stolen, and dissembled also." This, we note, was Israel's sin; there was social participation in the evil of one man. But in order to expiate Israel's guilt, the culprit had to be found. By a gigantic process of elimination the finger finally pointed to Achan. Joshua confronted him, exhorted him to confess, and got from him a complete story. Fully aware that looting had been forbidden, Achan's hands could not resist a goodly Babylonish mantle, two hundred shekels of silver, and a wedge of gold fifty shekels in weight. They were concealed in his tent, and after their recovery the thief and his sons and daughters, his tent, his livestock, "and all that he had" were brought to the valley of Achor. There he was burned, and they were buried under a rain of stones. "And Jehovah turned from the fierceness of his anger."

3

This is a bloody tale, and the telling of it for generation after generation served no idle purpose. In this case it is made clear that to take what in other cases were the legitimate spoils of war was forbidden. The sin was against Yahweh, the whole people were made accomplices of the crime, and lest it be lightly regarded, the family of Achan and his possessions were wiped out. Only the memory of the deed and the telltale cairn of stones in the valley of Achor remained. By the operation of primitive eugenics a thieving strain had been wiped out.

It is not our concern here to find in this story a pattern of the act of thieving that will fit all cases. War is a poor context in which to discover rules for or against personal behavior. Indeed, from a realistic point of view the whole campaign against Canaan was murder and looting on a grand scale. One does not bring moral judgments to bear on the destruction of Jericho. It is better to remember the reduction of its defenses as the result of seven days' marching and the blowing of rams' horns. If this was aggression, it was, to say the least, a romantic sort of assault. If the walls fell down, it was not the Israelites doing, really; and they could not be accused of evil if they had not actually done the deed. Of course slaughtering the inhabitants —well, that was the simple prudence of war. One kills or is killed. This, we say, is hardly the context within which we expect to find clearly stated moral maxims of universal validity. Nevertheless it is interesting that in the tale of Achan and his sin there were retained for generations to reflect upon, what to us are the obvious transcendent

181

and social, as well as the personal, components of stealing. All were revealed in his act: God, his own avarice, his fellows, his deep fear, and his dissemblings.

Of course by the time of the disastrous battle of Ai the Children of Israel had achieved sufficient organization to be able to take the land of Canaan by force. This required considerable co-ordination and laws strictly enforced. We must be allowed to assume that the business of ownership and exchange was under careful regulation, since no society has existed without an economic order predicated on these two elements. It is not surprising, therefore, that the formulation of the moral rudiments of their society should have included a commandment against stealing. The impossibility of social cohesion without respect for ownership of property had by that time been demonstrated.

Similarly we today protect private property.

> Taffy was a Welshman, Taffy was a thief,
> Taffy came to my house, and stole a piece of beef;
> . . . .
> I went to Taffy's house, Taffy was in bed;
> I took up a poker and flung it at his head.

This settles the matter very neatly. It doesn't ask why I should have had a leg of beef or why Taffy was impelled to steal it. He was a Welshman and a thief. When I sought to retrieve my stolen property, I found Taffy, until a short time before, hale and hearty enough to make off with two hundred pounds of beef, in bed, feigning illness no doubt, though of course his exertion may have prostrated him momentarily. But it made the administration of retributive justice easy. The poker was convenient, and Taffy was immobilized; so without a word of rebuke or request for an explanation I hit Taffy in the head. I am not sure what I did about the beef. Apparently I was satisfied with the results the poker had achieved, and I went home, the affair having been settled to the gratification of all. Taffy had learned a lesson. So had I. The neighbors with sides of beef at home were warned to be more careful than I had been, but they were also reassured that at least one thief had been taken care of. Maybe he was dead. If not he had a painful head to remind him of his folly. And above all, I was applauded for having dealt summarily with the lawbreaker. Thus private property as an institution was protected against Welshmen and thieves, and justified again within an even wider constituency.

4

Yet still we have thieves, big and little, individual, group, national. Is it because despite centuries of trial and error we are not truly convinced? Is all stealing one or another type of kleptomania? Why do men steal? What do we mean when we read, "Thou shalt not steal," and we hear it say a man has a moral right to property?

We are tracing out the doctrine of man that seems implicit in the Mandate to Humanity. He is the creation of God, and his purposes are assumed unto God. This involves his right to live and his right to be free, uncorrupted. His struggles to carry the burdens of these endowments are seen in his moral relationships with his fellows. It is hardly enough for him to be alive and free; he needs things to help him keep alive and to protect and assimilate his freedom. It would seem to be true then that there is an integral correlation between personality and property, between what a man has and what he is.

In man's subhuman associates there is a low-grade instinct of possessiveness. Sometimes it is concerned with things they make, a nest or a burrow, though after a season of use these are generally abandoned. Ants, bees, squirrels, and other provident creatures lay by stocks of food; but they are never for themselves individually but for the hill, the hive, or the total squirrel quotient in a particular neighborhood. The seasonal jealousies among male animals during mating and the fierce protectiveness of the mother while her young are dependent on her look like possessiveness. If they are, they are on a level so far beneath the human wish to possess as to be described better by another name.

Man, as we see him with the frame of reference of early Hebrew thought, was the creature of God, made in God's own image. The Jews never forgot that the earth was "the Lord's, and the fulness thereof; the world, and they that dwell therein." His ownership was postulated upon his creatorship. That which he made was his. It was the realization of this that dulled the edge of any compunctions they may have felt about expropriating the land of others. The world was the Lord's; they were the Lord's; what was the Lord's was theirs. Furthermore they were living under a commission that made them the agents of Yahweh in subduing and dominating the earth. This left little room for squeamishness or scruple.

Now either by analogy or by fact—it makes little practical difference which—man as well as God is known by what he owns. The body he owns identifies his species, the complexion he owns is a factor in determining his race, the language he owns as a childhood acquirement distinguishes his nation, and the amenities and arts he practices will largely classify his culture. Thus the biologist, the anthropologist, the philologist, and the sociologist have an easy time putting man in his proper categories. If he had nothing, he would be nothing. Does this describe personality in terms too gross to satisfy our pride?

It may be given a slightly different slant. If I go into a man's library and discover it preponderates in law books, I will know he is a lawyer. If his house or office contains no books at all, I shall conclude he is not a scholar. If what a man owns is computed in cattle, or cultivated farms, or agricultural equipment; or if he has factories and rail sidings and docks; or if he is attended by a nurse or two moving quietly in and out of clean-smelling rooms, I shall know what kind of an individual I am confronting. Even when a doctor raises cows for a hobby or a manufacturer buys and sells and fusses about with stamps, he does not disguise his real identity.

What is even more interesting is that not infrequently a change in man's possessions will change him. When he has little, he is nearly always a different sort of man than when he becomes rich. There are notable exceptions, but this is also due to something they have that determines the quality of their lives. When a scholar abandons his books to dabble in real estate or a parson steps down from the pulpit and into an insurance office, he is likely to become a different person. Not basically, for personality patterns do not so easily change, but superficially so that he becomes known not as a scholar but as a realtor, not as a preacher but as an underwriter.

There are some who say in a moment of extravagance or self-pity that they cannot call their souls their own. This is a type of poverty that is hard to come upon, but if it can be called up in imagination, it still would, perversely as it were, supply the necessary data for identification. For a soulless person is so different from everything else in the universe that it stands forever unaffiliated to anything else. This was Job's self-described predicament when he said: "And now my soul is poured out within me." An odd metaphor perhaps, but even the loss identified Job as a certain sort of man. And if it could be true that all a man had was his soul, here again his sole possession would distinguish him metaphysically from every other sort of creature. It would seem therefore to be true to say that in ways known to us and perhaps in ways beyond our knowing, what a man has determines what he is.

5

It needs to be said, however, that the way he comes by what he has is an important consideration in assaying his identity. The way Taffy acquired a quarter of beef identified him as a thief. How had the original owner got hold of it? Until we know that, we shall not be able to put him down as a cattleman, a butcher, a restaurateur, a big eater with a fondness for sirloin steak, or indeed a thief himself. This introduces the moral problem. It is not completely true to say that a man's personality is identified by what he has; the way he got it gives definitive quality to his identification. Thus considered some things he has are morally neutral. The color of his skin is his by the accident of birth; it classifies him as a Caucasian, but it allows him no moral advantage as a person, nor should he suffer disabilities because of it. If he claims that because he is white he is superior, by which he will perhaps mean morally superior, he is a fool. Could it have been established by legitimate means that all Welshmen are born thieves as they are born members of the white race, to retrieve from him the stolen goods might have been proper, but to hit him with a poker would have been unjust.

God, the ancients said, owned the earth because he made it.

> The sea is his, and he made it;
> And his hands formed the dry land.

This is one way by which possessions are to be legitimately owned. The house a man builds, the field he buys, the crop he raises, the

185

cloth he weaves, the tool he makes—these are his own. Not in an absolute sense, perhaps, for in every fabricated or cultivated thing there are elements that are given; and one who is deeply sensitive to the influence of things on personality will not forget this. By and large, however, there is consent to any title to ownership that rests on one's own productivity. This is somewhat qualified in a society the basis of which is communal, but for the moment I will allow the generalization to stand.

Now it is helpful, if we are to agree that man has a moral right to property, to discover the point at which the moral quality becomes manifest. The other two moral rights already discussed were seen to be related closely. The right to be one's self depends on the right to live. Does it follow that the moral right to property depends on the right to be one's self? The answer is Yes, in so far as the things he owns are part of what he is. It is implied in what has been said that to dispossess by force or stealth what a man legitimately owns is in a measure to depersonalize him, to disidentify him. Again this cannot be understood in absolute terms, but it is no accident that the Hebrew-Christian tradition, in which personality is elevated above society and conceived of in divine qualities, protects personal property as a moral right. The theft of Achan was a reproach to God, to Israel, and to himself. It made no difference that the loot belonged to an enemy. The owner of the Babylonish garment was entitled in that episode to the same sort of protection against looting that an Israelite was.

6

If the moral right to property is necessary in order that the moral right to freedom shall be exercised, it would appear then that the point at which one's property ceases to protect one's freedom, or becomes, in reverse, a barrier to his freedom, its possession becomes morally insupportable. It is not easy to draw a line here, and because of this, perhaps the moral implications of ownership are abandoned to the implications of power. The regulations devised to avoid economic chaos are far too often predicated on the cynical idea that what a man has, he can keep if he is able to, no matter how he got it. This erases the moral factor out of the equation, and the results is no answer at all.

186

Such considerations as these serve to point up the moral confusion that bedevils the economic disorder of our times; we are able to see more clearly why and how the ancient mandate against stealing seems to have less and less influence on the life of our times. Not that we are all turned thieves, but that we have not seen the deep moral significance in the relation between freedom and ownership, between the moral right to be free and the moral right to possess those things that enhance freedom.

The reason the difficulty is so complex is found in a factor which in itself is essentially simple. Man, confusing freedom with independence and autonomy, sees that the way to independence lies in the direction of having goods enough to buy release from contingency, and that autonomy is possible only for those who are materially strong enough to resist the rule of others. Thus he becomes dependent on the things he thought would give him independence and the victim of the possessions he thought would confer autonomy upon him.

There is no easy escape from these dilemmas, but moral dilemmas have never come equipped with safety devices. How is man to win freedom by abandoning things? This might well condemn him as a serf to poverty. On the other hand there have been genuine saints who have achieved their exalted spiritual status by the renunciation of possessions. On the contrary, one man who is genuinely free may have the capacity to make things serve his freedom, while his equally well-supplied neighbor will be observed under such a tyranny of things that his freedom is lost.

7

It is because the problem is morally so delicate that society has taken over its regulation and we live as individuals within economic orders more than within moral categories. Here, our pretensions notwithstanding, the basis is a less moral than a concern for security. There will be little argument as to the universal notion that security is very largely a matter of the abundance of the things that we possess. This is thought to be true of both the individual and society. Hence, in an always precariously poised position between want and surfeit, we will make the end of our striving the occasion of material

187

goods. Individuals talk about bank accounts and societies about standards of living. Both demand that laws be enacted and enforced to protect both.

At the same time society always holds in reserve the right to control individual wealth in the interests of social orderliness. It may have taken a long time to reach the point where this is society's right, but it is the basic presupposition of economic systems as opposed to capitalistic free enterprise and Marxist socialism. It cannot be gainsaid that in respect to our preoccupation with material goods it is not what separates us from the Soviet Union that appalls us but what we have in common. Our ideological differences are less to be feared than our practical agreement regarding the scale of human moral values. It is our relentless pursuit of security by means of material goods that drives us into head-on collisions. Peel off the rind of political ideology, democracy in one case and totalitarian dictatorship in the other, and the same fruit is exposed—man's engrossment with things.

This is not to say that there is nothing that truly separates us. On the contrary it is, or it should be, the moral tradition that underlies our culture that draws a line between us. It is possible to argue that the eighteenth-century concepts of freedom and equality, the inalienable right of a man to be himself and realize his fullest potentialities, have pervaded capitalism and left their deposit of humaneness and spiritual sensitivity. These elements are lacking in Marxism. They may not have forestalled the vulgarization of taste and debasement of human values in society, but they make possible the vocalization of protest when we discover their excesses. The Puritans demanded of the godly man that he must wear his wealth, if he had any, as a light garment which he could cast off if it were necessary for the retention of virtue. It may be that we of the West are spared something of the grosser materialisms by a certain basic detachment. It may be a subconscious nostalgia for the moral certitude the Ten Commandments once inspired. It may be there is still a sense of inner freedom that is suspicious of the trinkets, the gadgets, and the baubles of the world. We must be very circumspect in advancing such claims lest they prove illusory in the baleful light cast by the way we behave. Nevertheless it is the thesis of this whole inquiry that beneath the surface of our passing scene lies the granite foundation of an ageless ethical idealism that is never wholly lost to consciousness. As this is being written, the newspapers are recalling the fabulous William Randolph Hearst, whose death has released a spate of stories about him. Editors have decorously praised him, but the general impression one gets is that they are playing with a legendary figure, someone who despite his influence on the contemporary world has not been a part of it. None, so far as we know, has sought to justify his way of life. What justification is there for such prodigious wealth and prodigal self-indulgence in our times? If we think of him as belonging to a forgotten age, is it not because he seemed to have forgotten those moral constraints upon the accumulation and use of things to which we ultimately appeal for the security we need?

8

Just how far society can go in laying restraining hands on corporate or individual self-aggrandizement is the heart of the political struggle of our times. It is obvious that when one individual or a small group can by virtue of the power inherent in great wealth dominate a large segment of society, society can claim a right to limit that power. Morally the question may be somewhat simpler than its political aspect. No man has a moral right to corrupt another, or every man has a right to be free. He who adulterates that freedom is in violation of the Seventh Commandment, and on that basis moral judgment may be passed on the corrupter no matter how benevolent his despotism may pretend to be. The political aspect must be seen in the ways by which society can balance its obligation to protect man's moral right to own property, and its duty to protect the individual against trespass on his moral right to be free. We have not yet found an economic system that resolves this dilemma. Proudhon said that property is theft; Judge Gary of the U. S. Steel Corporation said the profits of capital belong solely to its owners. The Eighth Commandment said thou shalt not steal. That, I contend, touches the extremes of Proudhon and Gary and all the points between.

If society, whether it be the world community or its disparate cultural components, cannot successfully grapple with this problem by law, the problem will be seized by revolution. Indeed we are fairly well into this. There have been deliberate efforts to excite revolution by those who, promising political freedom, are denying the moral freedom that is tied into the freedom to own property. This is another way of saying what has so often been observed already here: that we see in our times a powerful, self-conscious political effort to repudiate the moral bases upon which our Hebrew-Christian culture has been erected. This assault has driven us to political resistance, not a little of which has itself been blind to the moral aspects of the struggle. An issue of the *Saturday Review of Literature* calls Americans to remember among other facts that "most people in Asia will go to bed hungry tonight. . . . Most people in Asia live in grinding poverty. . . . Most people in Asia believe anything different would be better than what they have. . . . Most people in Asia distrust people with white skins. Most people in Asia are determined never again to be ruled by foreigners." [1]

It is conditions such as these that are being exploited by those whose stake in world revolution is desperately high. These conditions, we are told, quite mistakenly, are the result of the imperialist exploits of the nations of the Christian West. We are proposing to prove our humaneness by programs such as E.C.A. and Point Four, and there is evidence that they have in some limited way achieved gratifying results.

These Asians, however, are impatient and distrustful, and for the moment, at the prompting of their self-appointed savior, are truculent and aloof. They are demanding the right to freedom and the right to the things that make freedom secure. If they think of winning them as Achan won a wedge of gold and Taffy won a leg of beef, there will be multiple destruction by fire and monuments of rubble and battered heads. This is the only way they can be gained if the moral right to ownership is not conceded to all men everywhere.

Perhaps we are safer in a moral isolationism that insists the Mandate was not for humanity but for our segment of the world's people only. If we are committed to this folly, we will have to defend our moral faith with weapons that yield little respect to moral law. That way lies tragedy too frightful to contemplate.

[1] "America and the Challenge of Asia," Aug. 4, 1951, p. 12. Used by permission.

That, however, is not necessary if we believe the opposite. "Thou shalt not steal" has not been abridged, nor has man abdicated his moral right to own the things that make for freedom and for peace. He needs to be reassured on another point, however: How does society propose to protect him? This introduces us to our fourth moral right—the right to justice—and invites a discussion of it.

CHAPTER XIV

The Right to Justice

MAN HAS a moral right to life, to freedom, and to property. These are three of the stout filaments that we have found woven into the pattern of the doctrine of man that is implicit in the Mandate. These rights are his because he is made by the Creator in his image and for the realization of his purposes. They can be abrogated finally only by the One who gave them.

This, however, does not complete the matter. Man lives within a society of his fellows. For a variety of reasons he will not find it easy to exercise his rights or to allow his brothers to exercise theirs. This involves him in moral conflict the issue of which is important for him as an idividual and for society. He will trust God for most of the time, but the more he knows about his fellows, the less certain he is about himself. Is there anything within the social plexus, achieved by experience or released by divine fiat, that stands above the flux of man-to-man contact and that offers him some surety that life is not indifferent to the ultimate issue?

This is the problem of justice. The Ninth Commandment says simply: "Thou shalt not bear false witness." This is clear enough; it means: speak the truth. Yet it is not clear always what the truth is, and some have argued that on certain occasions a lie is more honest than the truth. In a time like our own, characterized by one tough-minded realist as the Age of the Big Lie, we must proceed with caution if we want to tell the truth about truth.

When our commandment is set within the pattern of a moral

bill of rights, it receives a somewhat different emphasis. We can study it from the standpoint either of the liar who must be rebuked or of the man who is the victim of perjury. The former will hardly claim he has a right to lie; if he does, we shall suspect him at once of lying. The latter, however, can claim with our approval that he has a right to justice—that is, he need not be the victim of dishonest testimony.

1

This commandment is generally regarded as a proscription of dishonesty, particularly falsehood. So it is. As such it presents a fairly open and shut case. Without honesty character is disintegrated and society is impossible. Indeed it is or may be argued plausibly that telling the truth is the base on which all moral practice rests. There is good reason for referring to the Holy Spirit as the Spirit of Truth since truth is wholeness. Does not every immoral act begin with a lie? The liar lies to himself; he says what he is about to do is not evil. Whether he convinces himself matters little for he proceeds next to tell his accomplice or his victim that what they are about to do or what has just been done is not wrong. Here again the lie is a lie whether it convinces or not. The next step is lying to those who pass judgment on the evil deed. The sinner says he intended no evil or never thought what he was doing was wrong anyway. If his judges refuse to believe him, he will perhaps lie to himself again to prove that he was the victim rather than the aggressor in the act; and if he is ostracized by his fellows or otherwise penalized, he will endlessly feel sorry for himself and glut his self-pity with lies about his persecutors.

This is what the lie does for the individual; for the community it is equally demoralizing. The liar, once he is known as such, shuts off communication between himself and those he has deceived. Once a person has been victimized by an untruth, he will forever suspect the liar no matter how complete he may say—or even prove—his reformation to be. Trust is impossible. One liar in a community can wreck it. Hitler mobilized Germany and boasted that he did it with a big lie endlessly repeated. Part of our trouble in the rehabilitation of Germany has been our fear, always beneath the conference table, that these former followers of the big liar are not yet trustworthy. We may reproach ourselves for our suspicions, but the fear of being taken in by another lie will keep them alive.

The lie, again, is the poison that corrupts all man's moral rights. Has a man a right to life? "No," says the liar—nor to integrity, nor to property. These are all extrapolations of his puny self; they are the illusions of pride. Or they are the bourgeois superstitions of capitalist society or, as Nietzsche said, the collective egotism of the feeble. So if the liar prevails, the rights go; and man and orderly society go with them. No wonder the devil is called the father of lies and is doomed in the final settlement to spend a perfidious eternity in perfervid fire. "Thou shalt not bear false witness"; thou shalt not tell a lie. There is no appeal to that command.

2

What is implicit, we are convinced, in this mandate reaches beyond the proscriptions against the lie, basic as that aspect of it is. Man's moral right to justice, his right to defense against the perjured witness, his sense that though for a time righteousness comes on laggard feet and evil rides on wings, ultimately the balances will be struck and justice done—this sense, we say, man should have as a moral right. Otherwise the possession of all else he has is contingent on an unpredictable outcome. If he has no right to justice, he must have recourse to power on a lower level. This takes the human struggle out of a moral context and puts it into the arena where there is no rule except the will of the strong and no issue but the abitrament of naked force. Man's moral right to justice gives him no advantage; it takes from him disadvantage.

The development of the idea of justice among the Hebrews is a story too long to be told here. Unlike the justice implied in neighbor codes, designed primarily to protect society, justice with Israel was a reflection of the nature of Yahweh. Dimly apprehended at first, as all fecundating ideas must be, he came ultimately to be known as the God of justice. "All his ways are judgment" is a significant insight that points up the fact that he not alone *did* justice; he *was* judgment. "A God of truth and without iniquity, just and right is he." (Deut. 32:4.) This is a late estimate of the essential nature of Yahweh, an estimate we feel was put back by the editors into the Decalogue; but it must have had early adumbrations.

We have pointed to certain myths and legends in the ancient chronicle that gave vividness to the problems involved in man's moral right to life, freedom, and property. There is a charming story about the wise judgment of Solomon when he found himself caught between two anguished claimants to an unidentified babe. The ruse by which he discovered the real mother made justice possible, but we think the tale has been remembered more to glamorize the king than to implement justice. To know how this problem was ultimately faced and solved one must make a full study of the drama of Job. Here the issue between Job and Yahweh was justice. Bildad the Shuhite put the matter up to the wretched man whimpering amid a pile of ashes: "How long shall the words of thy mouth be like a mighty wind? Doth God pervert justice? Or doth the Almighty pervert righteousness?" (Job 8:2-3.) When the drama closes, Job has been convinced that his doubts were impious; and with a proper theatrical flourish the story ends with Job healthy, wealthy, wise, and full of days.

3

These, we say, represent long generations of thinking about justice; but it is possible to see its emergence in certain factors which, not so early as some have claimed, were far in advance of similar ideas developed in contemporary cultures. It is clear from the word "witness" in the command that the issue being dealt with was related specifically to the processes of the administration of law. The Hebrew word ed, "witness," is used everywhere with the same meaning: it connotes testimony offered in the administration of justice by law.

The Hebrew law, as already observed, had a unique pattern. God was both the author of the law and its final arbiter. Guilt or innocence was his to decide. This was saved from the sheer arbitrainess of fiat law by the participation of the people in its execution. Certain men were appointed to serve as judges. "Ye shall not respect persons in judgment; but ye shall hear the small as well as the great; ye shall not be afraid of the face of man; but the judgment is God's: and the cause that is too hard for you, bring it unto me, and I will hear it." (Deut. 1:17 K.J.V.)

In cases too difficult for the judges there was a sort of informal appellate court of priests at the place of the sanctuary.

If there arise a matter too hard for thee in judgment, between blood and blood, between plea and plea, between stroke and stroke, being matters of controversy within thy gates; then shalt thou arise, and get thee up into the place which the Lord thy God shall choose; and thou shalt come unto the priests the Levites, and unto the judge that shall be in those days, and enquire; and they shall shew thee the sentence of judgment. (Deut. 17:8-9 K.J.V.)

That the responsibility of the witness in the litigation was vested with a gravity only little less than that of the judges is shown by three facts. In the first place he never stood alone; there was always more than one witness called. Two were enough; three were better. Second, the witness was the executioner of the sentence (cf. Deut. 19:15-21). He knew that what he said involved him not only in the judgment rendered, but in the infliction of the penalty. In the third place, if during the trial it was proved that the witness had testified falsely, the punishment that his fraudulent testimony sought for the accused was visited upon him. One would be careful with his words if he realized that his hand was to execute a penalty if he was right and that he would suffer the penalty himself if he was wrong. It is difficult to imagine a stronger protection being erected about a man's testimony. When he was told that he must not bear false witness, he knew why.

4

The effort to secure honest and ample testimony before the judge was matched by the great detail in which the law was worked out. We assume, of course, that there was a long process of trial and error involved in securing such a tremendous corpus of statutes, but behind it all was the consciousness that men were not to be regulated by caprice or circumstance but by an authentic and impartial law that had its origin in Yahweh. Indeed the concept of God as the embodiment of law, or of law as the manifestation of God, was not only unique among primitive cultures, but goes a long way toward explaining the cohesiveness of the Hebrew people, their sense of mission and destiny, and their history. Their line has often been frayed, but it has never been broken.

One needs only to give casual attention to the laws preserved in Exodus, Leviticus, Numbers, and Deuteronomy to be impressed with the determined effort that was made to see to it that nothing in human experience was left unregulated. At the same time, with a fine sense of realism, it was recognized that justice is beyond the reach of legal fallibility and opportunities were provided for the treatment of doubtful or inadvertent guilt. Notable were the cities of refuge to which those could flee "which killeth any person at unawares." Particularly important was the emphasis on the superiority of law to the accident of birth or status. There were, to be sure, perversions of this principle; but symbolic of its rigor was the belief that Moses, the lawgiver, was denied entrance into the Land of Promise because in a moment of anger he had, as the words are put in Yahweh's mouth, "trespassed against me in the midst of the children of Israel at the waters of Meribah of Kadesh, in the wilderness of Zin; because ye sanctified me not in the midst of the children of Israel" (Deut. 32:51). There is, therefore, grandeur touched with pathos in the picture of Moses ascending to his death in solitude on the side of Mount Nebo. The vista of the new land stretched out before him; there was, no doubt, in his heart the stirring of the persistent dream. He had blessed his restless people in anticipation of taking leave of them, insisting on the sanctity of the law: "Jehovah came from Sinai. ... at his right hand was a fiery law for them" (Deut. 34:2). Then, bowing to the law he had honored, still a man in full physical vigor, he died. "And the children of Israel wept for Moses in the plains of Moab thirty days: so the days of weeping in the mourning for Moses were ended." (Deut. 34:8.) His was an epic accomplishment, judged by whatever standards, and must not be allowed to drop out of sight in any effort to assay the relevance of the great Mandate to the culture of our times.

5

To us who live in a law-minded, if not a legalistic, age the correlation of penalty and crime in the ancient law seems uneven and much of the time inexact. The idea of requital, the *lex talionis*, made inequities unavoidable. An eye for an eye is by no means a certain formula unless a technical knowledge of optics is presupposed. It would be necessary, if we followed it today, to have an optometrist attached to every court, and in case it was a tooth involved, a dentist. The subtleties of measurement in almost any attempt at retribution

197

are sufficient to defeat it, and this came to be increasingly realized until it was modified in one of the most famous words of Jesus. Also capital punishment seems to us to have been excessive, but this has been amended in our penal practices only within the past one hundred years. Its difficulty is rooted in the fact, already discussed, that it is essentially a violation of man's moral right to live. The implications of this are still short of realization even in our legally sophisticated times.

When, however, we set alongside the lofty legal concept of Israel the concepts underlying the law systems of other early cultures, we see its dimensions in clear perspective. Primitives invest all behavior with occult properties. A man is good or bad because of beneficent or malevolent spirits in possession of him. Therefore when he is suspected of crime, occult methods are used to detect guilt or innocence. We are all familiar with ordeals by fire and by water, by poison and by bleeding. Ripley's "Believe It or Not" depicted recently a lie detector currently in use among the Luba tribe in Africa. A murder suspect is forced to smoke a pipeful of tobacco and red pepper, and he is put to death if he coughs even once. This trusts the modern addiction to smoking where belief in spirits languishes. We wonder what will happen to the administration of justice among the Lubas when a pipe mixture is found which is guaranteed against a cough in a carload. That there was no such phase in the evolution of law and penalty among the Hebrews is something we cannot say, but it is manifest from such early records as we have that to them the ground of justice was in the fact of God and with them the administration of justice was in the hands of men. This is of the greatest importance both in the history of law and in the development of the idea that man has a moral right to justice, that he was to be protected with great care against the false witness. How else, we may ask, shall his prior rights to life, freedom, and property be defended against caprice or conspiracy?

6

We have said that this moral right along with others inheres in the basic fact of God; it is derived from the hypothesis that man is the created image of God. Only thus can man be adjudged competent to participate in the administration of justice, to be a witness for or against his fellow before judges or priests qualified in the law. For this reason also magic is abjured in the detection of guilt. A witch doctor did not bleed a fowl to lead him to the evil eye that had caused a death; nor did the sage consult the auguries in the sky. The witness was called before the judge to give testimony. There was certainly risk in this, but it was surer proof that the blood of a chicken or the flight of birds, and the witness knew that the culprit had a moral right to justice and that he, therefore, must not bear false witness.

Nevertheless it is not as easy to understand justice as of the very nature of God as it is to see life, freedom, and property within the divine nature. Justice is in its simplest terms, the fair treatment of all in terms of agreed-upon laws. What does this mean to God? He is transcendent to law as he is also beyond the necessity of fair treatment. It sounds little short of childish to say that God has a moral right to justice and shares this with his created image. And yet on sober reflection is it not necessary for us to say exactly this and even more imperative that we shall act it? God is transcendent to law; this means that we cannot conceive of him as imprisoned by restraints that are not of his own making. Here we are not speaking of God and what we call natural law; that is a metaphysical problem. Our concern is with God and moral law. The essence of this is that guilt is punished and innocence is rewarded and that every possible effort is made to establish each before its just consequence follows. Within this area we can arrive at conclusions that are simpler than the requirements of metaphysics, for the reason that the questions we ask are simpler. God, said the ancient Hebrews, had covenanted with his people. This was a covenant of law, not of whim. Whether or not man treated God with justice, in terms of the covenant commitment, God would respond unerringly in terms just under law. "God," said the author of the letter to Titus, "who cannot lie, promised [it] long ages ago." (Tit. 1:2.)

7

We find ourselves on steadier footing when we raise the question about man and his right to justice. Why does he have a feeling that this is properly due him? Initially, of course, we must give place to the conditioning that predisposes him. If he has any instinctual predilections, they are very dim. A mother bear will slap her cub, and he will whimper his protest at the indignity. Crows will punish a member of the flock for failure at the sentinel's post. Whether these are adumbrations of guilt and penalty or merely prudence taught by the necessity for survival is anybody's guess. Being human animals we will attribute analogous responses in our experience to higher sensitivities. Certain it is that children very early manifest a sense of hurt at what they cannot understand and react ingratiatingly to reward, even though it be nothing more than a word or a smile.

It is not difficult to trace this embryonic sensitiveness as it grows with the increasing depth of self-consciousness. The sulky child is reacting to what he feels is an injustice done. Given time the sulk may become a dominant pattern until the adult goes about with a chip on his shoulder to warn those who would take advantage of him, or becomes the inveterate self-pitier who thinks the world owes him a living and is in default on its payments. It can even become a deep wound that exhibits itself in paranoia. Not only is life unjust; it is deliberately malign.

How far this is to be understood in scientific terms as an innate sense of justice and desire for it—or the wish to be treated fairly— it is not our responsibility to say. At the same time we can note that it is plausible inference from the moral sense with which man seems endowed. Moral relations are man-to-man relations. If there were no order in human society, there would be no law, and if no law, no measure of justice or its lack. But all societies are organized, and all human contacts are within the pleuxus of law. It is inescapable therefore, that individual units in the group who are aware of the order that controls their lives should be equally aware of the disorder that denies them justice. In practical terms it would seem to make little difference how the sense of justice as a personal right comes about, whether it is congenital or contrived. It is the anthropologists who tell us that while objective concepts of right and wrong differ in cultures, the sense that there is a distinction and that it is right to be right and wrong to be wrong is exhibited among all people, whether primitive or sophisticated. Unhappily, it is observed, the primitive tends more to follow what he regards as the right than his sophisticated opposite number. Taboo protects him; he is afraid to be wrong. We—if we may call ourselves sophisticated—regard taboo as nonsense and the fear of being wrong the complete negation of sophisticated liberalism.

It is the feeling that man has a moral right to justice that enables him to share the responsibility of its administration to others. God is the transcendent and ultimate judge before whom all injustices must be redressed. Man as surrogate judge and witness shares this responsibility on the mundane level and within history. Were we not so accustomed to it and the never-ending convocation of courts and the routine of litigation, jury duty, and judgment, we would see it in its magnificent dimensions. What, after all, is more monstrously presumptuous in man than that he should sit in judgment on his fellows? Nothing, unless it is his claim that he has, because of what God and he are, a moral right to have justice awarded to him.

8

The practical result of this has gone very deep into the culture of the Western world. There has never been the fatalistic outlook on life that has blighted some other peoples. This is not to be said vaingloriously but with a due sense of gratitude. We simply do not believe we have been condemned in the nature of things to poverty, ignorance, sickness, indignity. To be sure, we have moments of dismay and longer periods of anxiety or even despair; but the confidence that beneath the surface of the momentary discomfiture the energies of rectification and redress are waiting to erupt—this confidence is unbroken and undiscouragable.

Politically it expresses itself in the concept of democracy, for what is this great ideal but the objectification of our sense of a moral right to justice in a political order designed to make it possible. We ask for democracy no halo it does not deserve, but within it the words "Ye shall not respect persons in judgment; but ye shall hear the small and the great alike; ye shall not be afraid of the face of man" (Deut. 1:17) have a familiar, contemporary sound. They may be flouted or forgotten for the moment, but if they are ever lost, our structure of law will collapse irremediably, and with our law gone, our culture will disappear.

9

Thus viewed, the Ninth Commandment provides its tenet to the doctrine of man we have been putting together. Man's origin and destiny are in God; within the complex of human society he has four moral rights: life, freedom, property, justice. About these has been woven the pattern of the culture that we call free, democratic, capitalist, under a system of law that applies equally to all.

I have been concerned all through this inquiry to point out the way in which the culture of the West is threatened and to ask whether in the face of moral indifferentism and the aggressive amoralism of the Marxist philosophy we have reason for believing our culture, based on this Mandate and the doctrine of man implicit in it, can survive. We indulge ourselves no complacency because of the records of the past. The Soviets say there is no history; our weathering of former storms is illusion; we are decadent and soon to die at the impartial and unfeeling hands of the dialectic of history.

The answer to this is the answer of faith. Meanwhile it is necessary to ask whether we believe in the moral right to justice for all men. The Soviets endlessly nag us with their incorrigible insolence about capitalistic and white man's justice. They promise to the world justice under totalitarianism, and we promise freedom under democracy. Freedom sometimes has seemed at loggerheads with justice, and great pretense is made of the absolute impartial justice under the despotism of the East.

It is not my purpose to argue these points here. Let it be said that it is most unlikely that justice as a moral right can be recognized in a political philosophy that regards morality as a bourgeois superstition. Nor do we believe justice will have much meaning if it is not part of a doctrine of man that conceives of life, freedom, and property as man's indefeasible moral rights. Are these also bourgeois superstitions, soon to be discarded by the victorious "people" of the world?

In the meantime it is imperative that we remind ourselves how limited is the operation and extension of justice throughout the world. We have a fondness for saying that we got our laws from the Romans and our jury system from Magna Charta, and we assume that these provide a basis and a pattern of administration that will save us from the grotesque distortions of justice that have afflicted the rest of the world. This is interesting and more or less true, but in the present world situation simply to congratulate ourselves about it is frivolous. The narrowed circumference of the world makes new demands on the West and asks new implementation for our ideals. For justice is indivisible; it cannot live in segregation or fragmented. We are compelled by the exigencies of history to affirm and effect the moral right to justice for everybody.

We need to be reminded that the world revolution that shakes creation was not created by Russian totalitarianism. It is the result of economic, political, and emotional factors which with great shrewdness are being exploited by the Soviets. In the article quoted in the preceding chapter there are other items we are asked to bear in mind: "Most people in Asia cannot read or write. . . . Most people in Asia have never known civil liberties. . . . Most people in Asia believe that freedom or free enterprise means the freedom of Western colonial powers to exploit Asians." [1] The major emotional drives in that part of the world are compounded of defiance of the white man's power and hatred of the white man's pride. It is these, and not our moral rights, that they know; for our power and pride have enforced the status of political and racial inferiority that they are determined to cast off, while our moral rights to life, freedom, property, and justice have been kept at home to supply the cohesion that has made us strong.

This is not the whole story and therefore not the true one, but it is what they are saying, and for them it supplies the spiritual energies of revolution. No repeated assurances, by word or foreign-aid allotments, can cancel the history of the imperialism of two and a half centuries; nor will it abate this growing hostility. We have not yet abandoned the role of the dispenser of charity to the wretched and— so we secretly suspect—the undeserving. If charity is odious, is our calculated political prudence any less so? No matter if we can say with honest certainty that the illiteracy and the undemocratic social patterns and the mistaken notions about the intentions of the West are not our fault. We must ask a deeper question; it is the question the Marxists have been shrewd enough to ask while we have been making pronouncements. The question: Is there justice in the wealth

[1] *Loc. cit.*

and power of the West and in the poverty and feebleness of the East? If our appeal is to power, we will make justice the slave of power; if our appeal is to morality, we shall make justice the servant of ethical idealism. If we are unable to become the agents of justice—universal justice, and we are under no illusions as to what that involves—as we have been the exemplars of power, we shall see the hordes of restless and angry Asians sucked into the vortex of Communist absolutism or drawn off into new forms of despotism and terror equally grotesque and suicidal.

This is the aspect of the world beyond our borders that lays siege to our souls. It is not very far beyond, and the time grows short. But within our borders the same question is being asked by the dispossessed, the discriminated against, the disillusioned, and the fearful. Once again it is these who often lend a ready ear to those who scoff at our moral idealism and expose our moral insincerity. Do we believe that man, every man, because of what he is, has moral rights that are inalienable? We who have enjoyed these rights answer for our faith. Can we answer for the doubts of others?

Let us be careful; we must not bear false witness, either by flattering ourselves or by disparaging others. The issue is too grave, the crisis too close. If we speak, we must be brief and our words must be free of every shred of pride or cant. Dare we go back across the centuries to appropriate anew one of the great words by which we have lived so long?

CHAPTER XV

Covetousness

"THOU SHALT NOT COVET thy neighbor's house, thou shalt not covet thy neighbor's wife, nor his man-servant, nor his maid-servant, nor his ox, nor his ass, nor anything that is thy neighbor's."

After what we have been studying, these words seem almost an anti-climax. Covetousness is a state of mind; it is a compound of appreciation and attraction, the components of which cannot be sharply enough defined to show where one ends and the other begins. Nor do we feel—and "feel" is the proper word to describe our response to these affiliated moods—that there is anything inherently wrong in either of them or in their combination. The opposite of covetousness is indifference or apathy, the moral quality of which is also contingent. It appears at first glance, then, that it is not covetousness that is wrong but coveting the wrong thing that is wrong. Coveting the right thing is clearly right. The great apostle urged his Corinthian friends to "covet earnestly the best gifts" (I Cor. 12:31 K.J.V.), because he had found them coveting the dubious gift of tongues.

1

The catalogue of things that were not to be converted is not exhaustive, nor is any one of them per se a bad thing. This effort to legislate a state of mind contains an element of interest that is not contained in any of the other commandments. That the issues of life are out of the heart is axiomatic with us. That where our heart is, there is our treasure also is supported by all that we know of the human psyche. Have we encountered in this last commandment something that in relation to moral conduct reaches depth and subtlety we had not thought to find in the ancient mind? This may serve to rebuke our pride in our modern knowledge of ourselves, or it may enhance the importance of the Mandate for our times. It should, of course, do both. Or we may say, as we have the right to do, that it represents the editorial transposition of an insight lately arrived at to an earlier period when it could hardly have been given such explicit form. We see here the relation of desire to evil act. It is not original with us. How early it emerged into a position of influence in thought about morality, it is idle to speculate. We are still a covetous breed. If we feel superior to the primitives at the feet of Sinai, we will do well to check our credentials.

There is a literary interest suggested by the words translated "covet." The Old Testament has two: *chamad*, which connotes simple desire; and *avah*, which means to desire for selfish reasons. The first of the Greek words similarly rendered is *zeloo*, already encountered in our study of the Second Commandment. It is Paul's word—"covet earnestly"—cited above. The other is *epithumeo*, which comes very close to our word obsession, a desire that has slipped the leash of rational control and has run wild. Thus in the biblical record we find the idea expressed in terms that reach all the way from the simple wish to the obsessive compulsion. *Chamad* is the word used in the Tenth Commandment. This being the mildest word it excites the least suspicion. Perhaps for this reason it invites closer study.

Of all these words it can be said that they are in themselves morally neutral. Obsession may be dangerous, but it can also be glorious. Without the compulsive neurosis of Michelangelo we would not have had his art, and suppose Wilberforce had never coveted freedom for the slaves, who, though they also had coveted it, were powerless to win it. This is to say that the disposition of the spirit called covetousness acquires its moral colors by passing through the subjective spectrum. *Chamad* by itself is the simple desire to possess something. How is it refracted into its dangerous and morally evil spectra?

206

2

Once again refer to the rudiment of desire in the instincts with which animals are endowed. They are unaware of them, but they become dangerous the moment instinct is thwarted. The satisfaction of hunger, sex, and companionship does not puzzle the wolf; it compels him, and he will develop ingenious tricks if necessary to get what he needs.

His human superior calls these instincts "drives" and will credit them with as much intensity as is necessary to flatter him. Thus the big eater is compensating for a subconscious sense of loneliness. The delicate eater, perversely, is satisfying a need to call attention to herself. If one loves "not wisely but too well," it can be explained as glandular hypertrophy or the subconscious striving for masterfulness. So on and on our explanations go, always in the general direction of satisfying our individual and generic ego. Again there is nothing wrong in this of itself. There are certain physical and psychological necessities that vitality demands. The man without desires is no man, and he will not be an animal very long.

3

We may go a step further and say that desire is clearly of the essence of the divine nature. "We love," said the ancient seer of Ephesus, "because he first loved us." (I John 4:19.) He wrote as a saint and as a psychologist, dealing with the love of God in the former role and with the most imperious of human drives in the latter. What we call the will of God, or the purpose of creation, or the destiny of humanity, are only slight variants of the desire of God. In so far as man has the same desires, or different ones, he is simply exercising a capacity with which he is naturally equipped; he is acting as the image of God. If this is a mark of divinity in him, to erase it would be to reduce his status. There is a surgical procedure, adopted in cases of extreme emotional disturbance, that severs the connection between the lobe of the brain that supplies emotional stimulus and the lobe that supplies idea. This leaves the patient free of the dangers involved in emotional overstimulation but condemned, as it were, to live with ideas he doesn't care anything about. Those who would proscribe desire as something evil in itself would presribe spiritual lobotomy as a redemptive operation.

This is not so bizarre as it sounds. This endowment, so great in power and so profound in significance and consequence, has troubled the spiritually sensitive of all times. Allow that desire is evidence of the divine spark within man and that he must have it if he is to survive, nevertheless it is always restless and often unruly. Like a spirited horse, if it cannot be held with a stout rein, it were better dismounted. Pedestrian ambling is, in the mind of some, better than the hazard of the wild, headstrong ride.

The debate over this goes on endlessly between the resigned and the reckless. To the Buddhist all desire is evil, since if man had no desire, he would suffer neither glut nor emptiness, neither satiety nor frustration. Therefore divest the summer garment of desire. He is answered by the Persian philosopher bard who put it memorably:

> Come, fill the Cup, and in the fire of Spring
> Your Winter-garment of Repentance fling;
> The Bird of Time has but a little way
> To flutter—and the Bird is on the Wing.

The summer garment of desire and the winter garment of repentance may represent no more than taste in their wearers, but they are the symbol of an argument that will not likely be foreclosed before the bird has completed its flight.

Similarly in the Puritan revolution shape was given to man's inordinate desires in the seven deadly sins. It seems exaggerated perhaps to distort desire into such unlovely forms: greed, gluttony, lust, and pride are not good to look upon, and they are, after a fashion, deadly. But desirelessness is quite as deadly, and if one wants to die, is not desire already dead? This accounts partially for the resistance of spiritually wholesome people to the honest excesses of Puritanism, and for much of the hypocrisy of the spiritually sick.

4

Now what we encounter in the Tenth Commandment seems to be an answer of good practical moral sense to the extremes of both negation and unrestraint, and to the Puritan effort to escape a dilemma by changing words. The Hebrew mind did not dissociate man's desires from his essential nature, the character of which was determined by the creative act of God. Instead it presented the

Creator as a counselor admonishing man not to allow desire to become selfish, inordinate, covetous. Desire, given as a necessity, must not become an imperative; always a pleasant companion, desire is never a congenial master.

This is a delicate handling of what is often a clumsy moral problem. It does not, and in the nature of the case it cannot, peg the point at which the straight road of desire ends and the abyss of covetousness yawns. One may feel his temperature rising, but there is no thermometer to tell him exactly the danger point or how sick he is. Differences shade off delicately here. Should the fine frenzy of concentration an artist brings to the creation of a masterwork be allowed to pass over into the frenzy of debauch with which he may want to celebrate its nativity? Aesthetics are identified as a religion in some quarters; creative art is the highest devotion. Those who say this find it difficult to tell the point at which the moral disciplines of art become the immoral relaxation of the artist.

It is instructive to note the way in which the desire to realize fully the moral rights to which man is entitled can be corrupted by covetousness. The desire to live can become a fever of profligacy, to be free may by ever so slight a change of temperature become the wish to enslave others, the desire to own what one may rightfully possess may turn into the avarice that would dispossess others, and the right to justice may harden into claims for exemption and impunity.

We may indeed go beyond this. Is there any one of the other commandments that is untouched by uncontrolled desire? God demands of us absolute loyalty, but shall our desire for God run to irrationalism or fanaticism? God commands us to take his name on our lips with reverence, but does that mean that we must sit endlessly fondling a talisman or mumbling incantations? We are warned that there is much to be learned from our elders, but does this mean we must never make the venture that takes us far from them? And the Sabbath day must be kept holy. Surely this does not mean to stultify the day in stagnation. As a matter of fact, we seem to discover that the same caution that prevents desire from becoming covetousness must be exercised everywhere lest religion become fanaticism and morality a prison house.

5

The history of religion and morals in any culture widely reveals the problem that lies at the heart of the difference between desire and covetousness. It is the judgment of Arnold Toynbee that religion is the most important element in the societies that have developed during the last six thousand years, and he predicts that a thousand years hence the student of our current scene will be more interested in our religion than in our science or our wars. The societies that have died have been the victims of moral and religious disintegration within, and disintegration often begins in imbalances like that which converts desire into covetousness. Is it because religion degenerated as in Egypt into cultism and the occult art, or as in Mohammedanism into political expansion, or as in India into nihilism, or as in Rome into self-deification? A response to these questions lies beyond our province, but a correct answer would be helpful in any criticism that is made of the religion of the modern West. Have we struck a balance that gives us moral and religious stability, or is our equilibrium an illusion produced by inactivity?

The history of Israel is full of illustrations in point for the reason that the chronicles of her people were set within the perspectives of religion and morality. Thus David coveted his neighbor's wife and fell into sin and disgrace, and Ahab coveted the vineyard of Naboth and set going as lively an intrigue as is to be found in any lore, ending quite appropriately with the death of the villain. At what point did David's appreciation of Bathsheba's charms flame into lust? Could he have said? And when did Ahab's admiration for the well-tended vineyard of his friend sour into a scheming determination to expropriate it? Could he have said? Or recall the teetering up and down between the tendency of religion to formalize itself into sterility and the reaction that makes it much too simple a set of maxims. To the famous question of Micah: "What doth the Lord require of thee, but to do justly, and to love mercy, and to walk humbly with thy God?" (Mic. 6:8 K.J.V.), there is an answer. That, said Micah, was "what is good." Precisely, but was it *all* the Lord required? There was a need confronting Micah that could be met only by a quick resumé of what was good, but in moments of reflection the restless prophet had surely seen more in the nature of the moral struggle than was contained in his eloquent brevity. He would have answered his own question, we believe, with a qualified affirmative and perhaps gone on to explain that justice and mercy and humility are neither simple nor easy to the mind that takes religion and morality seriously.

6

We seem to have, therefore, in the Tenth Commandment a general principle with respect to the necessity for balance, applied specifically to the problem of desire. As normal desire may curdle into covetousness, so normal devotion may contort into fanaticism. Covetousness is evil because it is uncontrolled desire or desire off balance. Under its pressure a man may be driven to invade his neighbor's house in order to possess it, not simply to admire it and wish it were his own. His neighbor's wife and servants and animals will also fall under his appraising eye, not in approval but in avarice. What could have been the basis of happy neighbor relations, namely, an appreciation of what his neighbor had, becomes the source of lust and the determination ultimately to destroy his neighbor by taking away what he has. For it is not to be imagined that the neighbor, aware of the designs of his covetous friend, will hand him the key and tell him to help himself. Thus desire, which can be the bond of community, becomes covetousness and the destruction of fellowship.

Do we not have here a preview, so to speak, of what is and what has long since been recognized as the basis of all moral living: the regulation of desire? This takes us back to the matter of self-discipline again. Presumably Yahweh might have made a creature in whom all the equilibriums would have been automatically maintained. This would not have been man as we know him, nor do we believe he would have been created in the image of God.

We must not forget the divine intention to create a being who could become godlike in a society that was to be godly. A part of both of these projects was man's willingness to bring his will (his desire) into conformity with the divine purpose. He would need help, and more often than not he would seem to have failed himself and foiled God's intention. God is a God of patience and grace, and when man draws too near the point of danger, God will lay his hand on him in caution or restraint if man keeps himself nearby and sensitive to God's touch.

7

It is manifest that society organizes itself to control cupidity and greed. It is not always or uniformly successful. Indeed societies are often organized in order that they may covet and possess the things of other societies. This is the sorry lesson of imperialism; it is the specter that always haunts the pretentions of colonialism. Here again we see the problem of balance. Desire that is the impetus to social advancement may become the covetousness that creates enemies. It was altogether legitimate for imperial Japan to desire the raw materials she needed for her growing industrialization. In 1931 she leased vast areas in China for this purpose. At almost the same time a covetous military junta was itching to use simpler methods. We scolded them, and they pointed to our preferred position in world trade as the real reason for our self-righteous pose. Pearl Harbor was the issue of that. Japan coveted her neighbor's house and markets and raw materials. We do not well to be happy that she met the disaster that crushed her; we do better to ask how far our desires today are leading us into a maelstrom of covetousness on a world scale.

8

Within our own society the problem grows apace. What is more lavishly stimulated in our land than the itch of avarice, the greed of covetousness? This is strong language, and yet what more moderate terms will describe our prodigal spending on advertisements, a great deal of which is not only duplication; it is, what is worse, duplicity? As these words are being written, a nearby radio has been pleading with the American public to send in box tops, to make a down payment with an old radio (that's all you need, folks) on a new television set, to go out at once and buy something else that it appears everybody is buying because everybody else is. Except for its absurdity the most amusing and unpredictable battle in America today is the Battle of the Cigarettes. Each claims to be milder than its rivals; the solicitude of the fine tobaccos for the sensitive membranes of the throats of possible victims is deeply touching. How generous of some manufacturers to add half an inch to elongate the filter that

212

eliminates harmful carbons and burning oils. And they are mild. The purpose of the manufacturer's self-praise is neither disguised nor misunderstood. It is to create artifically a desire. One would think there were enough normal desires to control without creating others.

This, and what goes with it, is called a high standard of living. It is nothing of the kind. It might be more accurately called a high standard of luxury. It may be only a high standard of covetousness. The encouragement of covetousness takes its place alongside the inculation of patiotism. What is it that we boast about and cite as proof of our superior status among the nations? That we have the highest standard of living and that it can be higher. A three-hundred-billion-dollar income in 1952 was promised by ambitious politicians and salesmen. But this disturbs us a little. That's a lot of money, and too much money causes inflation, and inflation is dangerous. So in one sentence the politico praises our unlimited productivity and its cash earnings, and in the next he argues for legislation to remove our earnings in taxes and to restrict credit lest too much buying power should depress the value of our dollar. All the while the admen grind out their catch lines, the billboards prove they are right, and the radio sponsor challenges all competitors to duplicate his product at his give-away price.

This grows less and less amusing, for the incitement to covetousness is not designed for American eyes alone. If we could only show the depressed millions of the earth our store windows and warehouses, our transportation systems and our factories, they, with a united mind no political promises could produce, would rise and throw off the despotism that demands belt-tightening and rewards it with speeches about the decadent plutocracies of the West. We actually believe that by making enough people in the world sufficiently covetous of our houses, our wives, our gadget menservants and maidservants, our motorized oxen and asses, and everything that is ours, we shall split the iron curtain and break the iron bonds of tyranny.

This may all be true; the zest with which it is promised indicates we are either honest zealots or hypocrites. But there is a day that sooner or later will break upon us. What has been called "the nemesis of imperialism" awaits a world saturated with covetousness, if it can be put off that long. The sale of the gadgets we make is followed eventually by the sale of gadget-making machines. Finally our one-time market will be supplying itself and then, given time and a well-cultivated covetousness of its own, will have to seek markets for its own products. This was what Japan faced when the madness of Pearl Harbor was let loose. We had industrialized Japan at great profit to ourselves, but her standard of living could not absorb her consumer goods. We could buy them only in such variety and volume as would not interfere with the production of our own industrial machine and our use of its goods.

Add to this other complications of world trade. At last we find ourselves the creditor of the world. In order to re-establish themselves, most of the nations of Europe have adopted one or another form of socialism to bring production, consumption, and trade into order. This is in line with the second thing that Toynbee said must be done to save civilization: the discovery of a working compromise between the extremes of capitalism and Communism. Saved from the sort of destruction visited upon the ruined economies of Europe, we do not take kindly to the expedients to which others have had to resort. Our devotion to an ideology under which we have grown great leads us to distrust the practicability of any other. And yet we must bolster up these economies if they are to buy our goods. Here the effort to inculcate covetousness amounts almost to demanding imitation. This is an unhappy circumstance with which we shall have to learn to live if we cannot devise intelligent ways of changing it.

When finally the two titans of the modern world, clad in the clanking armor of their prodigious industrial power, finally meet to contest for the dominance of the earth, they shall do battle for either the markets or the hearts of men. It is not encouraging to face the fact that the adversary that strides the East like a colossus seems to speak more directly to men's hearts than we have apparently been able to do. We have created distrust, and this baffles and angers us. Is it not we who have been nurtured in idealism, who have believed in human decency and worth, in the superior values of the spirit, and in being friends with all men in a great world confraternity? Have we lost our faith in them now? No? Then why are we saying that our only available resources in the present struggle are the weapons our adversary understands? For a long time in our history we did not understand force as the solvent of the world's ills. Now comes an enemy who understands and has faith in nothing else, and, lo, his

214

faith suddenly becomes our own. This surely is one of the oddest ironies of history. It might be well if we could dismiss it as odd. We cannot; we must face it as sinister. By what sorcery has our desire, and theirs, become covetousness?

Once again this discussion seems to have led us a considerable distance from the almost gentle remonstrance of the Tenth Commandment, yet we have not wandered aimlessly. The Fifth Commandment, to honor father and mother, is the only one that carried a promise: long life in the land the Lord was to give them. What would have been the promise to the Tenth if such an addendum had been thought necessary? Honor to father and mother stands in stark opposition to coveting one's neighbor's house and goods. A promise would therefore stand opposed. Thus: "Honor thy father and mother and live long; covet whatever is thy neighbor's and die soon." There is something eerie in the directness with which this speaks to our generation. "So teach us to number our days, that we may apply our hearts unto wisdom." (Ps. 90:12 K.J.V.)

CHAPTER XVI

Conclusion

THIS STUDY of the Mandate to Humanity appears to have undertaken to restore a very large picture with ten small tubes of very old paint. It is therefore open to the criticism that the result exhibits colors paled by too great diffusion or the use of borrowed tints that were not in the original color supply.

Or it may be put another way. Twelve sound steps make up the tone scale of our music—seven whole steps, five half steps. They are visible in the white and black notes on a piano keyboard. Out of these tones comes all our music, from the simplest melody in monotone to the most elaborate theme in complex harmony. The average ear can catch a tune, it takes an expert to follow the counterpoint of a fugue, yet the genius who composes a symphony has no more notes to start with than the boy who whistles a song. Out of the clear moral tones of the Decalogue has been developed the symphony of ethical idealism which for centuries has given tempo and pitch to our life. When we have misplaced those notes, we have detected thinness and dissonance; when we have employed them richly, we have discovered the grandeur of moral and religious concord.

Can the picture be reduced to a focus that will sharpen its detail? Can the symphony be reduced to a thematic pattern easy to hum? In the seventh century B.C. the editors, already aware of the profusion of laws and the resulting diffusion of moral impetus, discovered

216

such a reduction in certain famous words concealed amid the mass of statutes they were collating: "Thou shalt love Jehovah thy God with all thy heart, and with all thy soul, and with all thy might." (Deut. 6:4.) "Thou shalt love thy neighbor as thyself." (Lev. 19:18.) Centuries later this was given its most famous form when an expounder of the law asked Jesus for a summary. He put these two commands together and added: "The whole of the Law and the Prophets is summed up in these two Commandments" (Matt. 22:40 Weymouth). To this I shall presently return for a final comment. In the meantime let me attempt a necessarily more extended digest of what our inquiry has brought us.

1

The Hebrew mind, whether by special endowment or the early cultivation of the disciplines of religious reflection, came to understand man in the cosmos within religious and moral dimensions. The former led ultimately to the concept of monotheism, the latter to the concept of a world community under the governance of the Eternal. Man's relation to God rested upon three factors: he was created by God in his image; his destiny lay in the divine intention; and he was covenanted to certain obligations, the fulfillment of which promised blessing and the repudiation of which promised misfortune.

Loyalty to Yahweh was in the beginning little more than the devotion of other tribes to their preferred deities, except that in the case of the Jews there seemed to be moral overtones to the ritual observances their religion demanded. It was never an easy matter to keep their devotion free of the corrupting influence of neighbor cults, but they were kept measurably faithful by the realization that their God had saved them from bondage in Egypt and had demanded in return that he should be their only God. This demand was sharply put and allowed no equivocation. In recompense he promised to reward their faithfulness and to punish ther defections.

The fact of the absolute sovereignty of Yahweh, however dimly understood, was the pedestal upon which was erected all moral obligation. It was because of the *living* God that they were not allowed to make effigies to solicit and satisfy their worship; it was because of the *creating* God who had rested that they must maintain

217

a day of rest, that natural alternation between movement and stasis, action and repose, that is the equilibrium of all life; and it was because of the *sustaining* God that they were to regard their parents with honor and give gravity to those continuities between the past and the future without which life could have no meaning.

Specific relations within their society were selected for moral regulation. It was forbidden that one man should kill another, that one man should corrupt or adulterate another, that one man should dispossess another; and that one man should bring perjured testimony against another. These, it has been argued in detail, were prohibitions against violation of the moral rights to which man as a creature of God is entitled. Positively stated these moral rights are to life, to freedom (or integrity or the right to be himself), to property, and to justice. These four propositions, combined with man's created relation with God, compose a doctrine of man that has informed the ethical idealism and social practice of the culture that has inherited and practiced it for centuries.

With great insight they pointed out that man's desire to achieve the fullness of the divine intention for him and society must be protected against the excesses that defeat it. The desire for sexual companionship, for companionship in toil, and for satisfaction in legitimate possessions must not become covetousness of one's neighbor's wife, his servants, or his property. The desire that is the spring of all conscious development too often became the covetousness that was the reversal of all progress toward community.

2

This, I have been saying, is the meaning of the Ten Commandments. The immense body of law that the growing society of Israel developed was their attempt to give explicit application of the great principles of the Mandate to every practical situation. As is often the case, laws sometimes became ends in themselves and their interpretation the vested interest of a class. It was inescapable that lawmaking and law keeping should have become something of a nuisance at times, and many of the resulting laws turned out to be so trivial as to be nonsensical and thus invite their breach. The tension between law and laws has always been a real one, nor is this altogether a bad thing. But it has made it necessary that the prophet should betimes rebuke the scribe, and has made it possible for common sense ever so often to put pedantry to flight.

Therefore as laws perennially need re-examination, the law needed fulfillment. This was done from time to time no doubt within the Hebrew tradition. It was generally the function the prophet appropriated for himself. Thus to First Isaiah the God who inspired a slave revolt in Egypt sought also to draw men to him by his holiness, to Jeremiah the God who had held children to account for their fathers' sins was also making every man accountable for his own through the mysterious monitorship of conscience, and to Hosea the God who punished adultery could purge the corruption by love.

These represented both the fulfillment of the law and the distillation of the laws. Each is a normal process and serves its particular purpose. It is to be expected therefore that when the Hebrew tradition passed through the alembic spirit of Jesus of Nazareth, we would encounter both processes at work. In the Sermon on the Mount he fulfilled the law; in answer to the familiar question of the lawyer as to the greatest command, he distilled the laws. The latter inclination is the more general. The desire of the mature and sensitive mind is to reduce experience, as far as possible, to its essence. Most of us have no acquaintance with or interest in the multitudinous compendium of rule, regulation, ordinance, statute, law, code, or constitution under which we live. Morality that is the meticulous and self-conscious observance of legal minutiae may keep us out of the hands of the police only to land us in the office of the psychiatrist. Observe how easily conscience becomes moral sclerosis and how this loss of flexibility means a diminution of its vitality.

When Jesus was confronted with the demand of the lawyer, his ready answer was put in words that may have been forgotten by his generation. It is interesting to note, however, that he did not respond in terms specifically relevant to the experience of his wilderness temptation. It is idle to ask whether he was ever confronted with solicitations to break the moral law of his people in terms of murder, adultery, theft, and perjury. The epic story of his moral struggle puts the issue in a different category altogether. He was, in effect, tempted to disorient himself from God. He had power; the sug-

219

gestion was that it be used against the manifest purposes of God exhibited in nature. God does not make bread of stones even to feed a famishing son. Should the Son, to feed himself? He had power; the suggestion was made that he use it to win men by trickery, a leap from the temple that involved no risk. God wins men, but not by fraud. Should the Son? He had power, the awesome power to redeem; and the suggestion was that it be exchanged for the power to compel by the laws of evil. God redeems but not by conciliating the devil. Should the Son?

To each sinister proposal his response was essentially the same: man lives not by bread alone but by the word of God; man attracts following not by fraud but by service; man is redemptive only as he lives within the orbit of loyalty to God, who alone is to be worshiped and served. In other words the moral obligations of Jesus were seen within the perspectives of his religious obligations to God. The completeness of his identification of himself with the sovereign God of his people indicates that he was proof against assault in those areas where other less completely committed men struggle.

3

It is this, we think, that furnishes us with the profound spiritual depth out of which his answer to the scribe arose. Divided roughly, I have said the Mandate has to do half with man's religious relation to God, half with his moral relation to men. When Jesus was to give his opinion as to the greatest command, he also put it in two parts; but he did not dissociate them. "Thou shalt love the Lord thy God with all thy heart, and with all thy soul, and with all thy mind. This is the great and first commandment. And a second *like unto it* is this: "Thou shalt love thy neighbor as thyself." Are they alike? Is love of God like loving one's neighbor? Is the completeness of our love of God, with *all* the heart, soul, mind, and strength, like loving one's self? If we were honest about it, would we not say, before we repeat the second command: "But the second is quite another matter"?

It is necessary to understand this if we are to realize, first, the completeness of the engrossment of Jesus with the will of God and, second, the meaning of the new commandment which throughout the New Testament appears as the Law of Love.

This new law infused the summary he gave of the law and the prophets: love God; love man. There are three things said of love: it is the first and great command, and it is a new commandment. First in importance: "Thou shalt have no other gods before me," meaning that man must love man was posited on the prior assumption that man loves God.

In what way was the law of love the great command? Simply that love is the only disposition of the soul that is great enough to enclose God and man in its circumference. It has already been pointed out that hate, toward God and/or man, is a self-consuming fire, burning the soul's tinder with slow, sure incandescence. It cannot therefore be a disposition of the spirit for long, if at all.

And how was it a new commandment? This characterization comes from the end of the first century. (John 13:34-35.) Did it have the aspect of novelty then? Historically it was old; love is not a discovery of the Christian Era. Does this not mean, then, that love has to be learned afresh in every context, where it is necessary? Every social and individual contact must have it *de novo*. There is no depositary from which this energy can be drawn, no surplus of love generated by others to be appropriated by those who have a current deficit. And does not the exercise of love as the determinative principle of one's life always impart the aspect of novelty to the situations in which it operates? Twenty centuries have heard of the forgiveness of enemies, but when we see it actually today, we react as if it had never happened or been thought of before.

4

Now we believe in ways we have been too long realizing that without the activation of love the Ten Commandments are forever inert. By love we do not mean the filial or domestic experience or the romantic rapture; we mean the creative will to good; it is generosity, a compulsion to seek for others what they need, the giving of one's self to another in a creative, ameliorative, or redemptive act. Thus understood, not only is love the fulfilling of the law; it is the precondition of the law. Only such love can make real our submission to the absolute sovereignty of God. Otherwise it will be submission under duress, which is slavery. For what other purpose is man to preserve the rhythm between restlessness and rest if not to allow love its sabbath interval of regenerative quiet? Only love can impart to the honor we bear our parents the quality that will make it acceptable to them. Otherwise it will be sycophancy. Only love can give meaning to our moral right to life. One might even ask if a loveless person has not already, by himself, violated the right. What is freedom without love to save it from introversion or the illusions of independence and autonomy? What is the use of a moral right to property if love is not present to monitor its uses? And what of justice? Prior to the effort to have justice done is the will to good that compels one to desire it. Justice divides in the interests of fairness; love unites in the interests of fellowship. One's claim to a moral right to justice would go unheeded were there not love in the hearts of those on whom the levy was made. So we see love manifest as the only seedbed within which all of man's religious and moral responsibilities can grow, as well as the flower and fruit of their growing.

And what of covetousness? At last we have come upon the energy that both activates desire and lays it under restraint. Covetousness is desire drained of love. There is a way in which a man can respectably love his neighbor's wife, and his maidservant, and his house, and everything that is his neighbor's. This will be love without covetousness, desire elevated and controlled by the will to good. Those who truly love—that is, those who are obedient to the first, the great, the new commandment that fulfills the law—seek not to possess the object of desire, but to perfect it. On this law hangs all the law and the prophets.

5

I have summarized the sweeping implications of our ten simple axioms of religious and moral command, and have looked briefly at the fulfillment that the religious and moral influence of creative love brings to Sinai's mandate. It remains to be asked in what ways, if any, this has particular significance for modern culture.

We must not make the easy mistake of thinking that our age witnesses the first assault ever made against the framework of Hebrew-Christian ethical thought and practice. The story of the experience of Moses, freshly equipped with moral wisdom graven by the finger of the Almighty in imperishable stone, descending from the summit of revelation to the levels of realism, encountering the people in whose interests he had been in awesome tryst with Yahweh, debauching themselves in the worship of a calf—this is the symbol of a struggle that has never been resolved. In anticipation of seeing God descend upon the mountaintop in a thick cloud, they had sanctified themselves and washed their garments. But the sound they heard was thunder, and Moses was delayed. They could burnish a god of gold that would shine instead of hiding in a heavy cloud. And why not dance? Was it not more diverting than standing in awed silence, waiting for a voice?

Such symbolism is significant to those who are aware of the pull and tug between man's innate need for divine guidance and his restless impulse to provide it out of his own resources. It is the spring of inner confusion. Aaron, when he saw the calf, erected an altar before it and proclaimed a feast to Yahweh. If the chief priest could make a mistake like that, why blame the people who, having brought peace offerings, sat down to eat and drink in ritual worship and then promptly "rose up to play"? It is not only that moral guidance so often seems an imposition from the outside; it is something that may be casually set aside when one wants to rise up and dance about the thing his hands have fashioned for himself.

This is the condition to which religion and morality are addressed, this is the need which of itself is the proximate credential of all codes. This also is the reason why every culture carries within itself the infection of its own death, so that if left to itself, it will lose first its energy and at last its life. To maintain sufficient depth and distance to the perspectives within which we look at our times is therefore the primary necessity. The disclosures of Congressional commissions investigating crime on both the gangster and the government levels must not allow us to forget that there were group and personal mischief-makers in the First Congress, under our first president, that caused a cry of protest against corruption and scandal. The proposal that a code of ethics be drawn up by Congress for its own regulation may indicate a low level of moral sensitivity in that body. An article by a U. S. senator suggests as part of the swearing-in procedure a pledge to observe a ten-point code he calls a Congressional Ten Com-

mandments. While this code is designed to condemn ethical transgressions in that body in recent years, he is careful to say: "I shall
go further and attest to the fact that I have seen more moral courage
displayed on many issues by many on Capitol Hill than I have seen
in thirty years of experience in and around the business community." [1]
This is not the first time the moral problems of government have been
the subject of concern. Plato, who did a turn unsuccessfully as the
ruler of Syracuse, reflected at length upon his experience and concluded, in one of the greatest treatises on government of all times,
that only the king and the sage should be allowed to govern, the
masses of the people to have no loftier responsibility than tilling the
soil. We do not think the senator's decalogue will do what Plato's
Republic could not do, but there is nothing wrong in trying. The
problem, as we have seen in our study of the Mosaic decalogue, lies
on deeper levels.

Senator Benton compares the moral level of Congress with the
business community to the disparagement of the latter. Here again
it is easy to assume that because business is bigger and more dominant
in modern life than ever before, it is for that reason ethically less
sensitive. The size of a sinner has scant relation to the dimensions of
his sin. Power corrupts; this we have been endlessly told, but because
corruption is a qualitative matter, we shall be slow to accept the statement that big power means bigger corruption.

One might go on to needless lengths in an analysis of all the components of our culture, art, entertainment, education, diplomacy, the
press, and so on, in the attempt to assess their ethical quality. No
doubt we would find very depressing evidence of disintegration if
not indeed of moral decline. A study made of the incidence of dope
addiction among teen-agers, of cribbing at West Point, and the gam-
bler's "fix" in intercollegiate athletic contests concluded simply that
young people in a tense age are trying to adjust themselves to the
times, and the times aren't very good. At the same time we do not
think that the threat to the Ten Commandments comes from this
direction. The chilly winds of moral indifferentism have always
blown across the exposed cultural landscape. If they blow colder and

[1] William Benton, "A Decalogue for Members of Congress," *The New York Times
Magazine*, Aug. 12, 1951, p. 23.

224

the temperature falls, we will wrap ourselves in the momentary warmth of reforms or new codes; but we shall not change the wind's direction or create a summer of moral security out of "the winter of our discontent." We may wait in awe before some new mountain of revelation, but too soon we may dance again about some revelation of our own cleverness.

6

No; materialism, secularism, immoralism, or whatever name we may choose to represent the things we deplore about our times, the condition is implicit in history's flux. This is not pessimism, which sees a situation and despairs of it; it is a mood, whatever it may be called, that sees a situation and resolves to live with it constructively if possible; if not, to live anyway. We will neither wring our hands nor run. When we view life and destiny within the religious and moral circumference of our Hebrew-Christian tradition, we will see elements that transcend the human struggle and that pass the ultimate judgment upon it. This will steady us in unsteady times. When that understanding is truly lost, our culture will have changed so radically that it will no longer bear any resemblance to the tradition that has so long sustained it. Whether it will, in losing that identification, acquire a higher quality, or whether it will die, as other cultures have because their characters were radically altered, is the question that may be answered within the next century.

Next century: such a foreshortening of the interval of destiny needs justification. It lies, we believe, in the acceleration of all social movement due to the shrinkage of the world community and the speed of communications. Not only are we nearer everybody else and therefore collide more often, but we have better devices for shouting at them when they get too close and for warning them that we are more and more suspicious that our collisions are not accidental but are deliberately aimed at crippling or destroying us. We all seem to be doing this to our neighbors. To be sure, there are moments of respite when we can talk amiably over cable and radio to those who will listen with diplomatic restraint. But our temper is rarely relaxed. It is increasingly the pattern of our conversation to be suspicious of our friends as well as our adversaries. It is not overdrawn to say that distrust is the preponderant mood of international and intergroup relations, rising from our uncertainties about our pact fellows in Europe to the all-out disbelief of our enemies in Asia. This is to be expected in a tense world, but the velocity of our asservations and denials, crackling through the shrinking air envelope that encloses the planet, adds greatly to the danger of saying the wrong thing, or the right thing at the wrong time. The voice of America sincerely offers peace; the Kremlin jams the air waves. The Kremlin offers peace; the White House jams the proposal with denunciations of insincerity. Tempers have no time to cool; we are too close for comfort, and being uncomfortable we talk too much. This is a condition that never before existed. Technology that has made us neighbors has not made us friends, and there is nowhere to go, no more spacious or undisturbed neighborhood for our occupancy. This shortens the time element within which the destiny of our culture is to be decided.

The second factor which foreshortens the interval is the deliberate attempt of the Marxist culture to destroy the bourgeois culture of the West. To some the word "destroy" is too strong; there should be reassurances from history that no culture has been able to destroy another simply by assault from without. This is all well and good for us, but it does not make sense to a culture that assumes there has been no history up to now: and therefore the so-called lessons of so-called history are all sheer illusion. Furthermore, we are told that there can be no reversal of the forces that, released only through the dialectic movement of matter, are for the first time creating history. If this proletarian revolution depended solely on a philosophy, it might be relatively harmless since there are few who are interested in philosophizing. But with a shrewd recognition of the plight of the world's dispossessed and exploited, the Communist totalitarians have offered a political program that is grounded less in word than in bread. The world's population has always, within what we call the historical period, for the most part been hungry and sick. For this reason it has been easy to despoil. Now they are being told that for a price that looks cheap alongside a picul of rice—simply going along with the commissar—they will never be hungry or sick again. Until we have been hungry, we will do well to withhold our scorn of such easy faith. Add to this the fact, more and more widely known

226

among the people of earth, that technical skill is available for the abundant production of food and medicines if only those who own them, meaning the capitalist West, can be forced to release their selfish control. The stake of a full belly is worth risking everything for. World revolution is not too costly. Thus the famished and the feeble are swept into the turgid stream of upheaval, caring nothing about Marx so long as his apostles will promise them the things by which physical life is sustained.

7

There is another aspect of this that comes closer to our whole study than the factor of proximity and communications, and response of the hungry to the promises of revolution. We have been concerned to understand the great religious and moral principles contained in the Ten Commandments. We have also pointed out that the new Marxist culture as embodied in Soviet totalitarianism repudiates history as illusion and religion as superstition. It is not so easy, however, for it to repudiate law, since law is the order of any society. Is there something here that seems to be new in the history of culture?

Our law rests on a moral base. Blackstone's commentaries move from that assumption to the more specific applications of law. This moral aspect derives from the a priori hypothesis that man is a responsible creature, and this notion comes from the ancient doctrine of man that we have found in the Mandate to Humanity. Since man is morally responsible, he will be held culpable only if it is established that he has intended the misdeed for which he is charged. Society is penalized as much by manslaughter as by murder; it loses one individual. But man is not to be penalized as a murderer if his slaughter of his fellow was unintended. This puts a moral floor under all the processes of law. Only as man is morally culpable is he culpable at all. This is a fact of great significance.

A system of law that refuses to consider guilt in terms of morality must rest it on something else. If man is not responsible because he is a creature made in the image of God, his responsibility must lie in his being the creature of something else. There are two other alternatives: he is the creature of nature, and this provides the naturalistic

227

or humanist basis for law; he is the creature of society, and this locates the legal responsibility in social relations entirely.

With the former of these we are not immediately concerned. To a degree the locus of responsibility in nature and society intersect, but at other points they are distinct. Where nature is natural, society may be arbitrary. There are some who argue that more and more, naturalistic presuppositions are determining the interpretations of law in our culture. We must leave that to more expert analysis than we can give it. When, however, we see society the determinant of legal responsibility, particularly as it is concreted in the state of Communist absolutism, we discover something that has for the first time become articulate and aggressive, within the last century.

The individual, we are told, is solely and completely the product of his social environment. His ideas as well as his habits are socially determined. He is therefore responsible only to the state which has given him birth, nurture, and character. Responsibility in this case is not moral responsibility. Here intention has nothing to do with the quality of his act; it is its social conformity or nonconformity that decides culpability or innocence. That is wrong that subverts or threatens the state. A man will be punished not for the intention behind his act, but for its objective conformity to the state's order. Moral guilt or innocence are meaningless; if his act violates the state, he is legally wrong. Hence a man is penalized not for what he does but for what he is not. If he is a faithful party member, he is right; a non–party member cannot be right. This is the legal basis of all totalitarianism. The Nazi government, proposing to be an Aryan society, made all non-Aryans guilty of a crime punishable by imprisonment or death. Such societies recognize no endowed rights; such rights as one may have are evolved and transitory. They can therefore be changed by society's will or evolution, and such changes as occur will alter the rightness or wrongness of the behavior of its individuals. In such a society the right to life is determined by the will of the state; freedom has no meaning but as conformity to the absolute order of the state; property does not exist as a private right, and the canons of justice are determined by the advantage that accrues to the state in a contested situation.

This repudiation of the moral basis of law is the most significant fact in Soviet Communism as it impinges upon our contemporary moral culture. Its logic demands the renunciation of all transcendant standards of value; its concept of man withdraws him from all conditioning influences save those that exist in society to shape his ideas and his behavior. The Mandate to Humanity which is definitive for our ethical culture is meaningless to theirs. It has, they say, created a powerful, arrogant, pitiless, exploiting civilization that is doomed to fall before the onslaught of a state created by the dialectic of history. This new state uses its individuals to secure itself and ultimately to rescue society from the disabilities of class differences, and yearns to enclose the people of all the world in its orbit. To refuse the offer is not merely to spurn it; it is to invite the inexorable destruction that befalls all those who defy the dialectic processes of history. Time and destiny are against us. This is what we are being told.

8

There are answers to this in any good analysis of Communism and Christianity. We lack nothing of wisdom to rebuke this heresy. But the time is short and forensics are a feeble resource when the world frets with revolution. This inquiry has been to discover the meaning of the ethical ground work of our Western world as contained in the Decalogue, and to ask its relation to contemporary culture. The relation is clear: the religious and moral ideology of the Hebrew-Christian tradition is the diametrical opposite of the irreligious and antihuman morality of the Marxist-Engels tradition. Never were opposites in the field of religion and morals, and therefore of law, so trenchantly exposed. Nor does history bear record of another culture like that led by the mirthless men of Moscow, so determined to have it out with its adversary.

This is not a reassuring picture. The pressure of materialism within our own culture, and of antidemocratic socialism outside it, converge upon the core of religious and moral faith which is its heart. As modern man finds himself caught between them, he will not find it easy to stand erect and undaunted. What if he falls?

All this was known, after a fashion, two thousand years ago. Man

229

needs more than law, or justice, or freedom, or possessions, or power; he needs even more than all these, were he ever so fortunate as to have them all. For he is the creature of God destined both to wretchedness and splendor—wretchedness because he is man, splendor because he is not only man. He cannot resolve this paradox nor pentrate its mystery.

Sometimes, tired of pretensions, he will become as a little child. He will hear an ancient story about the children of a far-off day who stood by a shivering, cloud-topped mountain and heard their Father asking them to love him. Or he will hear another Son talking to his confused friends and giving them a simple new rule to live by, a rule that children understand. Or he will read a poem about love, written to some Corinthians, and be glad of the confident conclusion of an old man that love never fails.

Sophistication shrinks from the self-abnegation that love demands. When therefore it can rise to it, it is all the more impressive. Thirty years ago Bertrand Russell's eloquent pessimism was the pride of the disillusioned and the cynical. He spoke of the "noonday brightness of human genius" as destined to perish in a universe in ruins. Recently, with a simplicity that was in marked contrast to his sophisticated style of former years, he concluded a series of lectures at Columbia University on "The Impact of Science on Society" and said man must do three things: abolish war, distribute power evenly, and limit population. How are these things, which might correctly be described as secular social goals, to be achieved? "The root of the matter"—remember this is Bertrand Russell talking!—"is a very simple and old fashioned thing, a thing so simple I am almost ashamed to mention it, for fear of the derisive smile with which wise cynics will greet my words. The thing I mean—please forgive me for mentioning it—is love, Christian love, or compassion. If you feel this you have a motive for existence, a guide in action, a reason for courage, an imperative necessity for intellectual honesty." [2]

Sinai is too far beyond the horizon for us to see, and if we could see it, its summit would still be mantled by cloud, for no man can see the face of God and live. But it is not too far away to hear. Those who in the din of our troubled times turn an ear toward it will still detect, not the sound of thunder, but a still, small voice, patient and sure, with the undiminished authority of yesterday, today, and forever, saying: "Thou shalt have no other gods before me."

"He that hath ears to hear, let him hear."

[2] *The Christian Century*, Nov., 1950.

Scripture References

234

Index